# THE COLOR OF CRIME

# The Color of Crime

*Racial Hoaxes, White Crime, Media Messages,*
*Police Violence, and Other Race-Based Harms*

THIRD EDITION

Katheryn Russell-Brown

NEW YORK UNIVERSITY PRESS
New York

NEW YORK UNIVERSITY PRESS
New York
www.nyupress.org

References to Internet websites (URLs) were accurate at the time of writing. Neither the author nor New York University Press is responsible for URLs that may have expired or changed since the manuscript was prepared.

Library of Congress Cataloging-in-Publication Data
Names: Russell-Brown, Katheryn, 1961– author.
Title: The color of crime : racial hoaxes, white crime, media messages, police violence, and other race-based harms / Katheryn Russell-Brown.
Description: Third edition. | New York : New York University Press, [2021] | Series: Critical America | Includes bibliographical references and index.
Identifiers: LCCN 2021003108 | ISBN 9781479801749 (hardback) | ISBN 9781479843152 (paperback) | ISBN 9781479802739 (ebook) | ISBN 9781479888504 (ebook other)
Subjects: LCSH: Discrimination in criminal justice administration—United States. | Crime and race—United States. | African American criminals. | Racism—United States.
Classification: LCC HV9950 .R87 2021 | DDC 305.8—dc23
LC record available at https://lccn.loc.gov/2021003108

*The Color of Crime (Third Edition): White Crime, Media Messages, Police Violence, and Other Race-Based Harms* is in the *Critical America* Series.

New York University Press books are printed on acid-free paper, and their binding materials are chosen for strength and durability. We strive to use environmentally responsible suppliers and materials to the greatest extent possible in publishing our books.

Manufactured in the United States of America

10 9 8 7 6 5 4 3 2 1

Also available as an ebook

# CONTENTS

# Introduction

These are not the best of times. It is 2021 and the world is living, surviving, and dying through a pandemic. Most of us have been touched directly or indirectly by the COVID-19 virus. Many people have suffered a punishing blow. In the United States, millions of people have been diagnosed with the coronavirus and hundreds of thousands of people have died of complications from the virus. COVID-19 has wreaked a particular havoc against African American and Latino communities. Members of these groups are disproportionately front-line workers—as food service workers, meatpacking plant employees, health-care aides, and service industry workers. In some cities and states, Black Americans have been more than twice as likely to contract and die from the virus. The racial disparity highlights entrenched racial fault lines that meet at the intersections of race, socioeconomic status, gender, neighborhood, and health care. The racial toll has been particularly stark for people awaiting bail, awaiting trial, and serving time. The coronavirus has provided an undeniable inflection point we can use to assess how race matters in our understanding of criminality, criminal imagery, harm, and justice. Early on, we were instructed to wear face masks when out in public and to maintain a social distance of at least six feet from other people. Black men quickly noted the potential danger of wearing face masks. Aaron Thomas's comment keenly summarizes the existential conundrum:

> I don't feel safe wearing a handkerchief or something else that isn't clearly a protective mask covering my face in the store because I am a Black man living in this world. I want to stay alive but I also want to stay alive.[1]

The COVID-19 crisis helped to unmask a particular racial havoc. Four months into the pandemic, another social problem took center stage: police killings. The disproportionate rates of Black people killed by police is not a new phenomenon. However, in 2020, the murder of

George Floyd became a rallying cry, precisely because it demonstrated the deadly consequences of treating Black skin as dangerous and a proxy for deviance. This videotaped proof was unavoidable as millions of children, young people, and adults were home from work or school, with limited options for entertainment. Floyd's killing sparked worldwide protests and demands for transformative changes in policing agencies across the United States. Millions of people took to the streets to protest and march against the killing, shooting, and profiling of African Americans. There were rallies in small towns and large cities, in majority-White communities and majority–of color communities. The marches were largely led by a multiracial group of young people and included a vast range of participants—including college students, high school students, frontline workers, community activists, professionals, and retirees. Public artwork and murals featuring the victims of police killings, including Floyd, Breonna Taylor, and Ahmaud Arbery, were widespread. In some cities, protesters gathered to remove or vandalize statues of Confederate soldiers. In stark contrast to the 1960s civil rights protest marches, which involved mostly Black Americans, the majority of the marchers in 2020 were White. On the news, many of them could be seen chanting, holding, or wearing the words "Black Lives Matter." Since then, Derek Chauvin, the officer who kneeled on George Floyd's neck for nine minutes and twenty-nine seconds, was convicted of second-degree murder, and awareness of the frequency of police killings has penetrated the nation's collective consciousness.

Overall, this book reflects and critiques this nation's racial history and how this history informs our current criminal-legal practices and understandings of race, law, and justice.

## Book and Chapter Overview

I initially wrote *The Color of Crime* to address the many unanswered questions I had about race as a law student and later as a graduate student. I attended law school to learn about the intersections between law, race, class, and justice. Likewise, when I returned to graduate school for a doctorate in criminology, I presumed that my studies would focus on how and why race matters in the administration of justice. In both instances, I was frustrated with the slim pickings of course work, assigned readings, and the infrequent and unnuanced discussions on these seminal topics. Beyond addressing my own queries, this book's modest objective is to offer students and interested others a richer and fuller backdrop with which to understand and critique the US criminal-legal system. This work is part of my ongoing academic expedition—a project designed to enhance race and crime literacy. The material in this third edition is both forward and backward looking. It keeps an eye on the historical development of America's systems of policing, courts, and corrections, *and* it analyzes contemporary applications of racialized systems, practices, and labeling in the system.

There are eight chapters, including six completely updated chapters and two new ones. Chapter 1, "Definitions, Statistics, and Issues," provides an overall grounding for the book's material. It defines the central terms and themes discussed throughout the book, such as "race" and "crime," and offers a historical backdrop for them, including the terminology and definitions used to allot racial groups in the US Census. As noted, the chapter includes charts and tables that clarify the impact of race and racial disparity in the US correctional system.

Chapter 2, "Media Messages," takes a measure of how racial groups of color are portrayed in the mass media. Specifically, it explores how Indigenous Americans, Asian Americans, Latinos, and African Americans are portrayed by the media, including television and movies. Today there are many more faces of color in the mainstream media. However, the substance and breadth of these roles raise interesting questions. The chapter discussion identifies some remarkable trends in these portrayals, including how some groups of color (e.g., Native Peoples and Asian Americans) are rarely seen or heard but are "represented," and framed without being at the decision-making table.

Chapter 3, "History's Strange Fruit," considers the deep, long-standing and intentional associations made between race and criminality—through law and legislation, political actions, religion, and science. The chapter sets out the historical role of race in the development and operation of the US criminal justice system, from the slave codes to Jim Crow legislation. This history is used to identify the operating principles that are necessary for establishing an equitable criminal justice system. These justice principles establish the groundwork for the text's assessment of the degree and forms of bias within the US justice system.

Chapter 4, "Racial Discrimination, Racial Profiling, and Racial Monitoring," explores the various ways that racial bias manifests in the court system and how researchers measure the existence of racial discrimination. This chapter looks at research on how race impacts various stages including arrest, pretrial detention, conviction, and sentencing. It examines how racial discrimination is understood and assesses the value of traditional tools of analysis. The chapter also takes a look at the prevalence of "racial hall monitors," the name assigned to White people who have taken it upon themselves to monitor the goings and doings of Black people. These monitors ramp up the perils of what has been labeled, "Living While Black."

Chapter 5, "Racial Hoaxes," examines more than one hundred cases involving a false allegation of criminality against someone based on his or her race. Racial hoaxes are used to cover up actual crimes and to fabricate crimes. A few of the most well-known include cases involving Susan Smith, Charles Stuart, Tawana Brawley, Jussie Smollett, and in 2020, Amy Cooper. False allegations of crime, particularly against Black men, are more common than we might hope. The chapter analyzes the social, political, and legal harm done by hoaxes, regardless of the rationale for the hoax. The final section considers whether hoax perpetrators should face greater punishments for filing a false police report.

Chapter 6, "White Crime" addresses and assesses the practice of labeling crimes by the race of the offender. The discussion centers on the reality that only some racial groups are regularly identified as tied to criminality in general or to particular crimes. Crime committed by Black people is labeled "Black crime," yet crime by Whites is not accorded a similar race label. The chapter considers crimes that would fall within a category of White crime. It also considers whether racial labels should be attached to crime and, if so, which crimes it should encompass. The chapter concludes with a critique of James Q. Wilson's argument that White racism is caused by high rates of Black crime.

Chapter 7, "Race and Crime Literacy," makes the case that there is an identifiable body of material that a person should be familiar with to have a working knowledge of race and crime issues. This progressive extension of E. D. Hirsch Jr.'s argument for a "cultural literacy" rests on Judith Shapiro's writings on "sociological illiteracy." The chapter identifies over one hundred important names, cases, terms, phrases, and concepts that should be considered part of this body of knowledge.

Chapter 8 presents a futuristic, outside-the box social tale. "The Soul Savers," which takes place in the not-too-distant future, features a society struggling with social problems involving race and justice. An earlier version of the story was published in Michigan Journal of Race and Law in 2020. The objective of the tale is to have readers reflect on the material presented in previous chapters and interrogate the hypothetical scenario through the lens of the text material. The story pushes readers outside their comfort zone as they evaluate and critique the plausibility of racial, social, legal, and political realities depicted in the tale. The story also interweaves issues and practices that are already on the horizon for processing people through the justice system. "The Soul Savers" is an ode to the power of storytelling to get us to see what is right in front of us. It is a nod to Professor Derrick Bell's remarkable legal tale, "The Space Traders."

Two appendices are included. Appendix A includes summary data on race and crime (as part of the material discussed in chapter 1). The tables provide insight into racial groups' rates of involvement in arrest, prison, jail, probation, and parole. Appendix B provides summaries of the racial hoax cases discussed in chapter 5.

## Studying African Americans and Crime

For many years, academics have pushed to move race analyses beyond the Black-White dichotomy. Part of the difficulty in making more inclusive assessments is that groups of color cannot be accurately discussed as a single entity and then compared with Whites (another socially constructed racial group) or one another. Each racial group has had a unique experience with the American system of justice. For instance, Native Peoples, from their earliest encounters with Whites, had their land stolen and were stripped of their language and lineage. A complex and contorted three-level legal system exists to adjudicate Indian legal affairs. In contemporary times, American Indians, who make up less than 1 percent of the US population, have the highest rates of victimization. Unfortunately, these findings are not new.

Although some common themes of racial oppression apply to Blacks, Latinos, Asian Americans, and Native Peoples, the way the criminal law has been used to marginalize each group is notably distinct. Latinos and Latinas, the largest US group of color, have disproportionately high rates of arrest and incarceration. Members of this group acutely face the interrelated issues of immigrant rights and racial profiling. Asian Americans, approximately 6 percent of the US population, are often cast as being involved in human trafficking or gang-related offenses. Given these distinctions, lumping Blacks, Latinos, and Asian Americans together when discussing crime remains problematic. More research must be devoted to each of these racial groups. More research by and about Native Peoples is greatly needed. Notably, scholars Sarah Deer and Marianne Nielsen have made inroads in this area. The primary and unapologetic focus of this book is on the relationship between African Americans and the US criminal-legal system. However, this book includes many discussions about and references to other groups of color as well as Whites.

## Memory and Racial History

As the world continues to turn, and we continue to make sense of where we stand on issues of race and crime, we must place history at the center of this learning. The following statement by Nelson Mandela highlights the significance of memory and justice.

> In the heart of any individual, family, community or society, memory is of fundamental importance. It is the fabric of identity. At the heart of every oppressive tool developed by the apartheid regime was a determination to control, distort, weaken, even erase people's memories. . . . The struggle against apartheid can be typified as the pitting of remembering against forgetting.[2]

Memory is a funny thing. We like to believe that our memories are an accurate reflection of the way things were. When it comes to historical memory, however, the truth of the matter is often fleeting, distorted, and incomplete. As it turns out, to tell the truth about the past is not so easy a task. Our stubborn memories are clouded in myths and silences, and oftentimes with a stubborn insistence to put on a happy face.

On issues involving race and crime, we consistently wring our hands, point fingers, and cover our eyes. Whether it is racial profiling, capital punishment, media representations, police brutality, rising incarceration rates, or racial hoaxes, as a society we are uncomfortable reviewing the country's racial record. Our ever-ready attempts to run interference between the past and present reduce our racial history to a disembodied mass of curious data. The United States' racial history and its impact on the legal system, however, do not go away simply because we ignore them. The proverbial tree that falls in the forest while no one is present does make a sound—a loud, crushing one. Luckily, many people seek to make some noise and give history its due weight in analyses of contemporary conditions. Count me in.

*The Color of Crime* is devoted to remembering. The task of remembering is work indeed. As Nelson Mandela cautions, vigilance is required to fight against practices that dismiss or disappear histories. Through an analysis of cases, ideological and media trends, issues, and practices that resonate below the public radar, this text "remembers" race. *The Color of Crime* acknowledges and explores the tacit and subtle ways that deviance is systematically linked to people of color, particularly African Americans.

1

## Definitions, Statistics, and Issues

Definitions belong to the definers, not the defined.
—Toni Morrison

This chapter provides readers with a foundation for thinking and talking about race and crime. This chapter addresses salient race and crime topics, definitions, terms, and data that lie at the heart of the book's race and crime analysis. This overview examines the history of official racial categories, the development of criminological perspectives on race, and the racial labels assigned to various groups. This chapter, which introduces many of the concepts that are detailed in later chapters, provides a foundation and point of entry for understanding the fraught relationship between race, crime, and justice in the United States. Readers are encouraged to refer back to this chapter. Appendix A, "Data Snapshots on Race and Crime," provides tables that summarize various data on the criminal-legal system, including racial breakdowns of who is in prison, jail, on probation and on parole; data on interracial versus intraracial criminal offending; and who is most likely to serve time behind bars. These tables, too, are reference guides for the subjects discussed throughout the book. Let's begin with a look at the seminal terms, definitions, and concepts that set the stage for a contemporary assessment of how race influences and undergirds the US criminal-legal system.

### Defining Race

It is widely known that race is a social construction. Definitions, assignments, and assumptions about race are based upon a mix of factors, an amalgamation of social beliefs, historical precedent, a nod to biology, and political will. We need look no further than the myriad ways in which US racial categories have changed over the centuries. Within this evolving social construction, every person is accorded a race. This chapter begins with a look at the evolution of race—how race has been built.

The evolution of racial labels has been guided by three overarching historical realities and principles. The first principle is that historically there has been an established racial hierarchy, with Whites at the top, Blacks at the bottom, and Asians, Indigenous Peoples, and Latinos positioned in the middle. Whites promoted a racial hierarchy, which was supported by a multilayered system that provided "proof" of racial difference. This includes researchers who devised studies to show that Whites were the superior race and politicians who created laws that separated groups by race under the theory that racial interactions between Whites and Blacks would somehow taint and ultimately destroy Whiteness.

The second principle is that Whiteness represents a "pure" racial category, one unfiltered by other racial groups. This point is underscored by the extreme lengths to which the US Census went to define Whiteness as a pristine racial group, exemplified by its adoption of the "one-drop rule." According to this rule, a person with any ancestor of African descent was Black. The one-drop rule was adopted during the antebellum period. By law, the child of a Black enslaved woman who had been raped and impregnated by her White owner was considered Black. Thus, the one-drop rule worked to increase the number of slaves. Anyone not completely White was Black. The rule was premised on a belief that only White blood could be harmed or somehow tainted by mixing with the blood of other racial groups. The rule is known by various names, including the rule of "hypo-descent."[1] The one-drop rule was codified into law and all official government documents, including the US Census. The one-drop rule continues to be in effect, not as law but social custom, and thus it continues to shape contemporary perceptions and understandings of race.

The third principle is that visual appearance is the cornerstone of racial group membership, particularly for Whites. For more than a century, Census takers relied upon "visual inspections" to determine a person's race, supports the foundation for today's widely accepted connection between physical appearance and racial group membership. The shifting definitions of race offer significant insight into how society's perceptions of race have changed over the centuries. The next section examines how the Census has defined various racial groups at different times since the late eighteenth century.

## US Census and Race

In 1790, the US Census officially began collecting data on all citizens.[2] The ten-year assessment provides a racial snapshot of who resides in the country. It also tells us which racial labels were in use during specific periods. The guidelines published by the Census show how race has been measured over the years and chronicles the relationship between race and social status. These definitions of race determine how people are counted, how state resources are allocated, and how racial groups are perceived. The statistics set the baseline for assessing each racial groups' progress on social measures—including involvement in the criminal-legal system. Establishing the number of people in the United States who are Black, for instance, determines that group's level of racial proportionality (or disproportionality) in the court system. The definitions of race and the race categories that are used directly impact how we view the relationship between race and crime. Here are snapshots of some of the racial definitions used by the US Census for various decades. Table 1.1 shows the racial categories and number counts from the first US Census.[3]

TABLE 1.1. First US Census Racial Categories and Counts, 1790

| | |
|---|---|
| Free White males age sixteen years and older | 807,094 |
| Free White males under age sixteen years | 791,850 |
| Free White females, including heads of families | 1,541,263 |
| All other free persons | 59,150 |
| Slaves | 694,280 |
| **Total** | 3,893,637 |

In 1787, three years before the first US Census was conducted, the three-fifths compromise was adopted by the Constitutional Convention. Under Article I, Section 2 of the US Constitution, for purposes of taxation and representation, states were instructed to count each enslaved African as three-fifths of a person. Thus, enslaved Black people were not counted as full citizens (a compromise that provided a direct benefit to states in the Confederacy). Particularly notable, per the Census language shown in Table 1.1, people designated as slaves did not have an officially recordable race, gender, or age—in stark contrast to Whites. Racial language used in subsequent Census tallies makes clear that the goal was to maintain Whiteness as a closely policed, closely guarded racial category.

### US CENSUS DEFINITION OF "BLACKS," 1870

It must not be assumed that, where nothing is written . . . "White" is to be understood. . . . Be particularly careful in reporting the class Mulatto. The word . . . includes quadroons, octoroons, and all persons [who] have any perceptible trace of African blood. Important scientific results depend upon the correct determination of this class.[4]

The above language makes clear that "White" is not a default racial category. No one was presumed White. The 1870 Census definition of Blacks emphasizes the paramount importance of chronicling the degree to which a person was *not* White. The language outlines a racial hierarchy for people with both Black and White blood—a racial ranking within a racial ranking. Those with a relatively small amount of Black blood (e.g., octoroons) were shown preference compared to people who had more Black blood (e.g., mulattos).

The 1870 Census also made reference to Chinese immigrants. This was the first time the Census collected data on Chinese immigrants. Two decades later it initiated a count of Japanese immigrants. These new race categories resulted from the large influx of Chinese and Japanese people who came to the United States, primarily to the West Coast, to pursue economic opportunity after the US Civil War. Likewise, as members of varied ethnic groups arrived in the United States, the Census expanded its categories.[5] In 1920, for instance, the Census added categories for Hindu and Filipino.[6]

### US CENSUS, COLOR OR RACE, 1940

Any mixtures of white and nonwhite blood should be recorded according to the race of the nonwhite parent. A person of mixed Negro and Indian blood should be reported as Negro unless the Indian blood greatly predominates and he is universally accepted in the community as an Indian. Other mixtures of nonwhite parentage should be reported according to the race of the father. Mexicans are to be returned as white, unless definitely of Indian or other nonwhite race.[7]

This language underscores that anyone with non-White blood was considered nonwhite. These racial rules point to both a White and non-White racial hierarchy. It extends the one-drop rule to persons with Black and Indian blood, thereby mandating that those with mixed racial bloodlines allow one of them to trump the other. Most interesting is that Mexicans were designated as White.

## THE MODERN ERA

Beginning in 1960, the US Census allowed people to choose their racial group membership. This process of self-identification was a major shift from the previous practice, which allowed the Census worker to assign each person to a racial category based on a visual inspection. In another huge update, starting in the year 2000, people had the option of checking more than one box for race. This change was the result of years of protests by groups demanding that the government allow people with mixed racial backgrounds to select multiple races on the form. This development was also a direct challenge to the one-drop rule. Figure 1.1 shows the race question that appeared on the 2020 Census form.[8] Over the centuries, great shifts have taken place in how the Census defines and counts racial groups. Each Census represents society's contemporary understanding of race and how various racial groups fare relative to one another at that particular moment. In addition to the Census, the US Office of Management and Budget defines racial groups. Sometimes these racial categories converge and sometimes they diverge. The language used to categorize and count racial groups influences the political, social, and legal landscape. For instance, racial descriptions may reduce or expand the size of a group.

## DEFINING RACE, OFFICIALLY

In 1977, the federal government published official racial and ethnic definitions. Known as Directive No. 15, the statement detailed the racial and ethnic classifications for data collected by the US government. It included four racial categories (American Indian or Alaskan Native, White, Black, Asian or Pacific Islander) and one ethnic category (Hispanic). For twenty years, these were the official racial categories used at the federal level. In

**What is this person's race?**
Mark [X] one or more boxes **AND** print origins.

☐ White – *Print, for example, German, Irish, English, Italian, Lebanese, Egyptian, etc.* ↗

☐ Black or African Am. – *Print, for example, African American, Jamaican, Haitian, Nigerian, Ethiopian, Somali, etc.* ↗

☐ American Indian or Alaska Native – *Print name of enrolled or principal tribe(s), for example, Navajo Nation, Blackfeet Tribe, Mayan, Aztec, Native Village of Barrow Inupiat Traditional Government, Nome Eskimo Community, etc.* ↗

☐ Chinese ☐ Vietnamese ☐ Native Hawaiian

☐ Filipino ☐ Korean ☐ Samoan

☐ Asian Indian ☐ Japanese ☐ Chamorro

☐ Other Asian – *Print, for example, Pakistani, Cambodian, Hmong, etc.* ↗

☐ Other Pacific Islander – *Print, for example, Tongan, Fijian, Marshallese, etc.* ↗

☐ Some other race – *Print race or origin.* ↗

Figure 1.1. US 2020 Census Form, Race Question

1997, some slight revisions were made. Table 1.2 outlines the current racial and ethnic categories.[9] Overall, the directive adopts crude and illogical geographical boundaries for racial group membership. Of particular note, the racial definitions are not consistent across categories. For instance, it is not only a person's country or continent of origin that determines racial group membership. For American Indians, racial group membership is not the sole determinant of race. According to the language, a person's degree of community affiliation and attachment is used to determine whether they are officially American Indian. Also, the racial definitions for Black and White divide the continent of Africa. It appears that some North African countries are treated as "White," such as Egypt and Ethiopia. Others are classified as "Black" for purposes of determining racial group membership. In addition to concerns about the accuracy and consistency of these racial labels, other consequences result from these racial labels.

TABLE 1.2A. Official Racial and Ethnic Categories (Directive No. 15)

Racial Categories

| | |
|---|---|
| *American Indian or Alaska Native* | A person having origins in any of the original peoples of North and South America (including Central America), and who maintains tribal affiliation or community attachment. |
| *Asian* | A person having origins in any of the original peoples of the Far East, Southeast Asia, or the Indian subcontinent, including, for example, Cambodia, China, India, Japan, Korea, Malaysia, Pakistan, the Philippine Islands, Thailand, and Vietnam. |
| *Black or African American* | A person having origins in any of the black racial groups of Africa. Terms such as "Haitian" or "Negro" can be used in addition to "Black or African American." |
| *Native Hawaiian or Other Pacific Islander* | A person having origins in any of the original peoples of Hawaii, Guam, Samoa, or other Pacific Islands. |
| *White* | A person having origins in any of the original peoples of Europe, the Middle East, or North Africa. |

TABLE 1.2B. Official Racial and Ethnic Categories

Ethnic Category

| | |
|---|---|
| *Hispanic or Latino* | A person of Cuban, Mexican, Puerto Rican, South or Central American or other Spanish culture or origin, regardless of race. The term, "Spanish origin," can be used in addition to Hispanic or Latino. |

In an article analyzing how racial labels shift over time, Michael Omi addressed how race-related trends can impact Census data. He notes that over the thirty-year period between 1960 and 1990, there was a 255 percent increase in the American Indian population—a jump from over five hundred thousand to nearly two million people. It is unlikely that the population of American Indians increased so dramatically during these decades. More likely, changes in social attitudes took place over those years, resulting in an increased social acceptance of American Indians. The changes may have resulted from a rise in cultural awareness about American Indians or a belief that claiming American Indian membership would result in specific benefits.[10]

Another concern with the official definitions of race is the classification of "Hispanic" as an ethnicity, not a racial group. Accordingly, any

person of any race may declare Hispanic ethnicity. The labeling of Hispanic as an ethnic category raises three issues. One, why is Hispanic the
only ethnicity included in the directive? The United States has dozens of
ethnic groups. All racial groups have within-race ethnic groups and cultural divisions. Further, the "Hispanic" ethnicity distinction overlooks
the fact that Hispanics are also considered a racial group. Finally, the
categorization of Hispanic as an ethnicity is not consistent with other
official racial labels. For instance, the racial and ethnic designations and
definitions outlined in the directive differ substantially from the categories used by the US Census and the Uniform Crime Reports (discussed
below). How race and ethnicity are framed and defined by official agencies are a reflection of the political and social time period in which the
definitions were adopted. This discussion of how "Hispanic" is defined
in terms of ethnicity highlights the ambiguities of ethnicity. Like race,
ethnicity too is a social construct. It may refer to cultural practices, religion, and common ancestral origins. In terms of official categorizations,
ethnicity is framed as a label that Hispanics may opt into or out of.

### Who's White?

One major issue has been the categorization of Middle Easterners and
North Africans. Over the years, a growing number of people of Middle
Eastern descent have said that while they are expected to select "White"
as their race, they do not perceive themselves as White. Members of this
group say they do not fit into any of the other listed racial groups. In
response to these concerns, some organizations petitioned the Census
Bureau to create a new racial category, "Middle East and North Africa"
(MENA).[11] It is estimated that between three million and ten million
people would fit into this classification. A new category would allow
the Census to assess trends in health, employment, and education for
this group. However, other groups have argued that adoption of a new
racial group would have unintended consequences, such as allowing the
government to target and punish Muslims.[12] The United States declined
to add a new MENA category for the 2020 Census count.

Historically, Middle Easterners have identified as White. This is a
carryover from early legislation such as the Chinese Exclusion Act and
decisions by the US Supreme Court, which labeled Asians as aliens who

could not be granted citizenship. The Supreme Court's 1923 decision in *US v. Thind*[13] is a case in point. In 1913, Bhagat Singh Thind, a "high caste Hindu of full Indian blood," came to the United States from India to attend school. He received his PhD from University of California–Berkeley and in 1918 joined the US Army to fight in World War I. Thind was honorably discharged the same year. After the war was over, Thind applied to become a US citizen. His initial grant of citizenship was later denied. Thind appealed to the US Supreme Court and argued that, by law, he should be considered a White person. The US Supreme Court denied Thind's request, stating,

> What we now hold is that the words "free white persons" are words of common speech, . . . synonymous with the word "Caucasian." . . . [It] does not include the body of people to whom [Thind] belongs. . . . The physical group characteristics of the Hindus render them readily distinguishable from the various groups of persons in this country commonly recognized as white. The children of English, French, German, Italian, Scandinavian, and other European parentage quickly merge into the mass of our population and lose the distinctive hallmarks of their European origin. On the other hand, it cannot be doubted that the children born in this country of Hindu parents would retain indefinitely the clear evidence of their ancestry. It is very far from our thought to suggest the slightest question of racial superiority or inferiority. What we suggest is merely racial difference, and it is of such character and extent that the great body of our people instinctively recognize it and reject the thought of assimilation.[14]

The Supreme Court's decision reinforces the goal of protecting Whiteness as a racial category that is only available to a narrow group of people—those who are visually White and those with little to no trace amounts of non-White blood. The Court's language makes clear that Whiteness implies the ability to merge in with other Whites—to disappear into Whiteness. The Court decides that Hindus (unlike the English, French, German, etc.) are unable to accomplish this based on "clear evidence of their ancestry." The Supreme Court also suggests that it is not making a claim of White racial superiority—especially since the case was decided at a time when separate but equal was the rule of the day.

## Living and Representing Race

### The Susie Phipps and Rachel Dolezal Cases

Sometimes the legal and social rules on race lead to confounding results. Two very different cases highlight two very different problems associated with how race is socially constructed. Interestingly, both of these cases push us to consider whether one's racial group membership is genetically predetermined, a lifestyle choice, or something else entirely.

In 1977, Susie Phipps, a White woman who lived in Louisiana, went to the Bureau of Vital Statistics in New Orleans to obtain a copy of her birth certificate so that she could apply for a passport.[15] Upon receiving the certificate, Phipps discovered that she was listed as "colored." Phipps, who said she "was brought up white and married white twice," said she was shocked and sickened to learn of her official racial designation. It turned out that Phipps's great-great-great-great-great-grandmother was a Black woman who had been enslaved. According to Louisiana law, any person with one thirty-second or more of "Negro blood" was designated as "black."[16] In an interview Phipps said, "Take this color off my birth certificate. Let people look at me and tell me what I am."[17] Phipps sued Louisiana to have her racial designation changed to White. She lost, and the US Supreme Court declined to hear her appeal.[18] The Phipps case illustrates the maze of problems associated with social constructions of race and laws attempting to mark Whiteness as exclusive, including the possibility that a person could be surprised to learn of her own official racial designation.

In 2015, news outlets reported on a story about a woman named Rachel Dolezal, who claimed to be Black. Dolezal, who lived in Spokane, Washington was head of local chapter of the National Association for the Advancement of Colored People (NAACP). Her parents, however, said that she was White. Dolezal, who attended Howard University said that she identifies as Black and has "an authentic Black identity."[19] Dolezal was subjected to widespread criticism and scorn. She was forced to resign from the NAACP post and lost her part-time teaching position in Africana Studies at Eastern Washington University.

Some people expressed concern, not with Dolezal's affiliation or interest in issues involving the Black community, but with the fact that she lied about her racial heritage. In 2017, to secure work and avoid being associated with the racial controversy, Dolezal legally adopted an African name.[20] The Dolezal case is atypical in that it involves the reverse of what is known as "passing"—when a Black person with pale skin decides to pass or present themselves as a White person. From different angles, both the Dolezal and Phipps cases raise the questions "Who is Black?" and "Who is White?" Related to this, these cases ask us to consider whether a person can reject membership in a racial group because they prefer to belong to another racial group. These cases also point out how the connection to Blackness—from opposing ends—can be used to bolster racial status. In the case of Susie Phipps, she sought to distance herself from her Black ancestry, and in Dolezal's case she claimed Black skin for personal, social, and economic gain. In Dolezal's case, she claimed Blackness as a way to secure employment and community engagement. In 2020, another White woman, Jessica Krug, admitted that she had pretended to be Black for years. Krug was a history professor at George Washington University.

These cases highlight the reality that race is socially constructed. Although neither was legally entitled to claim the race of their choosing (Phipps was Black by law, Dolezal was White by law), they both would have been allowed to select their preferred race on an official record, such as the US Census. Both Phipps and Dolezal wanted a change: to live as a member of a different race than the one listed on their official documents. Their cases underscore the fluidity of racial definitions and their social and political meanings. The next section shifts the discussion to racial labels and which labels different racial groups prefer.

### Racial Labels

How society categorizes individuals and groups by race is complex and sometimes perplexing. For instance, one racial group may have a variety of labels (e.g., Black, African American, Negro, colored, etc.). A group's racial label may evolve over time and reflect the preference of the group or a label imposed from outside the group. For instance, Indigenous Peoples in the United States have been referred to by various names, including "Indigenous Peoples" or "First Nations,"[21] "Native American" or "American Indian," or by tribal affiliation.

For Asian Americans, prior to the 1980s, "Oriental" was commonly used to describe a person whose ancestral home was Asia. As well, in an earlier time, "mixed" referred to someone who had a White parent and a Black parent. Today, "mixed race" is used to refer to anyone with parents with a heritage of two or more races. A core question about racial labels is *who* gets to decide which name a racial group is called. Is it the racial group or groups that are in the majority, or the group being labeled? Here are some of the racial labels associated with various racial groups.

Latinos and Hispanics
>   Surveys indicate that Hispanics do not have a clear preference for a particular racial group label. A 2012 report showed that 25 percent said they preferred the term "Hispanic" or "Latino" to describe their group. However, 51 percent said they identify themselves based on their family's country of origin (e.g., Brazil, Mexico, etc.).[22] Approximately 50 percent said they did not have a preference for "Hispanic" or "Latino."

Native Americans, American Indians, First Nations, Indigenous Peoples
>   Studies indicate that Native Americans have varied opinions on the group's racial label. Polls indicate that some Native Americans do not have a strong preference for "Native American" or "American Indian." Instead, many group members identify themselves by their tribal affiliation. There is research indicating that some have a preference for "Native people" or "First Nation." Official government surveys, such as the Uniform Crime Reports, use "American Indian / Alaskan Native." In the most recent Census, the largest group of multiracial people in the United States were White and American Indian (50 percent).[23]

Asians, Asian Americans
>   More than 50 percent of all Asian Americans identify themselves by their ancestral home country.[24] Only 20 percent indicated a preference for "Asian Americans."

Blacks, African Americans
>   Blacks use "African Americans" and "Blacks" interchangeably. A Gallup poll found that over 65 percent of Blacks said they did not prefer one term over the other.[25]

Whites, Caucasians
>   "White" is the most commonly used term to describe Whites. In some instances, "Caucasian" or "European" is used. "White" is the preferred

term for official reports and surveys. Few studies have looked at which racial label Whites prefer. Some people have questioned whether it makes sense to refer to a group as a color (e.g., "White" or "Black"), when the people within these categories represent a wide range of skin colors. These concerns, however, have not diminished the use of "White." Both terms are holdovers from early racial language used in the US Census based on the one-drop rule.

The above discussions examine the evolution of racial definitions over time, including how official data classify and catalogue racial groups and how various racial groups label themselves. This history underscores a dynamic duality about race in the United States: race is a perplexing, real social phenomenon and a social construction. Racial definitions and categories are tied to and reflections of the social and political climate. Keeping this duality in mind is helpful when considering the history of race and crime research and contemporary statistics on race and crime.

## Historical Perspectives on Race and Crime

From the beginning, race has played a central role in the development of theories of crime and studies of criminality. Researchers in the United States and abroad looked for ways to legally and socially justify racial separation. A range of theories and perspectives were promoted to support the prevailing belief among Whites that they ranked above all other racial groups—socially, politically, physically, and intellectually. The theories and studies that supported racial ranking upheld the racial status quo. This section provides an overview of some of the more popular theories that indicated a link between race and criminal offending.

### Biological Determinism and Racial Ranking

For centuries, biological determinism was the rule of the day. It was preached as mainstream gospel that White people were intellectually superior to members of all other racial groups. When race was ranked, Whites were always placed at the top, Asians and Indians in the middle, and Blacks were always at the bottom. Not surprisingly, the prevailing view was not only that Whites were the superior race, but that all other racial groups were defective. The presumed inferiority and deviance of non-Whites was used as an excuse to treat them as second- and third-tier citizens. Mainstream science in the United States and abroad supported these racial rankings, which raises an important question about the early linkages between beliefs about racial superiority and research findings from the scientific community. Did the findings from science support racial rankings, or were the findings developed with the goal of providing a scientific—and thus more legitimate—rationale for continuing society's racial hierarchy?[26] The history suggests that the scientific research that "proved" White racial superiority and the conventional wisdom that Whites were the superior race were not happenstance. The new science—what many labeled "scientific racism"[27]—flourished and gave theories of racial difference a stamp of approval.

The emerging racial science in the eighteenth and nineteenth centuries allowed scientists to reach their conclusions and justifications about racial ranking and the relationship between racial groups from two distinct vantage points. The first, monogenism, was based on the belief that all races belong to one human species. This was rooted in religious doctrine and the belief that all mankind was created from Adam and Eve. According to monogenism, although all races come from the same source, over time some racial groups "declined."[28] This decline resulted in a racial hierarchy that placed Whites at the top, above the other, declining races. The second approach, polygenism, was based on the belief that each race is a separate, distinct species. Polygenism was widely adopted by eighteenth-century researchers who studied crime and deviance. Different racial groups were descended from different Adams. The non-White races ranked below Whites on the racial hierarchy scale.

During this period, numerous "scientific" studies attempted to gather empirical proof that non-Whites were inferior to Whites. In one study, French anatomist Etienne Serres set out to prove that Black people were inferior to White people. In his mid-1860s work, Serres hypothesized that the distance between the navel and penis would vary greatly between White men and Black men. White men, he believed, were more evolved and, therefore, as a group would have a greater distance between the two points.[29] Also during the 1800s, scientist Samuel Morton gathered more than six hundred human skulls to prove the validity of racial ranking. Morton believed that Whites were more advanced and would have larger brains when compared with other racial groups. In his published findings, Morton reported that Whites had larger skulls, followed by Mongolians, Indians, and Ethiopians. However, it was later determined that Morton had manipulated some of the data—he presented only those findings that supported his belief that Whites were racially superior to other racial groups.[30]

The Serres and Morton studies were both part of a larger group of racial research conducted by scientists in the United States and abroad. Each one was designed to validate the status quo: the second-class treatment of non-Whites. This research gave an empirical seal of approval to the social, economic, and political disenfranchisement of Blacks, Indians, and Asians. More to the point, this research, which imposed a racial hierarchy that placed Blacks at the bottom, has been used to justify racial discrimination and racial injustice in the criminal-legal system and beyond.

Outside of the mainstream, racially biased theories of criminality were subject to critique and challenge. Leading the charge was W. E. B. Du Bois.

## W. E. B. Du Bois: Pioneering Study on Race and Society

At the turn of the twentieth century, at the same time that theories of racial difference were the status quo, W. E. B. Du Bois began building a new sociological frontier. Du Bois, a young sociologist—the first Black to receive a sociology doctorate from Harvard—began research on Black offending in Philadelphia.[31] Du Bois noted that attempts to treat Black crime as something separate and distinct from White crime fueled beliefs that the former represented a pathology and the latter a social problem in need of intervention. Black criminality, he said, should be addressed by using the "the very remedies which the world is using on all submerged classes," with "goodness," "beauty," "truth," and "faith in humanity."[32]

In his wide-ranging work *The Philadelphia Negro*, Du Bois combined theory, empirical research, and statistics to develop an understanding of Philadelphia's Black community during the late 1800s. Du Bois's comprehensive study gathered data from more than nine thousand Black people who lived in Philadelphia. His findings offer a deep and broad look at Black life and an exploration of how crime is deeply rooted in social conditions. This groundbreaking Philadelphia study, however, was only one of his seminal contributions.

In fact, Du Bois's largest sociological gift was developing the first school of scientific sociology.[33] He developed this approach while working at Atlanta University.[34] Du Bois believed that in order for the newly emerging social sciences to be "scientific," they must be grounded in empirical research. Du Bois argued that social science should not be modeled after the natural sciences because there is a difference between human behavior and natural phenomena.[35] He was the first social scientist to create a sociological laboratory where empirical research was conducted to scientifically examine the causes of racial inequality. He believed that any claims of racial superiority or inferiority had to be empirically established and not scientific racism accepted as conventional wisdom.[36]

Many consider Du Bois's work essential to our foundational understandings of sociology. Elijah Anderson and others describe Du Bois as a "founding father" of sociology.[37] Historians have suggested that the predominant racial theories of Du Bois's day—which equated Blackness with inferiority—may explain why so many decades passed before he was acknowledged as a founding member of sociology.[38] Today, mainstream criminology still credits the Chicago School, led by Robert Park, with founding social disorganization in particular and modern sociology in general. Scholars have determined that Park was aware of and chose to ignore Du Bois's research, which had been completed more than two decades earlier.[39] Understanding the historical prominence of scientific research that promoted racial ranking helps make sense of contemporary attitudes and biases that link race and deviance.

In contemporary times there is no dearth of theories offered to explain the relationship between race and crime, how race impacts treatment of victims, and how race predicts the likelihood of arrest, conviction, and sentencing of defendants. For the most part, research on race and crime is focused on Blacks, sometimes on Latinos, and less so on Native Americans and other groups of color. Most notably, it is rarely focused on White criminality (see the detailed discussion in chapter 6). Some criminologists have argued that new racialized perspectives on the ways that race and crime interact are necessary to reduce disparities and enhance fairness within the criminal-legal system.[40]

## Discrimination and Disparity

The issues of racial disparity and racial discrimination are central to analyzing the relationship between race and crime. In some instances, these distinct concepts are treated as one and the same. They are not the same, though they may be causally related and may coexist. Distinguishing between them is important since they invite different policy responses.

Racial disparity exists when a racial group is represented in crime statistics at a rate much higher or much lower than its rate in the general population. A comparison between the rate of Black arrests and White arrests provides an example. In 2018, Whites constituted approximately 70 percent of all arrests. This means that Whites were arrested at a level that approximates their rate in the overall population (about 67 percent). In contrast, Blacks made up approximately 26 percent of all arrests. Since Blacks are approximately 13 percent of the US population, they are disproportionately overrepresented in arrest figures. When racial disparity exists, it signals that something is going on between race and crime, but it does not tell us the reason for the racial disparity. One way to think about racial disparity is that it operates as an alarm bell. However, it does not tell us why the bell is ringing. The disparity could result from a variety of factors. The reason for the disparity may be that the racial group offends at a higher or lower rate than its percentage in the overall population. Another reason for the racial disparity could be that the police target (or ignore) members of that racial group. It is also possible that a combination of factors is at work making it more likely that a particular racial group will become enmeshed in the justice system. Factors may include individual-level choices, systemic responses (e.g., police deployment strategies), and structural factors (e.g., low education, low employment, and high concentrations in poor neighborhoods).

Racial discrimination exists when there is evidence that someone receives negative treatment within the criminal-legal system based in part on race. Where racial discrimination exists, it is an indication that the court system handles people within it (offenders and victims) differently based on their skin color. The discrimination may be the result of the actions of individual actors or units within the system (e.g., a judge, a police officer, a lawyer, a juror).[41] Bias may also result from the structure of our system of punishment—for instance, how our justice system determines who is eligible for bail, or which types of crime are considered the most serious (e.g., white-collar crime compared with street crime). A system that operates partly based on a victim's or offenders' income is more likely to snare those at the economic bottom. This group is disproportionately more likely to include people of color. Chapter 4 considers issues of racial disparity and discrimination in greater detail.

### Implicit and Explicit Racial Bias

Another aspect of racial discrimination is whether it is explicit or implicit. Explicit racial discrimination refers to the negative (or positive) treatment given to a member of a group on the basis of race—for instance, a judge or corrections officer who expresses disdain toward Asians. Researchers can measure this type of discrimination when it happens at stages of the court system where race-related data is collected, such as arrest, bail, jury selection, and sentencing.

In many instances, though, racially biased treatment may be more subtle, even unconscious. In recent years, there has been growing attention to the issue of implicit racial bias, such as unconscious bias that indicates dislike of a particular racial group. Most people are not aware that they hold unconscious racial biases and that these biases can lead to racially disparate actions.[42] A growing body of research has demonstrated that implicit racial bias impacts decision-making in the criminal-legal system. For instance, studies indicate that citizens and police officers are more likely to associate Black people with crime than they are members of other racial groups.[43] Also, people are more likely to believe that an object held by a Black person is a weapon than an object held by a White person.[44] Given this, it is no surprise that studies using video simulations show that police officers and citizen participants resort to force more quickly when the perceived offender is Black.[45]

### Defining, Measuring, and Counting Crime

The two main sources of statistical information on crime in the United States are the Uniform Crime Report (UCR) and the National Crime Victimization Survey (NCVS).[46] Most assessments of the incidence and prevalence of crime across the nation are based on these reports. These data include state and federal crimes.

The UCR is an annual publication that provides a broad look at crime counts for various areas, including towns, cities, counties, states, tribal lands, universities, colleges, and the nation. Notably, these counts do not include information on race. The UCR also gathers data on persons arrested. These data are based on monthly reports submitted by more than twelve thousand law enforcement agencies. The annual reports on arrests include information on a range of factors, including race, sex, and age. This includes arrests for murder and nonnegligent manslaughter, forcible rape, robbery, aggravated assault, burglary, motor vehicle theft, larceny-theft, and arson. The UCR also collects data on crimes cleared and law enforcement personnel.

The NCVS was initiated to provide detailed information on criminal incidents, victims, and crime trends. As part of the NCVS, each year the Bureau of Justice Statistics interviews a representative national sample of approximately 160,000 people age twelve and older. The NCVS gathers information on crimes experienced by people in the household. The data include both reported and unreported crimes, and detailed information about victims, offenders, and the criminal incidents.[47] The NCVS data address a significant void since, in many instances, victims do not report crime. The NCVS captures statistics on crimes that were not reported to the police. Under NCVS reporting, the victim provides information on the offender's race. Notably, crime victims' perceptions may be skewed toward believing the offender was Black.

## What's Missing?

The UCR and NCVS data undoubtedly capture a major chunk of US crime. However, they do not present a complete picture of the nation's criminal activity. For instance, until recently there was a data gap on incidents involving police violence. Only in the past few years has the federal government gathered statistics on police use of force. Several years prior to this, the *Washington Post* began compiling its "Fatal Force" report, which provides detailed data on police killings by race, gender, state, and whether the victim had a weapon.[48] Lynching is another example of a crime for which there is no official data collection. As recently as

2020, the US Congress came close to making lynching a federal crime. The legislation, however, did not include a requirement of data collection.[49] The United States collected data on lynchings from 1882 to 1968 (see chapter 3 for a detailed discussion of lynching).[50] While the number of lynchings has declined sharply since the early to mid-twentieth century,[51] they still take place.[52]

When official statistics are collected for a particular offense it is a statement that the harm is important enough for the state to take notice and keep records. Arguably, the reverse is true; the failure of the government to gather data regarding a particular harm sends a message that the harm is insignificant in the eyes of the law and the justice system.

Another, much broader group of harms is missing from national crime data: actions that cause harm but have not been labeled criminal. These actions present a twist on the popular conundrum that asks us to consider whether a tree that falls in the woods makes a noise if no one is present to hear it. There are many examples of harms that fall within this definition. A racial hoax is an example of an action that causes harm but is not considered a crime. A racial hoax happens when someone commits a crime and falsely blames someone based on their race or when someone fabricates a crime and blames it on another person because of their race. Notably, the law does not uniformly criminalize the harm or impact of falsely accusing a person of a crime based on race (see chapter 5 for more detail on racial hoaxes).

The bottom line is that not every race-related harm is against the law. This fact should be part of the discussion and analysis of the limits of how national statistics on crime rates can help us understand the relationship between race and crime. Actions that are labeled as "crime" reflect society's values regarding which harms are important enough to punish. We might think of these uncounted crimes as part of the "dark figures of crime." They do not register on the criminal-legal system's radar because they are not counted as crimes.

## Why Study Race, Crime, and the Criminal-Legal System?

The material in this chapter provides an overview of important history, definitions, and issues that are connected to race and crime, and how various racial groups are processed by the justice system. Important questions remain: *Why* is it important to study race and crime? As a society, what do we gain from having deeper knowledge on this topic? Related to this, are there any costs or burdens associated with examining issues of race and crime?

## Benefits of Studying Race and Crime

Examining the connection between crime and race has many upsides. Race has played a key role in the foundation and evolution of the American criminal-legal system. This history has an impact on present-day beliefs and practices in the courts, in corrections, and by law enforcement. Therefore, taking account of race is necessary to understanding the role it plays in today's criminal law system. Also, there are stark racial disparities in how our criminal laws are applied. The rates of correctional supervision—prison, jail, probation, and parole—for Blacks and Latinos, for instance, are substantially higher than the rates for Whites. Ignoring or minimizing these disparities will not make them go away. Last, researchers and policy makers cannot enact laws and sponsor programs to address and reduce these disparities without race and crime data and research.

## Concerns about Studying Race and Crime

One concern about studying race and crime is that discussing any connection between the two may cause some people to think that something about race causes involvement with crime. Some people will assume (consciously or unconsciously) that discussing race and crime together means there must be a link between genetics, race, and criminality. This assumption is not surprising given the long history of attempts to find scientific proof of White racial superiority. Some researchers have continued to argue for a genes-crime-race connection. It appears that whenever issues of race and crime are discussed in the open (or behind closed doors), some people conclude that genetics explain or largely account for racial disparities in the criminal-legal system. There appears to be a generational resurgence and popularity of theories that offer biology or genetics as the primary explanation for racially disparate crime rates.[53]

A second concern about focusing on race is that it diminishes an intersectional understanding of how crime happens. Race is only one of the many factors that may explain an individual's involvement in criminal activity. Nonracial variables that are relevant to criminal involvement may include socioeconomic status, education, employment, age, and neighborhood. Criminology studies show that these variables are significant predictors of criminal activity.

A third issue relates to one of the core points discussed throughout this chapter: the fact that race is a social construct. Some people may have the viewpoint that because race is a social construction, this minimizes the need for discussions about race and crime. According to this logic, if race is not a real thing, then it should not be part of our analysis and discussions about crime. However, acknowledging the fact that race is a human creation—with definitions that have evolved over time—does not make race any less real. The fact that biological definitions of race are social fictions does not erase society's legal and political definitions of race.

The benefits associated with studying race and crime greatly outweigh the costs. One goal of this book is to demonstrate the value of openly addressing the relationship between crime and race in our justice system. As well, this book addresses the ways that race is linked with other crime-related factors and how society's decisions about punishment are tied to race.

## A Note on Terminology

Researchers, scholars, and laypeople have critiqued and questioned the racial fairness and equity of the American justice system. In the interest of accuracy and to avoid any implicit suggestion that the system is racially equitable, this book primarily uses "criminal-legal system" rather than criminal justice system. When discussing reports or studies, I use the racial terms employed in the cited research. When speaking more generally about various racial groups, the following terminology appears.

This book uses "Black" and "African American" interchangeably. Notably, "Black" includes a larger group of people than "African American," since "Black" is not limited to African Americans who live in the United

States and are descendants of enslaved people. "Black" includes people across the African diaspora, from Africa, the Caribbean, South America, and Europe. The terms "Latino" or "Latina" are used interchangeably with "Latinx." Both of these are preferred over "Hispanic." "Asian American" (rather than "Asian") is used to describe people of Asian descent who live in the United States. "Indigenous Americans," "First Nations," or "Indigenous Peoples" are the terms primarily used to describe groups also referred to as "Native American" or "American Indian." "White" is the preferred term to describe the US racial group in the majority, rather than "European" or "Caucasian." Where reference is made to a specific study, the racial terminology employed in the study appears.

2

# Media Messages

The medium is the message.
—Marshall McLuhan[1]

Pick a media platform, any one: television, radio, newspaper, magazines, books, Twitter, blogs, websites, or other social media. Each one has its own power and its own unique ability to make us see the world through a wide or specific lens. However, even with the acute rise in the number of media formats, the messages and images about race and particular racial groups are frequently stereotypical ones. Consider these broad racial truths or "media race-isms" about specific racial groups:

Indigenous Americans: Members of this group are rarely featured in national news stories, television series, movies, or commercials.

Asian Americans: They are infrequently featured in national news and entertainment stories. They are sometimes featured as media players (e.g., anchors, pundits, scholars).

Latinos: Members of this group have some presence in national news stories, as actors, athletes, entertainers, and journalists. They are infrequently shown as having a seat at the media table.

Blacks: Members of this group are regularly seen as news subjects,, news reporters, entertainers, athletes, and scholars.

Whites: Members of this group are the predominant face of US news, politics and entertainment. They are featured in every aspect of news production, as owners, reporters, producers, and subjects.

The above race-isms may seem to offer an unfairly harsh portrait of how race is represented across the media today. After all, much has improved over prior decades. People of color are regularly seen on television, in sitcoms, dramas, movies, commercials, and the news. Although this is true, not as much has changed as we might imagine, and the changes that have occurred are not as diverse as we might think. When it comes to race and crime, the media play a pivotal role in constructing and enforcing our collective racial consciousness. Media representations direct our beliefs about which racial groups are dominant, which ones are deviant, and which ones deserve the most or least attention by social institutions. As well, through media narratives we learn which racial groups constitute "good victims" and which symbolize the "likely criminals." In this way, the media operate in various capacities, as windows, tour guides, and mirrors.[2]

This chapter looks at the mainstream representations of Indigenous Peoples, Asian Americans, Latinos, and African Americans. The focus is purposely not on Whites, who are the dominant racial face in the media. They are the racial group with the greatest media visibility and representation across media outlets, particularly in television and entertainment. One study found that Whites (67 percent of the US population), comprise nearly 80 percent of the characters in top-rated, prime-time television shows. In addition to being disproportionately overrepresented in the media, Whites are more likely to be shown in positions of authority, as the main character, the person with the most desirable attributes, and as the character with the most screen time.[3]

## Indigenous Americans

Challenge yourself to come up with a recent news story involving Native Americans in the mainstream news. Push yourself to name a few prominent, living Native Americans. This will be a challenge for most people. As part of a class exercise, I ask my students to describe the prevailing images that come to mind for various racial groups. When asked about Native Americans, typical responses include, "spiritual," "alcoholic," "noble," "violence," and "gambling." Except for the latter, these descriptions reflect historical stereotypes of Indians.

Further, most students have a hard time naming an Indigenous person—in their communities, in their states, or at the national level. Over the years, my students have offered a handful of names, such as author Sherman Alexie, former congressman Ben Nighthorse Campbell, and Cherokee activist and tribal leader Wilma Mankiller. It is much easier for my students to name centuries-old Native people, such as Sitting

Bull, Crazy Horse, or Sacagawea. In 2021, Deb Haaland became the first Indigenous American named to a cabinet position, secretary of the interior. As is true for most of my students, most who are non-Indigenous do not personally know someone who is Native American.

More than 2.3 million people identify themselves as American Indian or Alaskan Native. This is approximately 1.3 percent of the US population. Given that Native Americans make up such a small percentage of the United States population, the prevailing perceptions are formed by media images and other forms of cultural transmission. As a result, the impressions most people have of Native Americans are not based on any actual exchanges or interactions with Indigenous group members.[4]

A 2018 report by the First Nations Development Institute and Echo Hawk Consulting looks at the representation of Native Americans and perceptions of them held by other racial groups. The report, *Changing the Narrative about Native Americans*, found that media attention about American Indians (when it exists) focuses on stereotypes or deficits.[5] It also finds that nearly 90 percent of the information about Native Americans included in states' school curriculum involves discussions of Indigenous Americans *before* the 1900s. In one startling finding, 40 percent of survey respondents did not know that there are still Native people in the United States. The Report concludes that Native Americans are largely invisible in contemporary society, do not control their media image, have a "deficit" public narrative, and are subject to political and legal decisions that are based on stereotypes. Researcher Paul Leavitt and his colleagues conclude that images of Native Americans are "frozen in time":

> [Native Americans] are rarely seen as contemporary figures in the media. . . . They are absent from depictions of mainstream public spaces, such as schools and hospitals, and from many professional positions, such as teachers, professors, doctors, and lawyers.[6]

An example of this is the image of a Native American woman with a feather in her hair that has been on the packages of Land O'Lakes butter for nearly a century. In 2020, the company decided to replace the image. The head of the National Congress of American Indians commented, "Americans need to learn the truth about the beauty and diversity of tribal nations, peoples, and cultures today."[7]

The prevailing invisibility narrative makes it harder to see Native Americans and easier to believe that they exist outside of and separate from mainstream society. The perceived spatial distance may support the idea that Native Peoples are somehow different. In fact, most Native Americans do *not* live on tribal lands or reservations—75 percent live in rural or urban locations.

In light of this discussion, which shows how Native Americans are portrayed as others, let's consider the Nike shoe specifically designed for Native Americans. In 2007, Nike introduced the Nike Air Native 7 tennis shoe, adorned with feathers and arrowheads.[8] The shoe led to debates about whether it reflects corporate cultural sensitivity, crass capitalism, or something else. Given that Nike does not make other race-specific shoes, this tennis shoe furthers the perception that American Indians are separate from everyone else—spatially and culturally.

The use of Native American names and images for professional sports teams, specifically for their names, logos, and mascots, has been an ongoing issue. Following decades of protests, in 2020 Daniel Snyder, owner of the NFL franchise then called the Washington Redskins, was pushed to change the team name and logo, yielding to pressure from corporate sponsors, including FedEx and Nike. For many Native Peoples, the term "redskin" is a slur. Historically, the term was a derogatory racial description.[9] It refers to the practice by Whites of hunting and killing Indians and providing their scalps as proof for the payment of a bounty.

Contemporary stories about Native Peoples often focus on gambling casinos. News stories also focus on fights to preserve sacred Indian lands. A recent example is the protest by Native Americans and others against the building of the Dakota Access Pipeline. Beginning in 2016, protesters rallied against the 1,172-mile pipeline, arguing that it was built through Indian reservations (including the Standing Rock Sioux), and that it had destroyed ancestral lands and sacred sites. Pipeline protesters also raised concerns about the possibility that the pipeline would contaminate the Missouri River, the water supply source for millions of Americans.

In 2004, the US Justice Department released a comprehensive report on crime and Native Americans. The study, a statistical profile of Indians from 1992 to 2002, revealed high levels of victimization for Native Americans. One startling finding was that Native Americans are two times as likely to be victims of violent crime (rape, aggravated assault, and robbery) as are African Americans. They are also the group most likely to be victims of interracial crime—harmed by someone who is not an Indigenous person. Not surprisingly, COVID-19 has had a severely disproportionate impact on Native communities as well. In some counties the death rate for American Indians and Alaskan Natives is four times greater than their percentage in the population.[10]

A 2017 study on jails estimated that in 2014 there were approximately 10,400 American Indians and Alaskan Natives in jail, approximately 1.4 percent of the jail population. Relatively little media attention that focuses on Native Americans addresses issues of crime and violence, nor does it highlight the fact that Native Americans are the only racial group subject to three separate criminal-legal systems—state, federal, and tribal courts.

All told, the story of Native Americans and mainstream media imagery is largely one of invisibility. The US Native American population is relatively small, and there are few well-known Indigenous people. As a result, ancient, decades-old representations of Native Americans persist. Further, non–Native Americans control and are responsible for the skewed mainstream images of Indigenous Americans. As noted, these images have real-life consequences for Native Americans, including policies, legislation, and legal decisions.

## Asian Americans

As media representations go, Asian Americans fare better than Native Americans. This is notable given that there are eighteen million Asian Americans—6 percent of the US population. One indicator of their muted media presence is that there are a handful of fairly well-known Asian American women and men. The short list for women includes actresses Sandra Oh and Mindy Kaling; comedians Awkwafina and Ali Wong; personalities Chrissy Teigen, and Jeannie Mai; and fashion designer Vera Wang. Representations of Asian American men are scarce across US media. There are few reasonably well-known Asian American men. The list includes actors Dev Patel, Aziz Ansari, George Takei, Ken Jeong, and Randall Park. Best-selling author and physician Deepak

Chopra is also a familiar name to many people. During his run for president in 2020, Andrew Yang was a media mainstay.

Asian American men often play characters who are romantically-undesirable sidekicks, workaholics, or technology geeks who are decidedly unhip. They typically do not get the girl but may help the White main character achieve his romantic or sexual conquests. While these characters may have positive attributes, they usually lack breadth. An example is the loyal but somewhat bumbling, date-challenged character such as Adhir Kalyan's character in the movie *Rules of Engagement*. Increasingly, more fully developed, sexually desirable Asian male characters are on display. Examples include Alexander Hodge's role on HBO's *Insecure*; Simu Liu's character in the Netflix series, *Kim's Convenience*, Robert Wu's character in the STARZ series *Survivor's Remorse*; and Kumail Nanjiani in the movie *The Big Sick*.

The one-drop rule (discussed in chapter 1) applies not just to people with mixed Black and White heritage, but also to some who have Black and Asian heritage. The rule appears to apply to golf phenomenon Tiger Woods. Woods, whose mother is from Thailand and father is African American. Although Woods, a four-time winner of the Masters Tournament, has spoken openly of his Thai heritage on his mother's side, most people classify him as an African American. This racial coding is a clear application of the one-drop rule. Racial labeling seems to have worked somewhat differently for tennis star Naomi Osaka. The 2021 Australian Open winner, who was born in Japan, has a Japanese mother and Haitian father. Osaka, who embraces her biracial heritage, is widely admired in Japan and the United States. Some press reports on Osaka have noted her mixed-race lineage but do not always assign her a racial label, such as referring to her country of birth (Japan).[11] In contrast to both Woods and Osaka, US vice president Kamala Harris, who is also biracial (Indian mother and Haitian father), identifies as Black.

In the seven decades since television was invented, there have been only *three* television shows that have featured an Asian American family. Most recently was *Fresh Off the Boat*, which premiered in 2015. Before that there was *Dr. Ken*, a comedy show that ran from 2015 to 2017, featuring Ken Jeong in the lead role. Prior to these two was the show *All American Girl*, a 1990s comedy. The show, which ran for one season, starred Margaret Cho. In the 1960s and 1970s, Asian Americans were typically cast in stereotypical, subservient roles—for instance, Mrs. Livingston, the housekeeper and nanny on *The Courtship of Eddie's Father*. An exception is Don Ho's character in *Hawaii Five-O*, the 1970s television series.

Asian Americans are mostly absent from news stories as presenters and subjects of the news. They are cast as objects of both desirability and disdain. The desirability includes both sexual attractiveness (women) and intelligence (men). On the other side, though, is an image of otherness—as geeks and as foreigners. The standard media portrayals of Asian Americans were turned upside down with the 2018 movie Crazy Rich Asians. The movie was a huge success, earning more than $240 million. It depicts cross-cultural and cross-generational relationships between Asian Americans and Asians, features Asian men and women in romantic relationships, and has a range of multifaceted Asian characters. There's a similar representational breadth in the 2019 film Always Be My Maybe, which has two Asian Americans playing the romantic lead roles.

Another common representation of Asian Americans is as the "model minority." According to the model-minority myth, Asian Americans are hardworking, smart, and respectful of authority. This description places Asians atop other groups of color. This casts a negative light on Blacks, Latinos, and Indigenous Americans, because it suggests that they should be more like Asian Americans. Media portrayals of Asian American men are more likely to fit the myth than portrayals of Asian American women. Many Asian Americans reject the model-minority stereotype as inaccurate and divisive within the Asian community and across racial groups.

An example of this division is the reaction to the 2014 lawsuit filed by a group of Asian American students against Harvard. In *Students for Fair Admissions v. Harvard*, Asian students said that their race played in role in the application process, in violation of the 1964 Civil Rights Act. They presented data showing that Asian students had higher test scores yet greater rates of rejection, and the lowest "personal rating" scores of any racial group. The judge found that Harvard did not discriminate against Asians in the admissions process. Citing benefits of diversity, the judge stated, "It is not yet time to look beyond race in college admissions," and that diversity "will foster the tolerance, acceptance and understanding that will ultimately make race conscious admissions obsolete."[12] The case, a challenge to Harvard's affirmative-action admissions programs, highlighted some interracial tensions between Asians and members of other groups of color and intraracial tensions between members of the Asian community.[13]

In 2020, one of the biggest threats to representations of Asian Americans came from the coronavirus pandemic. COVID-19, widely believed to have originated in Wuhan, China, was called the "Chinese virus" by then–US president Donald Trump. Language like this caused some people to blame Chinese people and other Asians for the deadly virus. As a result, anti-Asian acts of aggression climbed rapidly in the United States, with rising numbers of incidents in which Asian Americans were physically attacked, spit upon, verbally harassed, and subjected to online threats and taunting. In 2020, the Center for Extremism and Hate reported a 150 percent increase in anti-Asian hate crimes. In 2021, a White man went on a killing spree in Atlanta and killed eight people, including six Asian women. The deadly attacks took place at three nail spas.

The dearth of Asian American representations suggests that "Asian American" has a monolithic meaning. This one-box-fits-all category reduces Asians to a single group and obscures the fact that—in addition to China, Japan, and Korea—Asia includes Vietnam, Cambodia, Indonesia, Singapore, Malaysia, Thailand, Taiwan, Laos, India, and Pakistan. These countries are not culturally interchangeable.

## Latinos and Latinas

At 18 percent of the US population, Latinos and Latinas are the country's largest group of color. However, given their numbers, they have a relatively small presence in the major media as news reporters and entertainers and influencers. In recent years, their greatest presence has been as news subjects, particularly on immigration-related topics. During Donald Trump's presidency, for instance, he called for building a wall to keep Mexicans from entering the United States. He also called for policies that made immigration more difficult and ultimately punished Mexicans who sought to enter the United States, including the policy of separating children from their families upon entry to the country.

There are a number of high-profile Latinos, primarily entertainers. A list of well-known Latinos includes America Ferrera, Gina Rodriguez, Eva Longoria, Sofia Vergara, Salma Hayek, Rita Moreno, George Lopez, Jennifer Lopez, Gloria Estefan, Alex Rodriguez, and Pitbull. Latino politicians include Juan Castro, Julian Castro, and Alexandria Ocasio-Cortez.

Few TV series have centered on a Latino family. *Jane the Virgin*, which starred Gina Rodriguez, aired from 2015 to 2019, and the Latino reboot of *One Day at a Time*, starring Rita Moreno, was on from 2017 to 2019. There have been Latino and Latina actors cast as leads on some shows, including *Magnum P.I.* and *Modern Family*. Prior to these shows there was an even smaller presence of Latinos on TV. There was *Ugly Betty and The George Lopez Show, which* featured a Latino family. In the 1990s, Michael DeLorenzo co-starred on *New York Undercover*, the first show to have lead co-stars who were Black and Latino. *Chico and the Man*, which ran from 1974 to 1978, was the first television show with a Latino lead actor, Freddie Prinze.

Representation of the Latino community has not been much better in movies. They comprise under 5 percent of on-screen movie roles, which is notable given that Latinos and Latinas are responsible for nearly one-fourth of all ticket sales.[14] With the relentless media focus on relationships between Blacks and Whites, Latino people are frequently overlooked as part of "official" media portrayals of race. An example of this omission involves a PBS documentary on World War II produced by Ken Burns. During previews it was observed that the film made scant reference to Latino veterans or their contributions to the war. Following a great deal of criticism and pressure, Burns ultimately agreed to feature narratives from Latino and Indigenous American veterans, including on-camera testimony, personal archives, and combat history.

Latino people, like Asian Americans, are often cast as outsiders, foreigners, low-wage workers, or criminals. National and regional media discussions about the Latino community often revolve around issues of immigration, specifically illegal immigration and border patrol along the southwestern US states. This includes discussion of proposed legislation designed to address border security—to keep out those who live south of the border. It also ties to arguments about bilingualism—for instance, whether the United States should be an "English-only" country and whether Latinos are unfairly burdening social services and the public school systems. Latinos as a group are often discussed on the news but are not always direct participants in these conversations. Recent years, however, have seen increased visibility for Latinos. This racial chatter happens in varied media arenas, including the Sunday morning news shows and the late-night talk shows. Latinos are also second in line—behind African Americans—as the face of the feared American criminal.

## African Americans

The media offers a mixed bag of images of African Americans, who constitute 13 percent of the US population. Since the 1980s, African Americans have had a huge media presence, as athletes, actors, comedians, singers, lawyers, public intellectuals, talk-show hosts, journalists, professors, entrepreneurs, authors, doctors, and artists. Annual polls show that Americans consistently place African American celebrities on the list of people they most admire, including Oprah Winfrey, Barack Obama, Michelle Obama, and Michael Jordan. At the same time, African Americans are also on the list of the most reviled celebrities, a list that includes Bill Cosby and O. J. Simpson.

Today's reality is in stark contrast to earlier times, when it was rare to see Black people on television. On this topic, Oprah Winfrey has said that when she was growing up in the 1950s and 1960s, a family member would announce, "Black people on!" so that everyone in the house could come witness this unusual event.

At its inception, television operated as a segregated space. It was surprising to see people of color, and when they did appear, they were reduced to stock, stereotypical roles. For African Americans this meant playing the butler, maid, chauffer, or entertainer. There were some firsts. In the 1950s, crooner Nat King Cole was the first Black person to have his own television show. *The Nat King Cole Show* premiered as a weekly fifteen-minute variety show. The broadcast, however, was short-lived. Advertisers shunned the show, fearful that southern audiences would boycott their products.

In response to the long-standing barriers to entry, Black people developed their own organizations to showcase their talent. This was true for sports, where the Harlem Globetrotters, the Negro Leagues (baseball), the United Golf Association, and other organizations were created to provide a space for Black athletes. Filmmakers also developed Black creative spaces. The works of pioneering Black film directors, such as Oscar Micheaux, Tressie Souders, Clarence Muse, and Melvin Van Peebles, offered more nuanced portraits of Black life.[15] The Black press—particularly newspapers and magazines—was instrumental in providing an authentic, and informed presentation of African American life. In the 1950s, the TV program *Amos and Andy* provoked a great deal of criticism for its portrayal of Blacks, leading to a boycott by the NAACP. The show, which had the catchphrase "Ain't dat sumpthin'!," was viewed by many as a form of minstrelsy with portrayals of Blacks as dishonest, greedy, and moronic.

During the 1960s, African Americans were an increasing presence on television, primarily as entertainers or professional athletes, on shows such as *The Ed Sullivan Show* and *The Tonight Show* with Johnny Carson. In the following decade, TV series featured Blacks in lead roles, including Diahann Carroll in *Julia* and Bill Cosby in *I Spy*. Some shows centered on African Americans, including comedies *Sanford and Son, Good Times, What's Happening!!*, and *The Jeffersons*, and *Soul Train*, a music dance show. Blacks, however, were more likely to be part of an ensemble cast—for example, in *Room 222, Welcome Back Kotter, Hill Street Blues*, and *Benson*. Black actors found some roles available in mainstream Hollywood movies, such as *Sounder, Lady Sings the Blues, Claudine*, and *Mahogany*. Daytime soap operas also began to include more African Americans. Comedian Flip Wilson had a popular weekly variety show.

During the same period, there was a sharp rise in "Blaxploitation" films such as *Shaft, Superfly*, and *Coffy*. Many Black people decried these films as perpetuating negative stereotypes and one-dimensional portrayals of Black life. Other Black film offerings, such as *Cooley High* and *Five on the Black Hand Side*,[16] sought to show Black life through varied lenses, including class conflict within the Black community and the strength of male and female friendship bonds.

The 1980s and 1990s saw a rise in the number of Blacks featured in the media—as sitcom stars, major recording artists, business owners, sports legends, new members of the middle class, authors of best-selling books, talk-show hosts, and Pulitzer Prize winners. During this period a range of television shows featured African Americans as lead characters, such as *The Cosby Show, Frank's Place, A Different World,* and *Living Single.*

During this same period, rap music became an increasingly popular music choice for American youth. Straying from its origins, rap, which began as fun and boastful, became a political force, then shifted to become gangsta rap. The lyrics were bold, angry, and in your face. The rap music video, which by then was a staple of cable television, featured barely clad women, young men with guns, and simulated sex. These images became a large part of the media's visual representation of African American youth. Many observers cried foul—to radio stations, music companies, and Congress.

Rap and hip-hop music continue to shape how Blackness is presented and consumed. Hip hop—the music, clothes, language, and affect—is a major US export. The music continues to face criticism for its language, depictions of women, and crass materialism—and emphasis on high-end designer clothes, expensive cars, mansions, and ostentatious jewels. Given the popularity of rap music and its influence, many people have appealed to rappers to present alternative, more complex faces of Black life. For many who listen to rap, particularly non-Blacks, the music may be the singular racial contact they have with African American life.

## Contemporary Black Narratives

In the first two decades of the twenty-first century, there have been at least three phenomena that have led to a shift in public narratives about Blackness. The first event was Barack Obama's 2008 election as the first African American president of the United States. His presidency led to widespread discussions about race. Over the course of his two-term presidency, Obama and his Black family, who were the physical representation of the United States, played a dominant role in shifting the collective cultural consciousness around race (in ways both positive and negative)—more than any news show, court case, comedy show, social media thread, or movie.

Second, the release of two movies created additional stepping stones for an African American presence in the mainstream media. The first of these was Moonlight, which had an all-Black cast. The film tells the coming-of-age story of a young Black boy who is gay. The moving and riveting movie won the Academy Award for Best Picture in 2016. Two years later the release of Black Panther became a megacultural phenomenon. The film was a national and international sensation. The movie—featuring a nearly all-Black cast, with actors representing the range of the African diaspora—proved that people of all racial backgrounds would support a Black movie.

The third is the centrality of incidents involving violence against African Americans. The 2012 killing of seventeen-year-old Trayvon Martin by George Zimmerman was a catalyzing event that led to a national focus on the everyday perils African Americans encounter when walking, running, shopping, driving, gardening—"Living While Black." The subsequent high-profile videotaped police killings of African Americans resulted in a national rallying cry against excessive use of force by police and civilians. Trayvon Martin's case planted the seeds for the Black Lives Matter movement. Martin's killing and others laid the foundation for the public reaction to George Floyd's killing eight years later. Floyd, a Black man, was killed by a White Minneapolis police officer in broad daylight, in front of other officers and citizens. The videotape of the incident shows that officer Derek Chauvin held his knee on Floyd's neck for more than nine minutes. As he lay dying, Floyd calls for his "Momma," and said 27 times, "I can't breathe." The video of Floyd's death led to a seismic shift in the public conversation about the relationship between policing and African Americans—from a discussion about Blacks as perpetrators of crime to a discussion of Blacks as *victims* of state violence. In a verdict that surprised many, Derek Chauvin was convicted of killing Floyd on all three counts—second-degree murder, third-degree murder, and second-degree manslaughter.

## Trends, Issues, and Concerns

This section highlights some overlapping issues among racial groups and identifies some areas of concern regarding media representations. Given that people of color constitute more than one-third of the US population, it is troubling that so few minorities are visible within the mainstream media. Among all groups of color, some overlapping issues are present.

## MISSING PEOPLE

Some practices work to "disappear" people of color from the media. A particularly interesting example occurs when a television show is set in a geographical area with a large minority population but does not include them in the story. Two long-running series, *Seinfeld* and *Sex in the City*, were criticized for showing very little ethnic diversity in racially rich New York City. A much earlier series, *Magnum, P.I.*, faced similar criticism: the show, set in Honolulu, had relatively few Asian actors.

The fact that Indigenous Americans and Asian Americans are largely absent from the mainstream media does not mean that they are completely invisible. The dearth of representation by members of particular racial groups means that members of *other* racial groups will shape the less visible groups' public narrative. For instance, unflattering "jokes" by White comedians about Asian Americans (e.g., driving skills, speech patterns)are problematic because Asian Americans have fewer outlets through which to respond.

Allowing a racial group to be defined by members of other racial groups is problematic. The point here is not whether comedians or satirists should be entitled to say what they want to say. Rather, we should *notice* when a racial group does not have a self-determined media image. We should know the difference between a racial group that is able to successfully shape and mold its media image and one that cannot. Groups that fall into the latter category are unable to say who they are and are forced to occupy racial boxes—good, bad, or otherwise—created by members of other racial groups.

Another facet of the missing-people issue is that seeing an African American family is increasingly rare. Specifically, there are few representations of a family with a Black father, Black mother, and Black children. Again, this may be the media's attempt to highlight more diverse families. However, this trend raises concerns as to the message it sends about the Black family.

## LESS MEDIA OR MORE?

More than any other time in history, Black people today are often featured prominently across the media. However, portrayals of Blacks as buffoons and criminals persist. The new wave of Black images, which includes images of Black success, do not counterbalance images of Black criminality, because Black success is given a unique interpretation. In the minds of many people, particularly Whites, Blacks have already "overcome" and no longer have a legitimate basis for complaining about racism. In many instances, though, Black superstars may be treated as "honorary Whites."

A scene from Spike Lee's movie *Do the Right Thing* illustrates this point. In the scene, two young men, Mookie, who is Black, and Pino, who is White, discuss racism. Pino hates Black people and refers to them as "niggers." In an attempt to point out his racial double standard, Mookie reminds Pino that his favorite celebrities are Black (Magic Johnson, Eddie Murphy, and Prince). Pino responds, "They're not really niggers. . . . They're not really Black, they're more than Black."[17] Lee continued to explore the theme of racial representation in his movie *Bamboozled*. Lee's depictions of Black people force the viewer to consider whether the portrayals of Blackness in the early 1900s are demonstrably different from the portrayals in the late 1900s. Though there are more positive images of African Americans today than in earlier eras, racial images have not changed as much as we might presume. To some, Blacks who achieve large-scale success and acclaim—such as Oprah Winfrey, Barack Obama, or Beyonce—transcend their Blackness and ultimately become colorless. At the same time, those Blacks who conform to the racialized stereotypes are "Black." In this racial calculus, famous African Americans tell the story of racial progress. Blacks who are the face of the Black community are largely ones who live in the margins, those who are poor, downtrodden, or deviant.

Given this complex imagery, Black people are predictably viewed as emblematic of both success and deviance. The contradictory media representation of Blackness signals a double-edged resentment: the threat of Black crime and the threat of Black success. The result is cross-wired thinking about Blacks and Blackness. As is true for most Whites, most Blacks are neither super-successful nor super-deviant.

Today Blacks are ubiquitous across mainstream media. Two generations ago, it would have been hard to envision so many Black faces looking back at us from commercials, movies, newspapers, magazines, variety shows, comedies, dramas, reality television, game shows, soap operas, and broadcast news. All of this leads to the question of whether a more pronounced media presence is always a good thing. What is important to note about race and racial representation in the media, however, is not the volume of images but rather the substance of these portrayals. More media is not always better. Sometimes more is less. When the images are stereotypical and retrograde—such as "cooning" (think *Amos 'n' Andy*)—less is better. So, regardless of increasing representations of Blackness, the important question is whether the racial representations are an advance, a setback, or something else.

Though the media representations of African Americans have grown more diverse, Blacks are still the face of crime in America. For most of us, the media's overpowering images of Black deviance are impossible to ignore. These negative images have been seared into our collective consciousness. Therefore, it is not surprising that many Americans wrongly believe that Blacks are responsible for committing the majority of crime. The onslaught and disproportionality of criminal images of Black men cause many of us to *in*correctly conclude that most Black men are criminals. Most African American men are law-abiding citizens. These media images also make it hard for many people to believe that the overwhelming majority of crime is intraracial, involving an offender and victim who are the same race. Regardless of race, the person most people fear is a young Black man. This is what I label the myth of the *criminalblackman*.

Media and corporate enterprises responded swiftly after George Floyd's killing and the resulting social protests across the nation and around the world. Many companies said they would rethink and retool how they address race and racial disparities. Some took immediate steps by showing support for the Black Lives Matter movement. Some identified specific plans to improve and highlight diversity—increasing the pipeline for people of color—and promised to address systemic racism.[18]

## RACIAL AMBIGUITY AND RACIAL VENTRILOQUISM
Another aspect of examining how race shows up in media spaces is analyzing the presence of racially ambiguous people. These characters appear to be people of color, but their racial group membership is unclear. The viewer is not given any indication of the character's race. The presence of such characters provides diversity ; it is just not clear what exactly to make of this phenomenon. Perhaps this is the mainstream media's nod to the increasing numbers of mixed-raced

individuals, estimated to account for approximately 3 percent of the US population.

Racial Ventriloquism is another twist on the portrayal of people of color within the media. It can be called "racial ventriloquism" when Whites portray characters of color. The entertainment industry has a long history of this practice. Blackface routines were a Vaudeville staple. In the early 1900s, Al Jolson's "mammy" routine was well known. In film, Whites regularly portrayed members of other racial groups. In D. W. Griffith's film *Birth of a Nation*, White actors wore grease paint to portray violent, murderous Black people. White film stars, including Bob Hope and Bing Crosby, performed in Blackface. Whites regularly played Asians in films, such as in the Charlie Chan series. Silver-screen legends Katharine Hepburn and Shirley MacLaine both portrayed Asian women. Also, Whites were regularly cast as American Indians in films. In the 1950s, Burt Lancaster played a Native American athlete in *Jim Thorpe—All American*. Another example is Elizabeth Taylor, who played the lead in *Cleopatra*, the story of the Egyptian queen. In a memorable 1970s anti-littering commercial, a White actor portrayed a Native American, in full Native dress and head gear, who shed a tear after witnessing the impact of litter on the environment. Another example is the 1970s TV series *Kung Fu*, in which White actor David Carradine played the lead role as the martial artist. Singer Madonna was cast in the title role of *Evita*, the story of Argentina's Eva Peron. This phenomenon extends to animation. For thirty years, Hank Azaria, a White actor, voiced the role of Apu, an Indian character on The Simpsons.

This whitewash has not been limited to stage and screen. Prior to the 1960s, it was common for record companies to refuse to place Black recording artists on their own album covers. So-called race music was sanitized for White audiences with cover photographs of White women, landscapes, and other images deemed acceptable to White crossover listeners. The "cover" record represents another turn in the racial landscape of media representations. This occurred when a White recording artist—such as Elvis Presley or Pat Boone—would take a hit song previously recorded by a Black artist and rerecord it, with the goal of making it palatable to White audiences.

Whitewashing also works in ways that reflect skin-tone bias. For instance, sometimes light-skinned Black or Latina actors are selected to play darker-skinned characters. A contemporary example of this was the casting of light-skinned Latina actress Zoe Saldana to play singer Nina Simone, a dark-skinned Black woman. This casting decision led to a huge outcry, particularly on social media. Many expressed concerns that the selection of Saldana—who wore dark brown makeup, a prosthetic nose, and dentures—was performing a kind of Blackface. Similar questions were raised when White actor Joseph Fiennes was hired to play Michael Jackson in a film. Fiennes withdrew from the project following widespread criticism.

Let's consider three points in concluding the discussion of racial ventriloquism. First, one of the core concerns goes to authenticity. If the actor who portrays a person of color is of a different race, it is legitimate to ask whether they can bring adequate cultural, emotional truth to the role. Second, whenever a person of another race plays a character who is a person of color, that is one less acting job available for someone in that racial group. Third, and perhaps most important, racial ventriloquism is not a two-way street. If we get to a place where African American actors are playing White characters (in Whiteface?), this practice might be a less controversial one. Currently, though, race and skin tone matter in media representations of race. This issue has also been discussed in the context of movie roles by Black British actors Cynthia Erivo and Daniel Kalaluya. Both actors have played African American icons. Erivo has portrayed Harriet Tubman and Aretha Franklin, and Kalaluya has played Fred Hampton. In these instances, there were debates about the implications of not casting African Americans for these roles.

## Processing Racial Images

As you continue reading this book, please continue to observe the images of race presented by the media, including social media, television, movies, commercials, and the nightly news. Keep in mind what language is used to describe crime victims and offenders (e.g., "mentally ill," "good kid," "savage," or "honor-roll student"); which photos are used (e.g., graduation photo, mugshot, or family photo), and compare how much time the mainstream media spends on criminal cases involving people of different racial backgrounds. An infamous example of this took place in 2005, in the aftermath of Hurricane Katrina. There were photographs published of two separate hurricane victims wading through chest-high water with store products. The White people wading through water are described as "finding bread and soda from a local grocery store," while the young Black man "walks through chest-deep floodwater after looting a grocery store."[19]

### Future Media Messages

We regularly see people of various races, hues, nationalities, and ethnicities across the media. The material in this chapter pushes us to consider an alternative view of what these new, more racially diverse images mean. Although people of color are visible in various mediums, it is important to consider what these images show us and whether they offer new insights, challenge old stereotypes, or only appear to be something new. The discussion on media representations signals improvement as well as the need for more work to present accurate images of race.

3

## History's Strange Fruit

Southern trees bear a strange fruit
Blood on the leaves and blood at the root
Black bodies swinging in the Southern breeze
Strange fruit hanging from the poplar trees
—"Strange Fruit," Abel Meeropol

While many continue to debate whether the US legal system is fair and just, there is little debate about the system's racist origins. An evaluation of the workings of the contemporary criminal-legal system is incomplete without a consideration of its historical practices and their underlying rationales. In fact, how the US system of laws and punishments operates today is directly linked with how it worked two centuries ago. The operation of the system in place today bears a striking resemblance to the one that existed generations ago.

A review of history is essential to an assessment of racial progress. It is also necessary for an understanding of whether and to what degree past race-based practices still exist within our current system. This approach also allows us to identify the minimal components necessary for a racially-equitable system of punishment. The history of African Americans and the law provides the overarching framework for this discussion.[1] This examination includes some consideration of how other groups of color—specifically, Latinos, Native Americans, and Asians—have fared within the American legal system.

### Slave Codes, Black Codes, Black Laws, and Jim Crow

From 1619 to 1865, slave codes embodied the criminal laws that were enforced against enslaved Africans. Virginia was the first state to adopt this type of legislation. Though codes varied by state, they were uniform in their objective: to regulate slave life from cradle to grave. These statutes not only set forth the applicable law, but in their totality they prescribed the social boundaries for Black slaves. In addition to restricting the daily life of enslaved Blacks, the codes established laws regulating the business of slavery, including which human beings were sold, the hours they could be forced to work, who was responsible when they were injured, the punishment for stealing enslaved humans, and the reward for capturing enslaved persons who escaped.[2]

The harshest criminal penalties were reserved for actions that threatened the institution of slavery, such as slave rebellions. Enslaved people who attempted to escape could face death. Between 1852 and 1862, Harriet Tubman, who escaped to freedom, returned to help more than sixty other enslaved people reach free soil in the North. Tubman, the most famous "conductor" of the Underground Railroad, made nineteen trips. Her success in shepherding people to freedom—as she says she never lost a passenger—made her a "most wanted" person by those trying to capture Black people who fought against bondage. Bounty hunters were promised a large reward for Tubman's return—dead or alive.

Whites feared that those held in bondage would unite and fight against their enslavement. This fear was so widespread that it was considered at the Constitutional Convention and later included within the US Constitution. Under the Fugitive Slave Act, the militia could be ordered to stop invasions and to suppress "insurrections." Whites who acted to undermine slavery—those who helped enslaved people learn to read, organize escapes, and arrange abolition meetings—faced severe penalties under the various slave codes.

### Bloodlines

During the time of slavery, race was used as a political, economic, and social weapon—a marker to determine which racial group would dominate and which racial groups were to be dominated. Whites placed themselves atop the racial hierarchy through a raft of laws that detailed who could *not* be classified as White. Anyone who had even a trace amount of Black blood was precluded from claiming Whiteness. The obsession with racial purity—monitoring the boundaries of Whiteness—is exemplified by laws that measured Blackness and Whiteness by degrees of Black blood. According to the one-drop rule, a Black person was any person with any known African Black ancestry[3] (see chapter 1 for more detail).

Thus, even someone who had more White relatives than Black ones—for instance, someone with one-fourth Black blood (a "quadroon")—was classified as Black. This rule worked to the benefit of White enslavers, as the child of an enslaved person and a slaveholder was a slave. The codes not only created a racial caste system under which Whites and Blacks held separate statuses; they also created an in-between tier for "others," such as mulattoes. An enslaved person's punishment might be determined by his "degree of Blackness." For example, some slave codes excused or reduced a mulatto's punishment if she or he had a White mother.[4] Though slave codes rarely made explicit reference to Native Americans, they too were enslaved and subjected to the inhumane rule of the slave codes.

## Punishments

Table 3.1 shows how Virginia law imposed punishment based on the victim's race and the offender's race. As indicated, enslaved people faced death for numerous criminal offenses. Harsh sanctions, such as brutal public executions, were imposed to keep slaves in their place. Under Maryland law, for example, an enslaved person who was convicted of murder was to be hanged, beheaded, and then drawn and quartered. Following this, his head and body parts were to be publicly displayed. Deterrence is one possible rationale for such a punishment, but the harshness of it suggests that something much larger was at stake: the preservation of White economic dominance.

TABLE 3.1. Criminal Penalties by Race during Slavery, in Virginia.

| Crime | White Offender | Enslaved Black Offender |
|---|---|---|
| Murder (White victim) Petit treason[a] | Maximum penalty, death | Death |
| Murder (Black victim) | Rarely prosecuted Hard labor or death | Whipping (if prosecuted) |
| Rape (White victim) | 10–20 years, whipping, or death | Death or castration[b] |
| Rape (Black victim) | No crime | No crime, exile, or death[c] |
| Assault (White victim) | 1–10 years (if intent to kill) | Whipping, exile, mutilation, or death |

a Murder of a slave owner.
b Same penalty for attempted rape.
c If rape victim was a *free* Black woman, penalty could be death.
Source: A. Leon Higginbotham and Anne Jacobs, "The Law Only as an Enemy: The Legitimization of Racial Powerlessness through the Colonial and Antebellum Criminal Laws of Virginia," North Carolina Law Review 70 (1992): 969–1070

## Criminal Penalties by Race in Virginia

Enslaved Africans faced other barbaric sanctions, including iron branding. Sometimes a letter was burned onto a slave's cheek or forehead to represent the crime committed (e.g., "R" for runaway). Another form of punishment consisted of placing enslaved people in the gallows or requiring them to wear heavy (e.g., five-pound) collars around their necks. Another punishment was to send them to the pillory for offenses such as hog stealing. Their ears were nailed down and later cut off.

Whippings were common. Sometimes referred to as lashes, whippings were administered to the bare back with a leather strap. As brutally depicted in the TV miniseries *Roots* and the movie *Sankofa*, and as hauntingly described in author Toni Morrison's *Beloved*, some slaves were whipped so severely that their backs were disfigured beyond recognition. A number of slave code offenses, such as using abusive language or preaching without permission, mandated thirty-nine lashes.[5] Although some Whites believed that administering more than thirty-nine lashes at one time violated Christian tenets, untold numbers of enslaved people were subjected to whippings of more than one hundred lashes.

Those held in bondage lived with the constant fear that at any time they could be accused of and punished for offenses they did not commit. They also lived with the knowledge that if they were the victims of assault, there was no opportunity for redress—no slavery ombudsperson. The slave codes of most states allowed Whites to beat, slap, and whip with impunity. In *State v. Maner*, an 1834 South Carolina court held that it was not a crime for a White person to assault an enslaved person.[6]

In some instances, however, Whites did face punishment for extreme acts of brutality against enslaved persons. They were punished, however, not because they violated a person's human rights—enslaved people did not have legal rights—but because they had interfered with another person's property rights. For example, under a nineteenth-century South Carolina law, a White man found guilty of killing an enslaved person could be fined. The fine was paid to the owner, not the kin of the murdered person.

## Sexual Assault Crimes

Interracial sex assaults offer the best example of how racial double standards worked under the slave codes. An enslaved Black man who forced sex with a White woman faced the most severe penalty, and a White man who forced sex with an enslaved Black woman faced the least severe penalty. As Table 3.1 indicates, a Black man could be killed for having sexual contact with a White woman. There were more Black men executed for raping a White woman than there were Black men executed for killing a White person.[7] White fear of Black male sexuality is the only possible explanation for why the rape of a White woman by a Black man was the only crime for which castration could be imposed under Virginia law. The fear of Black male sexuality coexisted with the widespread belief in Black inferiority.

The prohibition against interracial liaisons was based on the view that Whiteness and personhood were inextricably linked. Enslaved Black men could never attain manhood. Therefore, Black men had no business with White women. Laws prohibiting interracial intimacy were the first line of defense against race mixing. It was assumed that a White woman would not consent to sex with a Black man. Laws outlawing interracial marriage served as a second line of defense.

The sexual assault of a Black woman was not a crime under most slave codes. This was a crude reflection of the reality that slave women were sexual and economic property. If a slave master wanted to force sex on his human chattel, this was perfectly legal. The number of mulatto children born to slave women was tangible evidence of this practice.

Some codes, though, did punish White men for having sex with Black slaves. In *In re Sweat*, a 1640 Virginia case, the court determined that a White man had impregnated an enslaved Black woman who was owned by another White man. For this race-mixing crime, the White man was sentenced to do "public penance" at a church. This was a slap on the wrist compared with the punishment that the slave woman received. The woman was tied to a whipping post and beaten.

In addition to the ever-present threat of being raped by White men, Black female slaves had a further burden to bear. It was also not a crime for one slave to rape another slave. The formal legal system might be invoked, however, if an assault caused an injury to the slave that hampered her ability to work, because this amounted to economic interference. In Virginia in the 1800s, some case reports involved a Black male slave charged with raping a Black female slave. In the one case that did result in a criminal conviction, the male slave was removed from the county.[8]

Several rationales have been offered to explain why slave codes neither acknowledged nor sanctioned equitably the rape of Black women. One reason is that slave women were viewed as naturally promiscuous, making forced sex a legal impossibility.[9] Another reason is that the rape of a slave woman did not usually threaten the maintenance of slavery. In fact, if the rape resulted in offspring, this meant one more child was available for slave labor. Finally, there was little awareness or concern at the time about the physical and emotional trauma caused by rape. All these rationales allowed slaveholders to remain psychologically detached from the harms of slavery and physically bonded to the permanence of the institution. Faulting Black women slaves for being victims of sexual assault allowed Whites to assuage the moral offense and harm of their actions. This reasoning represents an early and classic example of blaming the victim.

In addition to prohibitions against interracial sex between Black men and White women, the slave codes punished Blackness in many different ways, making certain activities criminal only when committed by someone Black. For instance, a slave who "lifted his hand against" a White Christian or used "provoking or menacing language" against a White person faced a punishment of thirty-nine lashes. It was also an offense for seven or more Black men to congregate, unless accompanied by a White person. Under many slave codes, a free Black person who married a slave became a slave. Some states made an exception if the free person was a mulatto who had a White mother.

At their core, the codes explicitly denied slaves political, social, and economic equality. Slaves could not themselves own property. They could have pets, with the permission of the slave owner, who was the legal owner. Slaves could be mortgaged and sold. They could not enter into contracts, including marriage, without the consent of their owners. Not surprisingly, slaves were barred from holding elected office, another example of how the law was used to criminalize Blackness. Only convicted White criminals were barred from holding elective office. Black people who had never been convicted of a crime were treated like Whites who had been.

Enslaved Africans were not the only race singled out for punishment under the codes. As noted earlier, Whites who acted to thwart slavery could face serious sanctions. In Mississippi, for instance, a White person who taught a slave to read or helped a slave obtain freedom risked being fined, imprisoned, or possibly executed. Some states barred White abolitionists from jury service, some sentenced White women to prison for marrying Black men, and others fined White women who had children by Black men. Notably, if an enslaved woman became pregnant by a White man, he was not guilty of any crime.

## Slave Patrols: The First American Police Officers

Slave patrols or "patterollers" operated to keep a tight rein on slave activity. Whites greatly feared slave insurrection, and the slave patrols were established to monitor and quell suspicious slave conduct. Slave patrols, enumerated by the slave codes, were the first uniquely American form of policing. Slave patrollers, who worked in conjunction with the militia, were permitted to stop and search slaves and their living quarters. They were also permitted to beat slaves who did not have proper written permission to be away from their plantation. Patrollers stormed slave cabins to search for runaways, weapons, and any evidence of literacy, such as books, writing tools, and paper.

Patrollers frequently physically abused slaves, whipping the men and beating and sexually assaulting the women. Many states explicitly protected assaults by slave patrols from criminal punishment. For instance, in North Carolina the patrollers were not liable for punishing slaves unless their actions showed malice toward the slave owner.

Whites were expected to serve in slave patrols. In South Carolina and Georgia, Whites were required to serve. In Alabama, slaveholders under the age of sixty, and all other Whites under the age of forty-five, had to participate in the slave patrols. By the mid-1850s, the patrols existed in every southern colony.[10] The work of the slave patrols was considered low status, and often fell to non-slaveholding Whites. As interest and compliance with serving on patrols declined, money was offered as an incentive.

Not only did the slave codes create separate crimes and separate, harsher punishments for Blacks, but "justice" was meted out in special, racially separate tribunals. Slave tribunals were designed to uphold the rights of White slaveholders. In these courts, slave defendants had no right to a jury trial, could be convicted with a verdict that was less than unanimous, were presumed guilty, and did not have the right to appeal a conviction. Enslaved people could not serve as jurors or witnesses against Whites. So even in those instances when a person held in bondage was overworked, underfed, and brutalized, he had no legal recourse. His testimony was no good in court against a slave master. Under an 1818 Georgia law, an enslaved person was not allowed to be a party to any suit against a White man. The tribunals for Whites had starkly different procedural practices and guarantees than the slave tribunals.

Racism in the courts was not confined to the official court system. In some cases, Blacks who were charged with crimes were subject to "plantation justice." The codes gave slave owners private enforcement authority, allowing them to act as both judge and jury. Plantation justice was consistent with classifying certain human beings as property. It allowed enslaved people to be subject to various punishments, including lashings, castration (by knife), dismemberment (e.g., ears, fingers), and hangings. These laws sanctioned other forms of extrajudicial punishment, such as the hiring of bounty hunters to capture runaways. The return of the runaway was the goal. However, some wanted the return of human chattel dead or alive. Evidence that the slave was dead was satisfactory for some.

This discussion cannot adequately convey the harsh reality created, enshrined, and enforced by the slave codes. To say that the enslaved were viewed as less than human is a gross understatement. Animals had greater legal protections than enslaved Blacks, who ranked below dogs, cats, and other breathing, feeling animals. Horses and cows were legally protected against senseless cruelty.

In their totality, the slave codes reveal the vast difference in how Whites and everyone else fared under the law. Virginia legislation, for example, permitted slaves to receive the death penalty for numerous offenses. First-degree murder, however, was the only offense for which Whites could be sentenced to death. What was considered a crime, which court would hear which cases, which sanctions were imposed, and the applicable constitutional protections—were determined by race.

## Black Laws and Black Codes

Black laws existed during the same period as the slave codes. These laws governed the movements and actions of Black people in states and territories that did not have slavery. In 1804, one year after achieving statehood, Ohio was the first state to enact Black laws. Under Ohio's law, Blacks who entered the state were required to produce court papers proving they were free, register with local authorities, and find an Ohio resident who would sign a five-hundred-dollar surety bond. The bond guaranteed that they would be on good behavior and ensured that they would not have access to government supported services, such as public schools. Black laws were coupled with other laws that limited Blacks' social and political engagement, such as rules prohibiting Blacks from testifying in court against Whites, and prohibitions against voting. In addition to the hardship of meeting the entry requirements, White mob violence also discouraged free Blacks from entering Ohio and other states.[11]

On the heels of the passage of the Emancipation Proclamation in 1863, the ending of the Civil War, and the adoption of the Thirteenth Amendment, which abolished slavery, Black codes were enacted. In 1865, Ohio passed the first Black codes, laws that governed the movements of the formerly enslaved population. Newly freed Black women and men were given the right to marry and enter into contracts. In some ways the Black codes operated as both shield and sword. At the same time new rights were granted, laws were passed that minimized them. For example, vagrancy laws allowed newly freed Blacks to be arrested for the "crime" of being unemployed. Mississippi's statute was representative:

> All freedmen, free negroes and mulattoes . . . over the age of eighteen years, found on the second Monday in January, 1866, or thereafter with no lawful employment or business, or found unlawfully assembling themselves together . . . shall be deemed vagrants, and on conviction thereof, shall be fined . . . not exceeding fifty dollars . . . and imprisoned . . . not exceeding ten days.[12]

In an attempt to protect White laborers, licensing requirements were adopted that barred Blacks from all but the most menial jobs. For example, court approval and a fee were necessary to obtain a license to become a mechanic, artisan, or shopkeeper. Black people who were fortunate enough to obtain a license could lose it if there were complaints about their work. Laws criminalizing gun possession, voting, desertion, and assembly after sunset were also used to restrict Black mobility and employment. These codes were the post–Civil War incarnation of the Black laws.

In their totality, the Black codes created and supported a system of involuntary servitude, exactly what was prohibited by the newly adopted Thirteenth Amendment. Race discrimination worked in many ways. Blacks faced harsher criminal penalties than Whites. For instance, thousands of Blacks were executed for offenses that Whites were given prison time for committing. Further, White crimes committed against Blacks were largely excused. For instance, the Texas codes made it a crime for a White person to murder a Black person. Yet, in Texas, between 1865 and 1866, there were acquittals in *five hundred* cases in which someone White was charged with killing someone Black.[13]

Punishment was not limited to the courts or legal officials. The fact that former slaves now had rights was a rallying cry for White vigilantes, including the Ku Klux Klan (KKK). The KKK and its sympathizers were responsible for murdering thousands of Black people. In the 1874 case of *United States v. Cruikshank*, two Black men were ambushed and killed by more than three hundred Klansmen. After the attack, ninety-seven Whites were indicted on murder and conspiracy charges, and only nine went to trial. In all nine cases, the White defendants were acquitted of murder. Only three were found guilty of conspiracy to murder. Lynching, the hallmark of the Klan, introduced a new form of oppression against Blacks. This extralegal southern "justice" resulted in death for thousands of Black men, women, and children.

## The Lynching Ritual

Carried out as an extreme form of vigilante justice, lynchings rose to prominence after the Civil War. Though lynching victims were often selected at random, lynchings themselves involved a series of well-established ritualized sequences: selection of the victim, the lynchers, the location (based on the anticipated size of the crowd), and the method of death (e.g., hanging, shooting, burning). If the victim was to be hanged, the vigilantes chose a tree and gathered lynching implements—rope, wood, guns, kerosene, tar, and feathers.

Although most victims of lynching were Black, members of other racial groups were also lynched, including Asians, Mexicans, and Italians. In fact, around the turn of the twentieth century, the US State Department paid approximately half a million dollars in reparations to China, Mexico, and Italy on behalf of lynch victims.

Lynchings had the look and feel of a sporting event—a rigged, one-sided one—in which the outcome was predetermined. Entire families, including women and small children, attended lynchings. Sometimes schools and businesses were closed so that community members could watch the killing. Spectators arrived with food, drink, and spirits. It was not uncommon for White mobs, which sometimes included police officers, to gather to witness or participate in the murder.[14]

Some newspapers included lynching announcements. These advertisements provided the date, time, and location of upcoming lynchings. Referring to a particularly violent 1917 lynching, sociologist W. E. B. Du Bois wrote,

> A Negro was publicly burned alive in Tennessee under circumstances unusually atrocious. The mobbing and burning were publicly advertised in the press beforehand. Three thousand automobiles brought the audience, including mothers carrying children. Ten gallons of gasoline were poured over the wretch and he was burned alive, while hundreds fought for bits of his body, clothing, and the rope.[15]

Lynch victims, both men and women, were usually required to strip naked. Black men were usually castrated, and sometimes their bodies were used as target practice. The murderous assault ceremoniously concluded with Whites fighting over the remains of the Black victims. Teeth and other body parts were collected as souvenirs.[16]

What could trigger such a morbid and vile practice by Whites? Beyond a rumor that someone Black had committed a serious crime (murder, rape, robbery, or barn burning), there was an endless list of alleged offenses, as detailed in Ida B. Wells-Barnett's work:

- Being "saucy" (verbally disrespectful) to a White person
- Making lewd advances toward a White woman (e.g., whistling)
- Being related to someone suspected of committing a crime
- Being in the wrong place at the wrong time
- Insulting someone White (e.g., buying a new car)
- Engaging in boastful talk
- Defending oneself from physical assault[17]
- Expressing race prejudice

As these examples make clear, Whites did not have to have a legitimate reason to carry out a lynching. The oft-stated rationale was that it served as extralegal protection for White womanhood against the Black male brute. Lynching data, however, reveal that allegations of sexual assault against White women accounted for less than one-third of all lynch murders. Though the lynching ritual was offered up as a call to protect White women and thus the White family, this was simply a cover. The goal was to send a clear threat and promise to Blacks—to stay in their place, or else. The bottom line is that lynching was an unlawful act of violence used to enforce a White-at-the-top racial order. Being Black was adequate provocation for Whites to lynch. Lynching was an extralegal tool to punish Blackness and derail Black progress.

Counts vary as to the actual number of lynchings. The Equal Justice Initiative calculates that between 1877 and 1950 there were 4,075 lynchings of Black people in twelve Southern states. This is 800 more lynchings than previously reported.[18] Official US reports use a different time period and state that between 1882 and 1968, 3,449 Blacks were lynched. Data gathered by lynching historian Ida B. Wells-Barnett, who painstakingly collected newspaper accounts of lynchings that took place across the United States, suggest that official figures were gross undercounts. For example, Wells-Barnett's data show that between 1876 and 1892, 728 Black people were lynched.[19]

Table 3.2 highlights nineteen lynching cases from 1930. In several instances, White mobs forcibly removed Blacks from law enforcement custody—the courthouse or a jail cell—so that they could be lynched.[20] In many instances, Blacks were murdered by lynch mobs before they had been formally charged with any crime.

TABLE 3.2. Selected Black Lynchings, 1930.

| Alleged Crime | Method of Lynching | Circumstances |
| --- | --- | --- |
| 1. Rape/murder | Burned to death | No formal arrest |
| 2. Murder | Shot to death | No formal arrest |
| 3. Rape | Shot to death | Removed from jail |
| 4. Rape | Burned to death | Jail where Black man was held was burned down. His burned body was removed and left in Negro section of town. |
| 5. Murder | Shot to death | Body was tied to a car and dragged through town. Later, body was burned in front of a Black church. |
| 6. Rape | Shot and stabbed to death | Lynch mob broke into jail and removed victim. |
| 7. Rape | Shot to death | No formal arrest |
| 8. Rape | Shot to death | No formal arrest |
| 9. Murder | Shot to death | Victim had been arrested but was left unguarded. |
| 10. No crime | Beaten to death | — |
| 11. Rape/assault | Hanged | Removed from jail |
| 12. Resisting arrest | Shot to death | — |
| 13. Rape | Shot to death | Removed from jail |
| 14. Murder | Shot to death | Killed in jail |
| 15. Robbery | Hanged | Taken from police officers |
| 16. Attempted rape | Shot to death | Taken from police officers |
| 17. No crime | Shot to death | Victim (Black man) had been the star witness in a case against two White men charged with raping a Negro woman. He was shot to death in his home. |
| 18. Murder | Hanged | Removed from jail |
| 19. Rape | Shot to death | No formal arrest |

Source: Arthur Raper, *The Tragedy of Lynching* (1933).

Lynching photographs tell the remarkable, searing stories of the lynching ritual. The book *Without Sanctuary: Lynching Photography in America* by James Allen, Hilton Als, John Lewis, and Leon Litwack offers a stunning and sobering catalogue. One photograph shows a gruesome 1916 lynch-murder in Robinson, Texas. The charred remains of a Black man who was hanged are barely recognizable as a human body.

Nearly as startling as the lynching itself is the fact that the photograph was made into a postcard and sent through the US mail. The back of the postcard reads, "This is the barbecue we had last night . . . your son, Joe."[21] Lynching postcards, delivered by the US Postal Service, were commonplace.

Many of the photographs show scores of White men in shirts and ties and wearing hats—indicative of an important social event. The book's photographs also reveal the sizeable crowds that were frequently present at lynchings. Lynch-mob murders were held in various public places, including in town squares, on bridges, by the side of the road, and—in a cruel twist, as noted by legal scholar Sherrilyn Ifill—on courthouse lawns.[22]

Lynchings have been characterized as a perverse kind of public "performance." This description is rooted in the fact that some vigilante murders were held in public theaters—admission guaranteed a seat and, in some instances, a chance to shoot at the victim. During some of these illegal executions, audience members sang lynching songs. These macabre performances, taking place in one town, then another, bore continuing witness to the depth of White hatred of Blacks.

There were numerous anti-lynching crusades. Blacks and their allies waged fervent protests against lynchings. Notably, combating mob violence was the impetus for the founding of two stalwart civil rights organizations, the National Association for the Advancement of Colored People (NAACP) in 1910 and the Anti-Defamation League in 1913. The NAACP formed an anti-lynching group that worked for decades to gather information on lynching assaults. It also pushed for the passage of federal laws that would outlaw lynchings. The US Congress was repeatedly petitioned to intervene and adopt a federal law that would criminalize lynching. Not one of the bills became law. In 2005, nearly forty years after the last officially documented lynching, the US Senate issued a strong apology for its failure to enact legislation that would have protected Blacks from lynchings and criminalized the practice. This statement was the first time that Congress has apologized to African Americans. The Senate resolution noted the following:

- Lynching succeeded slavery as the ultimate expression of racism in the United States following Reconstruction.

- There were documented incidents of lynching in all but four US states.
- Ninety-nine percent of all perpetrators of lynching did not receive any punishment for their crimes.
- The first anti-lynching bill was introduced in 1900 by George White, a Black US congressman. Nearly two hundred anti-lynching bills were introduced in Congress from 1900 to 1950.
- Between 1890 and 1952, seven US presidents petitioned Congress to end lynching.[23]

Lynchings helped spur a mass exodus of Blacks from the South. For instance, in Georgia, between 1920 and 1930, over 260,000 Blacks migrated from the state. During the Great Migration, from 1910 to 1970, *six million* Blacks left the South for cities in the North, Northeast, and West.

Though nowhere on the scale of the postbellum period, lynchings still take place. The dragging death of James Byrd is a well-known modern-day lynching. In 1998, in Jasper, Texas, three White men chained Byrd to the back of a pickup truck, drove him around for three miles, and dumped what remained of his body in front of a Black cemetery. One of Byrd's killers had been a member of a White supremacist prison gang. Two of the killers were executed; the third is serving a life term. More recently, Ahmaud Arbery was lynched in 2020. Arbery, a Black man who lived in Brunswick, Georgia, was attacked and shot while he was jogging in his neighborhood. He was killed by two White men, one of whom was a retired police detective. The men said they believed Arbery had burglarized a home in the neighborhood.

Not surprisingly there has been a great deal of silence around lynchings. Families of lynch victims in particular, have not always wanted to recount or discuss these painful family memories. In 2019, in recognition of Black lynching victims, the Equal Justice Initiative opened a national memorial in Montgomery, Alabama. The six-acre memorial to racial terror–lynch victims recognizes the more than forty-four hundred Blacks who were killed between 1877 and 1950. The memorial site includes eight hundred six-foot-tall monuments. Each one represents a US county where a lynching took place. The names of the lynch victims are engraved on the steel columns. The site is the first national memorial dedicated to victims of racial terror–lynching incidents.

## Jim Crow Segregation Statutes

The slave codes, Black laws, and Black codes represent versions of state-sanctioned double legal standards. The term "Jim Crow," which came into common usage in the early 1900s, refers to laws that mandated separate public facilities for Blacks and Whites. Segregationist practices, however, came long before Jim Crow. For example, the Louisiana statute challenged in *Plessy v. Ferguson*, upholding racial segregation in railway cars, was enacted in 1890. One constant remained as the slave codes became the Black codes and the Black codes became segregation statutes: Blackness itself was criminalized.

Jim Crow also relegated other groups to second-class status. Other non-Whites, for instance, were not allowed to marry or live with Whites. An 1880 California law prohibited marriage between a White person and a "Negro, mulatto, or Mongolian."[24] Laws were also enacted to deny testamentary capacity. In the 1870 decision of *People v. Brady*, the California Supreme Court upheld the constitutionality of a law that prohibited Chinese witnesses from testifying against Whites.

At one time, Jim Crow signs littered the American landscape. There were all manner of signs: some printed on placards, some engraved on steel plates, and others written by hand. Signs were posted on highway roads, on wooden poles in front of stores, on doors inside buildings, and above water fountains. No space was exempt from Jim Crow's rule. Jim Crow was more than a directive determining access to particular locations. It was a cruel racial threat backed up by the violent force of vigilante mob rule. Jim Crow laws specifically targeted Native Americans, Asians, and Mexicans, in addition to Blacks.

An examination of the Jim Crow era reveals nothing approaching "separate but equal." A better description would have been separate and despised. Jim Crow rule was often displayed in crude and jarring directives:[25]

- "No niggers allowed" (store sign)
- "Drinking Fountain" (with arrows pointing in opposite directions for "White" and "Colored")
- "White Women, Senoras Blancas" (above restroom door at train station)
- "We cater to White only. Niggers, Mexicans and Puerto Ricans not allowed" (billboard)

- "White Baggage Room" (train station)
- "No colored allowed" (building plaque)
- "This part of the bus for the colored race" (city bus)
- "No dogs, no Negroes, no Mexicans" (sign posted outside store)
- "Negroes and freight" (railway sign)

Jim Crow's reach was so expansive that it held sway beyond the public sphere. Not only did Jim Crow laws determine which public facilities Blacks and other people of color could use; they also determined who could serve Blacks (and who Blacks could work with) in those facilities. For instance, there were laws prohibiting White female nurses from treating Black male patients, a clear indication of the taboo against interracial sex. There were also laws prohibiting Black teachers from teaching White students and White teachers from teaching Black students.

Segregation-era laws encompassed a broad range of social actions. Blacks could be punished for walking down the street if they did not move out of the way quickly enough to accommodate White passersby, for talking to friends on a street corner, for speaking to someone White, and for making direct eye contact with a White person. Jim Crow's unwritten rules of racial etiquette required that Black men refer to White men as "Mister" or "Sir." At the same time, however, Whites would commonly refer to Black men as "boys." The rules governing racial manners also required Blacks to step aside and bow their heads in the presence of Whites. These practices were humiliating for Black people, as my grandfather Charlie Russell Sr. could attest. Born in 1912 and raised in northeast Louisiana, he told stories of how as a grown man he had to step off the curb to accommodate an approaching young White boy. Likewise, my grandmother Katie King Russell, born in 1914 in northeast Louisiana, was allowed to purchase clothes from a store, but as a Black woman, she was not allowed to try them on prior to purchase. Once bought, they were final sales. No returns, no exchanges.

All the while, White fear of race mixing remained steadfast. The murder of Emmett Till is a prime illustration. Till, a fourteen-year-old from Chicago, visited Mississippi in the summer of 1955. He made the fatal mistake of speaking to Carolyn Bryant, a White woman, while shopping in a corner store. Till was kidnapped from his uncle's home by Bryant's husband and brother-in-law. After beating and shooting Till, they tied a seventy-five-pound fan around his neck and dropped his body into Mississippi's Tallahatchie River. Days later, Till's bloated, mutilated body was found floating in the river. After deliberating for sixty-eight minutes, the jury of twelve White men voted to acquit the men who lynched Emmett Till. In an interview published in *Look* magazine the following year, J. W. Milam and Roy Bryant confessed to murdering Till and provided details of the killing. In 2005, the US Department of Justice reopened the case. It was closed in 2006, with no new charges being filed.

Jim Crow's racialized system of social, economic, and political dominance supported the widespread White belief that no matter how much racial equality the US Constitution promised, Whites would never accept Blacks as their social equals. The following list includes some of the places and practices of racial segregation and underscores the pervasiveness of Jim Crow:

| | |
|---|---|
| Beaches | Parks |
| Cemeteries | Phone booths |
| Chain gangs | Prisons and jails |
| Courthouses | Public transportation |
| Golf courses | Restrooms |
| Hospital wards | School textbooks |
| Hotels | Schools |
| Libraries | Swimming pools |
| Lunch counters | Theaters |
| Orphanages | Water fountains |

Ostensibly designed to outlaw racial interaction in public places, the long arm of Jim Crow reached private areas as well. Anti-miscegenation and anti-cohabitation laws made it unlawful for Black and White people to marry or live together. The 1967 case of *Loving v. Virginia* involved a marriage between a Black woman and White man. After marrying in Washington, DC, the couple returned home to Virginia. A grand jury charged them with violating Virginia's anti-miscegenation law: "Intermarriage prohibited . . . It shall hereafter be unlawful for any white person in this state to marry any save a white person, or person with no other admixture of blood than white and American Indian."[26] The US Supreme Court held that the Virginia law deprived the couple of liberty without due process, in violation of the Fourteenth Amendment's due process clause.

The 1954 *Brown v. Board of Education* decision did not eradicate racial segregation in public education or public spaces more broadly. Attempts at desegregation frequently inspired a pro-segregation response. In 1957, Montgomery, Alabama, passed the following ordinance: "It shall be unlawful for white and colored persons to play together . . . in any game of cards, dice, dominoes, checkers, pool, billiards, softball, basketball, football, golf, track and at swimming pools or in any athletic contest."[27] This ordinance is notable for its degree of specificity regarding the social interactions of Whites with non-Whites. This legislative mandate to separate sports by race mirrored the rampant segregation that existed in organized sports. During this period, professional sports were almost entirely segregated by race. By necessity, Black sports leagues were created; the Negro Leagues for baseball, the Black Fives, and the United Golfers Association are some examples.

A look at Jim Crow legislation does little to indicate the severe toll these laws exacted on Black life. Not only did Jim Crow regulate Black movement; it confined aspirations and tamped down life opportunities for Black Americans. Jim Crow simply reflected the majority belief that the proper place for Black people was one tier below White people. The manufactured rationales included suggestions that Blacks were separated from Whites for their own good. With the backing of the federal government, the states, and private businesses, Jim Crow predetermined where Black children could be born, where they could go to school, which neighborhoods they could live in, what jobs they could hold when they grew up, whether they were eligible for health insurance, which restaurants they could frequent, which motels they could patronize, and whether they could secure an automobile or home mortgage loan (and at what rate).

"Sundown towns" were another widespread and deeply rooted segregationist practice. Blacks, Latinos, Native Americans, and Asian Americans were intentionally and systematically barred from thousands of towns and cities across the country. These White-only towns have two distinct characteristics. They are indeed all-White and have race-based policies in effect that bar Blacks from living in the town and prohibit them from remaining there after nightfall. In his book *Sundown Towns*, sociologist James Loewen details these communities. He estimates that from 1890 to 1968 there were more than fifteen thousand sundown towns in the United States.. The number of sundown towns have dwindled, but they have not completely disappeared.[28] Enforcement of sundown laws often leads to violence, injury, and death to "trespassers."

The legal death knell has sounded for Jim Crow. The civil rights movement of the 1950s and 1960s led to the passage of legislation including the 1964 Civil Rights Act and the 1965 Voting Rights Act. Unfortunately, other manifestations of racial bias and violence persist. What remains is the need to address the question of what components would constitute a racially equitable criminal-legal system.

Each legal scheme—slave codes, Black laws, Black codes, lynching, and Jim Crow—evolved directly from its predecessor. That is, the language of the slave codes is echoed in the language of the Black laws. As well, the text of the Black codes are reminiscent of the slave codes. As these structures of punishment were adopted, the goal was the same: to regulate, control, and suppress Black activity and advancement.

## Criminal-Legal Justice Principles

Can anything be learned from the slave codes, Black codes, Black laws, and Jim Crow? These systems of punishment are object lessons in how not to structure a racially fair criminal–legal system. Antebellum and postbellum criminal law stood as the antithesis to a racially just system. Today, almost four hundred years after White settlement in North America, seven justice principles appear to offer the minimal conditions required for a racially equitable system of justice:

TABLE 3.3. Justice Principles

| | |
|---|---|
| Principle 1 | Race does not impact whether a person is stopped, searched, or arrested by police. |
| Principle 2 | Race does not impact whether a person will be charged with a crime. |
| Principle 3 | Race of the defendant does not impact whether he will be found guilty of an offense. |
| Principle 4 | Race of the defendant does not impact his sentence. |
| Principle 5 | Race of the victim does not impact whether a defendant will be charged with a crime. |
| Principle 6 | Race of the victim does not impact whether a defendant will be found guilty of a crime. |
| Principle 7 | Race of the victim does not impact the sentence the defendant will receive. |

These justice principles are not exhaustive. They provide a useful threshold test and marker for measuring the impact of race in criminal-legal processes. The principles identify basic requirements, since it is hard to imagine a fair legal system that does not adhere to each one. The principles make clear that justice and racial bias cannot coexist. The existence of racial discrimination, at the individual and structural levels, threatens the possibility of justice.

The chapters in this book analyze various aspects of race and the administration of justice, including application of criminal laws, and how race and crime are framed in public discourse. These justice principles provide a reference point for evaluating whether today's US criminal-legal system operates in a racially fair manner. Keep these in mind as we move to a discussion of racial profiling.

4

# Racial Discrimination, Racial Profiling, and Racial Monitoring

Study after study shows that Blacks and Whites hold contrary viewpoints about the fairness of the judicial system. Whites are more likely to believe that the system works for them, and Blacks are more likely to believe that it works against them. Two common expressions capture these opposing viewpoints: "There may be a few bad apples, but overall the system works" (Whites), and "Justice means 'just us'" (Blacks). Like Blacks, members of the Latinx community believe that they are more likely to experience racial profiling. Interestingly, where Blacks and Latinx people see racial bias, Whites tend to see "rational discrimination." Based on direct and indirect experiences, Blacks and Latinos are more likely than Whites to report that they have experienced unfair treatment by the police. In the months following George Floyd's death, poll data showed that an increasing percentage of Whites reported that police killings of Black people was a problem and indicated support for the nationwide protests.

Research on racial discrimination clearly supports the conclusion that isolated pockets of acute racial discrimination exist—for instance, drug-related offenses or capital punishment. The debate comes when researchers are asked whether the entire US criminal-legal system operates in a racially discriminatory manner. Many criminologists and sociologists answer with a resounding "yes." However, a vocal contingent of scholars reaches a "no discrimination" conclusion. This view is largely based on research that focuses on select stages of the criminal-legal system process, such as arrest, charge, sentencing, and conviction. Unfortunately, the potential for racial bias exists at many more points along the continuum. An expanded analysis would include, for instance, a consideration of prearrest actions, courtroom language, and postconviction decisions. By focusing on the bright lines of discrimination, criminology research tends to overlook these critical points. Until these other unmeasured stages are included within mainstream analyses, no conclusion can be drawn that the system is free of racial bias.

This chapter provides an overview of the current research on racial discrimination, outlines the criticisms of this research, and demonstrates why the most important informal stage—prearrest contacts with police—should be subject to official measurement. These findings challenge the mainstream view that racial discrimination exists only at certain stages of the system. Without expanding our assessment of racial bias, we miss and therefore cannot accurately determine its prevalence. The other points need to be measured and included within the calculation of how race affects justice. The discussion also includes a look at how racial profiling, ostensibly used as a crime control measure, works a rough justice on Blacks and Latinx people in particular, including the reinforcement of the *criminalblackman* imagery.

## Do You See What I See?

Depending on your vantage point, racial discrimination in the criminal-legal system might be considered a thing of the past, an entrenched contemporary reality, something that happens to "other people" (low-income people, persons of another race, people who live in other neighborhoods), a random and rare event, something that happens to the guilty, or a nagging side effect of an otherwise well-working system. These widely varying perceptions and experiences make it difficult for some people to see the racial discrimination experienced by some groups, and harder for them to hear the SOS call to address racial discrimination. Some racial groups, for instance, have more direct and more frequent negative interactions with law enforcement. These experiences create two different realities and understandings about how justice works, as described in the opening paragraph. Further, finding consensus on what steps to take is hard because so many different standards are used to evaluate whether racial justice exists. All told, these soup-to-nuts perspectives create a kind of blindness about the workings and viability of the system.

There are many reasons for the varied opinions regarding the racial equity of the legal system. Criminal justice researchers have some responsibility for this state of affairs. For decades in the post–civil rights era, mainstream research has largely concluded that racial discrimination in the judicial system is, with few exceptions, neither intentional nor widespread. What follows is a critique of this research, which makes a strong argument for reconsidering a "no discrimination" thesis. Notably, though, over the last decade, an increasing number of researchers—including criminologists, sociologists, ethnographers, anthropologists, and demographers—have focused on issues of racial disparity and discrimination within various social systems, and concluded that these systems operate in ways that keep marginalized groups tethered to the court system.

## Single versus Multistage Research

Many studies that purport to examine the existence of racial discrimination evaluate a single phase of the justice system. As a result, this research is arguably marred by tunnel vision. Research that analyzes race discrimination at a single stage of the system cannot detect racial discrimination that exists in other parts of the system. For example, a study of how race influences sentencing in State A may find no racial disparity. This finding, however, does not mean that State A does not have a racially discriminatory court system. Research may not indicate significant racial discrimination at sentencing, but discrimination may permeate other stages (e.g., prosecutorial charging and plea bargaining). In fact, relatively little research has broadly examined racial disparity in prosecution. Most of the studies focus on a single aspect of prosecutorial discretion (e.g., charge decision).[1] Prosecutorial bias might exist at stages of the system that are not subject to official measurement.[2]

Further, a study involving several criminal courts that overall finds no presence of racial discrimination may mask discrimination in a few of the courts. For instance, an aggregate analysis of the sentencing decisions of ten courts might indicate very little racial discrimination. A look at these ten courts individually, however, might reveal sizeable discrimination in two of them. Aggregate studies, therefore, may minimize the existence of race discrimination in sentencing. At best, single-stage studies provide important, though limited, information about the role race plays in the system; such studies cannot reliably answer the broad question of whether racial discrimination exists in the US criminal-legal system.

Multistage research promises a more comprehensive look at how system officials and the system's larger structure treat race. Although multistage research covers more ground than single-stage studies, the fact that discrimination is not evident at two or three stages (e.g., bail and sentencing) does not mean that it is absent from other stages. Additionally, single-stage and multistage studies cannot be generalized across states. In other words, a finding that there is no racial discrimination at the prosecutorial charging and sentencing phases in five states does not prove that racial discrimination is absent in the court systems of the remaining forty-five states. State variations—including differences in criminal code statutes, prosecutorial charging practices, jury-pool eligibility, and judicial selection—mean that the empirical findings from one state or county do not necessarily apply to different states or counties.

Researchers employ various methods, select different thresholds, and analyze different stages to evaluate racial disparity and discrimination. While some stages are rife with racially disparate outcomes that raise concerns about discrimination, the stage-based research approach discourages criminologists from making broad-scale conclusions about the degree of systemic racial bias. As a result, no consensus exists among criminologists and sociologists as to the severity of racial discrimination in the criminal-legal system.

## Defining "Disparity"

Another criticism of the research on discrimination is that it does not provide an accurate definition of "disparity." The term has been used to refer to whether a racial group is involved in the criminal-legal system at a rate that exceeds its presence in the general population. Using this formula for disparity, Black people, who constitute about 13 percent of the US population, are grossly overrepresented in arrest, conviction, and incarceration figures.[3] In the late 2010s, Black people account for approximately 27 percent of all arrests and overall approximately 32 percent of the correctional population (prison, jail, probation, and parole) (see Appendix A). Latinos account for about 18 percent of the US population and make up 26 percent of the state prison population and 32 percent of the federal prison population; thus they are also overrepresented in incarceration rates. In contrast, Whites are underrepresented in the correctional population: at 48 percent, their rate is far below their 67 percent of the US population.

TABLE 4.1A. Arrest and Incarceration, by Race

|  | White | Black | Hispanic |
|---|---|---|---|
| Crime Statistics | | | |
| Arrests[a] | 69% | 26% | 19% |
| Incarceration[b] | 30% | 33% | 23% |

a. Uniform Crime Reports, Table 43 (2019). The UCR classifies "Hispanic" as an ethnic group not a race, so a percentage of those classified as Hispanic are included in the White category.
b. Pew Research, Bureau of Justice Statistics (2017).

TABLE 4.1B. Indicators of Social Marginality, Proportional Representation by Race

General Statistics

|  | White | Black | Hispanic |
|---|---|---|---|
| Unemployment | 4% | 7.5% | 5% |
| Live below poverty line | 11% | 21% | 18% |
| Nonmarriage births | 29% | 70% | 52% |
| College degree | 36% | 22% | 15.5% |
| Married | 59% | 35% | 48% |
| Female head of household | 17% | 48% | 24% |

Note: Regarding within and across racial group comparisons: Data on arrests and incarceration reflect overall percentages, as in 69 percent of all arrests are of Whites. Data on all other factors represent within-group percentages, as in 4 percent of all Whites, 7.5 percent of Blacks, and 5 percent of Hispanics are unemployed.

Some researchers reject this conventional formula for disproportionality, preferring a more complex analysis. Why, they ask, should a group's percentage in the population be the baseline for determining disproportionality? Some researchers argue that we should expect arrest rates to mirror more the indicators of social marginality. Accordingly, the conventional measure of disproportionality is useful only if we assume that all racial groups are on equal social footing.

Table 4.1 provides information on select social indicators for Blacks, Hispanics, and Whites. When compared with Whites, Blacks and Hispanics have higher rates of unemployment and nonmarriage births, and are more likely to live below the poverty line. At the same time, Blacks and Hispanics are less likely than Whites to have a college degree or to be married. On these measures of social standing, the Black and Hispanic rates exceed the White rate. Notably, rates for Black nonmarriage births, female-headed households, unemployment, and poverty are more than twice the White rates. Given these data, is it surprising that Black arrest and conviction rates follow a similar pattern? Decades ago, noted criminologists Marvin Wolfgang and Bernard Cohen reached a similar conclusion:

> If a careful detached scholar knew nothing about crime rates but was aware of the social, economic and political disparities between whites and Negroes in the United States . . . what would be the most plausible hypothesis our scholar could make about the crime rate of Negroes? Even this small amount of relevant knowledge would justify the expectation that Negroes would be found to have a higher crime rate than Whites.[4]

Thus, indicators of social marginality, such as high rates of unemployment and crime, are interdependent, and we would reasonably expect them to be positively correlated. As unemployment rates rise, so do arrest rates.

The current definition of disproportionality is not so much misleading as it is incomplete. Perhaps disproportionality is best thought of as one of the many indices of social status, rather than as a definitive measure for crime rates. For instance, understanding why Black people offend at rates that exceed their percentage in the population requires a consideration of other factors that may have a direct or indirect effect on crime. The empirical reality is that race, poverty, employment, crime, marriage, and education are interacting variables. Whether a group offends at a high or low rate generally indicates how it will fare with other social indices.

Researchers have also considered other baselines for measuring the racial profiling of motorists. Various measures have been suggested, including the racial group's percentage of the driving population, percentage of those with automobiles, percentage of the population (in a select geographical area), and percentage of licensed drivers. There is no clear consensus among researchers as to the best measure for the baseline.

*Determining the Relationship between Disproportionality and Discrimination*

Another important issue is how racial discrimination and racial disparity are analyzed, comparatively, in the research. They are frequently discussed as if they are competing, antithetical phenomena. In fact, they coexist. Left-of-center critiques tend to focus on how racial discrimination impacts the people who are brought into the courts and corrections system. This includes a focus on the law, such as selective enforcement or disparate impact. Right-of-center analyses tend to focus on the disproportionately high rate of Black offending, overall crime rates, and recidivism rates. Despite these political distinctions, research shows evidence of racial discrimination against Blacks *and* evidence that Blacks disproportionately offend. The conclusion as to the precise relationship between disparity and discrimination varies based on research question, method of analysis, and data pool: disparity and discrimination may be correlated or causally related, or operate independently of each other.

The disproportionately high rate of Black offending may have caused many researchers to deemphasize racial discrimination. For some, disproportionate Black offending may be viewed as a justification for any racial discrimination that persists in the courts. The problem of racism in the administration of justice is too important to play second fiddle to other criminal justice system realities, including disproportionate offending rates. Whatever one's position on the disparity-discrimination debate, there should be unequivocal acknowledgment that racial discrimination and racial disproportionality both exist *and* that both are problems that must be addressed.

Even some researchers who embrace a no-discrimination thesis concede that disproportionate rates of offending do not completely explain the high rate of Black incarceration. In a seminal research study, criminologist Alfred Blumstein in 1993 determined that 20 to 25 percent of the incarceration rate for Blacks is *not* explained by disproportionate offending. He surmises, however, that a 20 to 25 percent gap is no great cause for alarm, because eliminating this gap would not change the incarceration picture dramatically. By Blumstein's calculation, the 20 to 25 percent of unexplained disparity between the arrest and incarceration figures represents about ten thousand Black prisoners.[5] Ten thousand prisoners may be a statistical drop in the bucket of the overall prison population (less than 1 percent); socially speaking, though, it is no small number. Ten thousand Blacks who may have been treated more harshly *because* of their race is proof of an enormous social problem. If an estimated ten thousand Blacks have been subjected to discrimination, some were unjustly convicted and unjustly sentenced to lengthy prison terms. Subsequent replications of Blumstein's work have found even greater rates of unexplained disparities.[6]

Further, the impact of race discrimination would extend beyond those Blacks who were its direct victims. This would include the economic and social impact on their families (e.g., children, spouses, and parents) and their communities (e.g., social services). By what logic could we excuse or, worse, ignore this unexplained 20 to 25 percent gap? Blumstein states that the high rate of Black incarceration is not the result of racial discrimination, which seems to be a pat dismissal of the cruel discriminatory fate of thousands of people. Blumstein likely did not intend to downplay the impact of racial discrimination. His analysis and assessment, however, greatly minimize the racial impact of incarceration.

Some researchers studying the disproportionately high rate of Black arrests have questioned whether it is caused by crime rates or other factors are at work. A few have suggested that the historical patterns and practices of the legal system itself may enhance the grossly disproportionate involvement of Black people in the criminal-legal process. National studies show that rates of drug use are similar across racial groups. However, FBI data for 2019 show that one-quarter of the people arrested for drug abuse violations were Black. One study found that Blacks were arrested for marijuana possession at a rate four times higher than Whites.

A look at the racial impact of the cocaine laws provides even further evidence of racial disparity. Studies indicate that more than one-half of all crack cocaine users are White. Blacks, however, are almost four times more likely to be crack cocaine defendants than Whites. In 2015, the Federal Bureau of Prisons reported that 88 percent of the people sentenced for crack cocaine offenses were Black and 4 percent were White.[7]

The US Supreme Court's decision in *United States v. Armstrong* highlights how certain kinds of race discrimination can elude traditional checks and balances.[8] In this 1996 case, the Los Angeles federal public defender's office argued that the US Attorney's office was selectively prosecuting Black defendants under the federal crack cocaine statute. The public defender's office, noting that the penalty for a crack conviction is much harsher under federal law than under California law, argued that Black offenders were being targeted for federal court. Under the mandatory federal crack law, a conviction for the sale of crack co-caine was punished one hundred times more severely than the conviction for the sale of powder cocaine (five grams of crack resulted in a five-year prison term, whereas it took five hundred grams of powder to result in a five-year prison term). In 1991, all twenty-four of the Los Angeles federal crack cases handled by the public defender's office involved Black defendants. The public defender's office requested records from the prosecutor's office reporting how many Whites and Blacks had been prosecuted in state court. The US Attorney's office was also asked to state its criteria for deciding whether to prosecute a case in federal court. The public defender sought to establish that White crack offenders were being prosecuted in state court because the penalties were less harsh.

The Supreme Court held that the defense would have to offer some minimal proof of racial discrimination *before* the prosecution could be legally required to turn over its case records. Not surprisingly, without the records from the prosecutor's office, the public defender's office was unable to meet this legal burden. The *Armstrong* decision does not mean that the US Attorney's office is not selectively prosecuting Black people in federal court. Rather, it means that the prosecutor can withhold evidence of it.

The *Armstrong* decision is just one example of a legal roadblock that makes measurement of race discrimination in the system difficult. The legal reasoning indicates that forms of discrimination that are hard to measure can escape penalty. *Armstrong* symbolizes the legal barriers to identifying race discrimination in the criminal-legal system, but empirical barriers also exist.

## Petit Apartheid

Criminologist Daniel Georges-Abeyie observes that mainstream measures of racial bias begin with arrest. He notes, however, that numerous opportunities for racial bias occur prior to arrest. One example is the point at which a police officer decides whether to make a traffic stop. This is an unmeasured stage, since most police departments do not keep data on the decision *not* to make a vehicle stop. Georges-Abeyie argues that unmeasured stages, such as prearrest activity by law enforcement, can have significant causal consequences, signaling a gateway for entry into the justice system. Georges-Abeyie uses the term "petit apartheid" to label race-driven practices that are not included within mainstream analyses of racial bias.[9]

Beyond prearrest, petit apartheid encompasses all court-related actions, including rulings made during bench conferences and in the judges' chambers. Analysis of the system would also include evaluations of how racial language is used in the courtroom to evoke racial imagery. Looking at how prosecutors use racial labels in their closing arguments (as either implicit or explicit allusions to the defendant's guilt)[10] offers another measure of petit apartheid. Analysis would also include a study of the less-than-favorable names that lawyers secretly give to their clients.[11] An analysis of petit apartheid opens the door to the previously unseen (because they were unmeasured) actions within the system— activities that happen in what sociologist Erving Goffman labeled the "backstage."[12] In the backstage, decisions and judgments are made beyond the public's view. An example of a backstage is a court ruling that happens in the judge's chambers.[13] Away from the courtroom and the jury, the language used by a judge and the attorneys might be overtly racial. Because this is not a public stage, it is unlikely that any racial bias would be uncovered. Bias that takes place on the backstage is harder to remedy. This discussion sheds light on previously closed processes and allows us to see *how* race matters in criminal law.

Discrimination in the postconviction phase has received increasing attention over the years. The Innocence Project assists prisoners who seek to prove their innocence through DNA testing. In 2021, the project reported that 375 people have been exonerated after DNA tests revealed their innocence, including 225 African Americans (60 percent), 117 Whites (31 percent), and 29 Latinx (8 percent).[14] The bottom line of Georges-Abeyie's analysis is that a look at the informal phases of the criminal-legal system would reveal a stark pattern in which people of color consistently and unfairly receive harsher treatment from legal officials (e.g., police and judges) than do Whites.[15]

A thorough assessment of the impact of race on the court system requires that we focus as well on the bookends—racial profiling and postconviction—as well as those stages that have been ignored in earlier research. Only then can we purport to have a more accurate picture of our court system's racial viability. The next section examines how police treat Black men prior to arrest. The discussion shows how this informal stage should be measured and the social, economic, and the sociological consequences of failing to measure it.

## African Americans, the Police, and Racial Profiling

As a group, African Americans, particularly men, have an endless supply of stories of police harassment. These incidents include being mistaken for a criminal, being treated like a criminal, publicly humiliated, and in some instances, called derogatory names. Often their encounters with the police arise from being stopped in their cars. Blacks are subject to vehicle stops for a variety of reasons, some legal, some not:

- Driving an expensive luxury car
- Driving an old car
- Driving in a car with other Black men
- Driving in a car with a White woman
- Driving early in the morning
- Driving late at night
- Driving a rented vehicle
- Driving too fast
- Driving too slow
- Driving in a low-income neighborhood known for its drug traffic
- Driving in an affluent neighborhood
- Driving in a White neighborhood
- Driving in an area where there have been recent burglaries
- Falling asleep while waiting in the drive-through of a fast-food restaurant
- Fitting the profile of a drug courier
- Violating the traffic code (e.g., failure to signal, excessive speed, exposed taillight)
- Driving with an air freshener hanging on the rear view mirror

Police suspicion is seemingly aroused by any activity involving African Americans and automobiles. It is so commonplace for Black men in particular to be pulled over in their vehicles that this practice has acquired its own acronym: "DWB"—Driving While Black.

Police harassment comes in many forms. One example is the frequency with which African Americans are stopped, questioned, and assaulted by the police as they go about their daily lives. In his book *Chokehold*, law professor Paul Butler provides a detailed look at the physical abuse Black men receive during routine police stops.[16] Racial harassment is often a fact of life for Blacks. "Living While Black" takes many forms, some mere inconveniences, some troubling, and others deadly. Numerous incidents involve Blacks who have faced police force while they were walking, standing in a vestibule, shopping, running, or sitting in an idling vehicle (see chapter 6 for a detailed discussion of police violence against Blacks).

There are, however, clear distinctions between police harassment and police brutality. "Police brutality" typically refers to the unlawful use of excessive force. "Harassment" covers a range of police actions, some lawful, some unlawful (e.g., conducting a stop on less than adequate legal cause). For many Black men and women, consistently negative encounters with the police have blurred the lines between harassment and brutality. For Black men, who are disproportionately more likely to be stopped by the police, each stop has the potential to result in police violence (see chapter 6 for further discussion). The frequency of contact between Black men and the police has led a generation of Black parents to have "The Talk" with their sons and daughters—concrete instructions on how to handle a police encounter without getting harmed. Studies attest to the fear and loathing that many African Americans have of the police.[17] Legal scholar Jerome McCristal Culp Jr. referred to this as the "rules of engagement" for Black men. According to Culp, these rules, taught to young Black men and boys over five years old, instruct that "at all times we [Black men] make no quick moves, remove any possibility of danger and never give offense to official power."[18] Law professor David Troutt offers the "law of mothers" to describe how Black women warn their sons and worry about their encounters with police.

Many Black men have developed protective mechanisms to avoid vehicle stops by police and to minimize the potential for harm during these stops. One shield they use is an altered public persona. This includes a range of adaptive behaviors, like sitting erect while driving, traveling at the precise posted speed limit, avoiding certain neighborhoods, not wearing certain head gear (e.g., a baseball cap), and avoiding flashy cars. Black men are used to structuring their encounters with police during car stops: placing both hands on the steering wheel, responding to an officer's questions with "sir" or "ma'am," and quite creatively, keeping the car radio tuned to a "non-Black" music station (e.g., classical, country, or rock). Black men are wise to take such measures because studies consistently show that a suspect's demeanor affects whether he will be arrested. Legendary trumpet player Miles Davis had a unique method for handling police harassment. To avoid being detained and questioned, Davis called and notified the Beverly Hills Police Department when he was leaving his home.

The different experiences that some groups have with law enforcement and their perceptions of those experiences may explain why impressions of the legitimacy and trustworthiness of police treatment vary by race. This is especially true regarding racial profiling. Studies indicate that personal experience and one's race affect one's perceptions about racial bias by police. For instance, Blacks are more likely to believe that they receive harsher treatment at the hands of police, are more likely to be critical of police, and are more likely to believe that profiling is widespread.

In addition to the experiences of the larger Black citizenry, Black police officers present an interesting twist on the issue of police abuse. They too have stories of abuse and harassment at the hands of other police officers (of all races). Out of uniform they are Black, not blue. The long list of cases involving Black undercover officers who have been mistaken for criminals by White officers illustrates this point.

Black distrust of the police, courts, and correctional system is not new. It is historically rooted in the role that police played in enforcing the slave codes, Black codes, Jim Crow segregation, and the ultimate form of vigilante justice, lynching. In his treatise on race in America, historian, Gunnar Myrdal reported that between 1920 and 1932, White police officers were responsible for more than half of all the murders of Black citizens.[19] Accounts also show that White police officers were often present at lynchings (see Chapter 3 discussion). Today, police brutality barely resembles its past forms. Many Blacks alive today, however, still remember the widespread, persistent, and inhumane abuse that Blacks suffered at the hands of police.

Further, only within the last fifty years or so have Blacks been allowed to police White communities on a wide scale. Into the 1960s, Black officers were viewed by Whites as second-class officers and were only allowed to patrol Black communities. "Separate but equal" meant that Black officers could not arrest White suspects. Police racial segregation was practiced in most large cities, including Miami and Houston. Millions of people alive today were alive when Black police officers were not allowed to police White communities. For many Blacks, police abuse, disrespect, and violence are not distant memories but rather part of daily consciousness. A consideration of this history helps to explain why Black skepticism of and disdain for police are continuing phenomena.

## Legalized Racial Profiling?

The "out-of-place" doctrine gives police legal support for stopping and questioning Blacks at a disproportionate rate. It allows police to use a person's race as a factor in making a stop when someone is in an area where another race predominates. A number of courts have upheld the doctrine as a useful police practice to stem crime. The doctrine arguably encourages police to view Black men as de facto guilty, without regard to legal indicators of criminal activity (e.g., reckless driving, speeding, completing a drug sale). It permits Blacks to be stopped at a disproportionate rate since there are far more White neighborhoods than Black neighborhoods. This practice also supports and perhaps encourages racial segregation—people should stay with "their own kind." We can only speculate as to the toll—spiritual, psychological, and physical—exacted on a group whose freedom of movement is consistently challenged.

In 1996, the US Supreme Court addressed the issue of pretextual vehicle stops. In *Whren v. United States*, the Court was asked to decide whether it is constitutional for the police to use a minor traffic violation to stop a driver whom they suspect of criminal activity.[20] Michael Whren and another Black man, James Brown, were stopped in a "high drug area" in Washington, DC. At this point, the officers had probable cause to believe that there had been a violation of the vehicle code. The undercover officers became suspicious of drug activity after observing Brown pause at a stop sign for more than thirty seconds, fail to use his turn signal, and take off at a high speed. One of the officers saw Brown looking in the direction of the passenger's lap. After they pulled the car over, drugs were found, and the two men were arrested.

In a unanimous decision, the Supreme Court held that as long as a traffic stop is based on probable cause, it is constitutional. A police officer's motive for the stop is irrelevant. In this case a traffic law had been violated, thus probable cause was established. Because the police do not stop most people who engage in the same conduct, the question arises whether Brown was stopped because he was Black. The direct and indirect experiences that Blacks have with the police affect their perception that the criminal-legal system is skewed against them. Court decisions such as *Whren* bolster this viewpoint. A complete assessment of the role that race plays in police stops requires the scrutiny of the actions of Black men *and* the actions of the police—and an assessment of reasonable response by motorists when they are unknowingly approached by undercover officers.

Many people would argue that it is unfair to blame the police for being suspicious of Black men. After all, Black men are disproportionately engaged in crime. It is reasonable, then, that the police disproportionately suspect them of criminal activity. Black men do commit street crimes at high rates that far exceed the percentage of Black men in the US population (approximately 6 percent). The important question is whether Black men are stopped and questioned by the police at a rate that greatly exceeds their rate of criminal involvement. If so, the high number of police stops is not legally justifiable.

## Floyd v. New York

Given the perception and prevalence of racial profiling, lawsuits against police departments alleging racially discriminatory practices are relatively rare. This is no surprise considering there is a high bar to hold a municipality liable for violating constitutional rights, such as unlawfully stopping members of a particular race. The *Floyd* case offers detailed insights into police stops made by New York City police officers.[21]

*Floyd* was a class action case that challenged the stop–and-frisk policy of the New York Police Department (NYPD). The seventeen plaintiffs— Black and Hispanic, men and women—argued that New York police officers targeted specific racial groups for stop-and-frisks, without adequate legal justification (e.g., "reasonable suspicion"), in violation of the Fourth Amendment's prohibition against unreasonable searches and seizures and the Fourteenth Amendment's equal protection clause. The plaintiffs filed their case seeking an injunction—a court order requiring that police stop any and all racial profiling practices. In making the determination, the judge considered the following facts and findings:

- Between 2004 and 2012, the NYPD made over 4.4 million stops.
- Over 80 percent of these stops were of Blacks (52 percent) and Hispanics (31 percent).
- Fifty-two percent of the stops resulted in a frisk for weapons. In only 1.5 percent of these cases, a weapon was discovered.
- Weapons were seized in 1.4 percent of stops involving Whites, 1.1 percent involving Hispanics, and 1 percent involving Blacks.
- Contraband was found in 2.3 percent of White stops, 1.8 percent of Black stops, and 1.7 percent of Hispanic stops.
- Twelve percent of the stops led to an arrest or a summons.
- In 2010, New York City's resident population was Whites, 33 percent; Hispanics, 29 percent; and Blacks, 23 percent.

After reviewing the findings, the judge found that the NYPD was engaged in wide-scale police stop-and-frisks based on less than legal cause, in violation of the Fourth Amendment and practiced racial profiling, in violation of the equal protection clause. The court found that the city of New York showed "deliberate indifference" toward the NYPD's practice of making stops and frisks without adequate legal basis and its practice of indirect racial profiling (by targeting Blacks and Hispanics for stop-and-frisks). Further, the judge noted, the court's role was "to judge the constitutionality of police behavior, not its effectiveness as a law enforcement tool."[22] The court mandated policy changes for the NYPD and the appointment of an independent monitor. The judge stated that the court was not ending the practice of stop-and-frisk, but rather was ending the practice of racially motivated stop-and-frisks.

The case highlighted the divergent viewpoints on which law enforcement crime control policies are acceptable. Michael Bloomberg, the mayor of New York during the time the case was litigated, defended the actions of the NYPD. In an editorial that appeared in the *Washington*

*Post*, he pointed to the success of stop-and-frisk as a crime control measure.[23] Bloomberg argued that since only 6 percent of the police stops were unjustified (approximately 264,000 stops), the judge should not have imposed a court-appointed monitor to check NYPD's stop-and-frisk practices. In 2013, the plaintiffs settled their case with the city of New York, and in 2018, the final report was filed. As Table 4.2 indicates, in the years leading up to and after the settlement, the number of stops sharply declined.[24]

TABLE 4.2A. Annual Arrests by Race

| | 2011 | 2013 | 2015 | 2017 | 2019 |
|---|---|---|---|---|---|
| | 685,724 | 191,851 | 22,565 | 11,629 | 13,459 |

TABLE 4.2B. Annual Arrests by Race

| | 2011 | 2013 | 2015 | 2017 | 2019 |
|---|---|---|---|---|---|
| Black | 350,743 | 104,958 | 12,233 | 6,595 | 7,981 |
| Latinx | 223,740 | 55,191 | 6,598 | 3,567 | 3,869 |
| White | 61,805 | 20,877 | 2,567 | 977 | 1,215 |

In each of the years, the findings show that two-thirds or more of the people stopped were innocent of any criminal wrongdoing. While the number of stops have dropped, Blacks still make up more than 50 percent of all police stops each year.

## Racial Hall Monitors

In recent years, we have witnessed a groundswell of cases involving private citizens who decided to take the law into their own hands and enforce racial boundaries. These cases involve White citizens who volunteer to act as "racial hall monitors" who jump into action when they see a Black person engaged in activity they deem unacceptable, or relatedly, when they believe a Black person is in a Whites-only space. Because these encounters often result in calls to law enforcement, these cases have a direct tie to racial profiling by police. Also, they operate in comparable ways to other forms of vigilante justice.

Race monitors are everywhere. For 2018 alone, legal scholar Chan Tov McNamarah documents ninety-two racial monitoring incidents (which he calls "racialized police communication").[25] The actions of race monitors are particularly insidious as they work outside of official legal channels. Race monitors may be neighbors, store clerks, coworkers, or complete strangers. Further, no one knows when a self-designated racial hall monitor will rear her head. They are an ever-present threat, and their actions are captured by various hashtag labels, including #ExistingWhileBlack, #BreathingWhileBlack, and #LivingWhileBlack. Racial profiling by the police and by self-appointed racial hall monitors deliver a one-two punch against Blacks' freedom of movement.

The most notorious and well-known of these cases has been dubbed "BBQ Becky." Jennifer Schulte, who at the time of the incident was a project manager at an environmental resources company, visited Lake Merritt in 2018. "The Lake," as it's known, is a scenic, three-mile, heart-shaped shoreline in the heart of Oakland, California. Each day it has hundreds of visitors, including runners doing early morning sprints, workers taking lunchtime walks, groups practicing Qigong, people on evening strolls, families feeding the ducks, and couples sitting on the grass. Sometimes people barbeque there as well. While there are designated areas of the park for barbequing, the signs are not always clear.

During her visit, Schulte approached a Black man who was barbequing and proceeded to tell him that he was not allowed to cook in the park and that she was going to call the police. He was soon joined by a friend, Kenzie Smith, who was also Black. The incident was filmed by Michelle Snider, Smith's wife. The police were on the phone with Schulte for three hours. After they arrived and evaluated her for a psychiatric hold, they decided to let her leave.[26]

There have been scores of other cases involving Whites who appointed themselves racial hall monitors and demanded that Blacks prove that they had permission to be in a particular place—demanding evidence of a racial pass key. Another example includes a 2018 incident in St. Louis, Missouri. It involved a White woman, Hilary Brooke Mueller, who unlocked the outside door to an apartment building. The man behind her, D'Arreion Toles, a Black man, sought to enter as well. She blocked his entry, saying she was "uncomfortable" with him coming into "my building." After he managed to move past her, she followed him through the hall, on the elevator, and to his door, insisting that he tell her which unit he lived in and repeatedly demanding that he display his key fob to prove that he lives in the building. The tenant, who managed to stay calm throughout the entire episode, told her, "Have a good night, ma'am. Don't ever do that again." Following the incident, Mueller was fired from her job as a property manager at another apartment complex.[27]

In another 2018 case, an eight-year-old Black girl was selling water on a San Francisco street. Alison Ettel, a White woman who lived in the neighborhood, said the girl was making too much noise. At some point, Ettel approached the girl and asked her to show that she had a permit to sell water. The girl's adult cousin videotaped the incident and posted it on social media. Ettel was dubbed "Permit Patty," and following the incident, several marijuana businesses cut ties with her medical marijuana business for pets. Ettel was forced to resign as CEO.[28]

A 2018 case nicknamed "Napping While Black" involved a Yale graduate student who fell asleep in the common area of her dormitory. The student, Lolade Siyonbola, had been writing a paper in the common room and dozed off after midnight. Another graduate student, Sarah Braasch, turned on the light and told Siyonbola that she could not sleep in the common area and that she had "every right to call the police." Siyonbola recorded her interactions with Braasch and the police and later posted them online.

These cases have key characteristics in common. First, racial hall monitors typically act alone. Second, in most of these cases, the White hall monitor is female, often in her twenties, thirties, or forties. Third, regardless of the evidence or the information the Black person provides, the racial hall monitor insists that the Black person has crossed some racial boundary—done *something* wrong. Fourth, the hall monitor believes she is performing a social good, a necessary and important deed for society. Fifth, the fact that most of these encounters were being videotaped did not deter the actions of the race monitor. Notably, these cases are neither region nor gender specific, as regards the victims. Black women, men, and children have been surveilled and questioned by racial hall monitors across the country, in large cities and small towns, in the North, South, and West. Although in many instances racial hall monitors were shamed on social media, the incidents continue to happen.

These cases bring to mind the "papers" that enslaved Blacks had to have on hand when they traveled to other plantations (discussed in chapter 3). Blacks had to prove they had permission to be in certain physical spaces. BBQ Becky and other racial hall monitors are modern-day patrollers. By their actions and their words, these racial monitoring incidents send an unmistakable message to Blacks in public spaces: "Get out! You're not welcome here."

Other problematic outcomes are tied to racial hall monitors. First, these instances of private racial profiling have problematic and potentially fatal consequences. With numerous national cases involving police violence against Black citizens, some of these racial do-gooders are fully aware of what might happen if the police are called: it could result in a Black person being harmed or killed.[29] Second, these incidents may reinforce the image of Black deviance by subtly encouraging the misguided racial hall monitor. Third, they further diminish Black credibility in public spaces by pitting Blacks against Whites in a losing battle of whose words will be believed. This harkens back to a time when the courts did not allow Blacks and other people of color to testify against Whites.

## Punishing BBQ Becky

The prevalence of BBQ Beckys (sometimes referred to as "Karens") poses a social and criminological problem. These self-appointed hall monitors cause harm, yet they do not face punishment. The absence of legal recognition that their actions are wrong makes their actions de facto legal. This reality may explain the prevalence of cases. With each instance of racial hall monitors, future BBQ Beckys become emboldened. Without consequences for these race-based intrusions, racial hall monitors are being tolerated, if not encouraged. In response to these types of cases, Grand Rapids, Michigan, passed an ordinance designed to address the harm of individual Whites setting racial boundaries. The ordinance makes it an offense for someone to assume a person has committed a crime based on their race. The goal of the law is to avoid biased and inaccurate crime reporting. Violators face a five-hundred-dollar fine.[30] In Oregon, Janelle Bynum, a Black state legislator, introduced legislation to make racially motivated 911 calls an offense. The measure allows victims to sue for damages. Bynum proposed the legislation after police were called on her while she was out canvassing neighborhoods. She said the legislation was designed to ensure that people of color can walk around neighborhoods without being harassed.[31] One researcher, who labels this phenomenon "frivolous race-based police calls," suggests that a law designed to punish these actions should impose a fine and mandate an apology, implicit bias training, and mediation.[32]

## The Police-Public Contact Survey

In 1999, the US Bureau of Justice Statistics began gathering data on police contacts with citizens. According to the 2015 data, police were likely to initiate contact with Whites and Blacks at equal rates (11 percent for both groups), and at slightly lower rates for Hispanics (9 percent). Overall, the figures show that 23 percent of Whites had contact with the police (citizen initiated or police initiated), compared with 20 percent of Blacks and 17 percent of Hispanics. Based on this, all three groups had engagement with the police within a fairly close range (17 to 23 percent), but what happens after the police-initiated stop is noteworthy. The study found that Black drivers were more likely than White drivers (4.4 percent versus 3.3 percent) to be searched by police. For Hispanics, the rate is 5 percent, the highest. Hispanics were more likely to be ticketed than Blacks or Whites, and Whites were more likely to receive a verbal or written warning than were Blacks or Hispanics.[33] For street stops and traffic stops, Whites were much more likely than Blacks and Hispanics to believe the stop was legitimate.[34]

## Traffic Stops Statistics Study Act and Other Data

Starting in 1997, Congressman John Conyers began introducing the Traffic Stops Statistics Study Act. Conyers, who was the longest-serving African American congressman before he retired in 2017, proposed the bill in response to a spate of high-profile cases involving police stops of famous Black men. The bill would have mandated that the US attorney general gather statistics on all routine traffic stops made by federal law enforcement officials. This would include information on the number of traffic stops, identifying characteristics of the persons who were stopped (e.g., gender, race, age), reason for the stop, whether contraband was found, and whether an arrest was made. The bill, which Conyers introduced each year, never passed.

A few years later, related legislation was introduced. The Traffic Stops along the Border Statistics Study Act was drafted in response to complaints that Latinx drivers were being targeted for vehicle stops and searches along the US-Mexico border. Since 2018, there has been increased tension around the official US response to border security. This tension is largely the result of US treatment of Central and South American immigrants attempting to cross the border to get asylum in the United States. As part of its crackdown, the US Border Patrol increased its searches of Greyhound buses and Amtrak trains. Reports show that border agents in some instances boarded buses and asked passengers to show proof of citizenship or asked select passengers for citizenship papers. Many of these practices are questionable, as US citizens are not required to carry citizenship papers. Also, many of the immigration crackdowns have occurred on buses far from the US-Mexico border—including in New York and Pennsylvania.[35]

### A Costly Enterprise

Racial profiling is not limited to law enforcement officers or self-appointed lay citizens. Racial profiling is a social phenomenon that can manifest itself in any instance involving discretion, power, and race. Among the many other forms of racial profiling are name profiling (e.g., Black-sounding names or foreign-sounding names), linguistic profiling, and accent profiling. These are a few examples of individual characteristics some people use as racial proxies to differentiate and discriminate against groups of people by race.

As this chapter makes clear, many social, political, and psychological costs are associated with race-related police abuse. Each case of police abuse or police harassment involves specific officers and specific citizens. However, these incidents have an impact far beyond the individual who has a run-in with law enforcement. For instance, one Black person's difficult encounter with the police is negatively reinforced when hearing of similar experiences other Blacks have had with the police. Each negative experience creates another building block in Black community folklore.

It is unrealistic to expect that the criminal-legal system's net will only capture the guilty. We would expect that *some* people, including some Blacks, who are not involved in crime would be mistakenly suspected of criminal activity. Notably, nearly one-half of all Black men believe they have been wrongly suspected of criminal activity when fewer than one-third are involved in criminal activity. To more fully explore this issue, research on racial disparity must be expanded to include analyses of prearrest police contacts.

Police practices that allow law enforcement officials to act on negative perceptions and stereotypes of Blacks will continue to broaden the gap between Black and White experiences and perceptions of police. For Blacks, race-based policies raise questions about the legitimacy of the police and further alienate them from the system. People who do not face the daily threat of being stopped, searched, or detained by police, largely oftentimes on the basis of skin color, are unable to appreciate just how emotionally burdensome these stops can be. To a person who is pulled over by the police once a month for no apparent reason other than his race, the stops take on an onerous feel. Race-based practices and policies pit law enforcement against minorities and create an unbreakable cycle. Racial stereotypes may motivate police to arrest Blacks more frequently, but the fact that Black men are disproportionately engaged in crime is not a justification for racial discrimination. High rates of Black arrests generate statistically disparate arrest patterns, which in turn form the basis for further police selectivity by race. As noted at the top of the chapter, what many Whites view as the police "doing their job" is viewed by many Blacks as harassment.

Beyond causing harm to Blacks and Latinx people, race-based police stops also harm society at large. There are social costs to perpetuating inaccurate stereotypes, including exaggerated levels of race-based fear and greater levels of racial scapegoating. Although Blacks are responsible for a disproportionate share of crime, they are not responsible for the majority of crime. Culp explains how race-based police harassment is a denial of civil rights:

The police and citizens have to figure out ways to allow me to have rights as a black male too. Every time there is a conflict between the rights of the majority and my rights as a stereotypical black male, my rights cannot always be subordinate, or else I have no rights at all.[36]

Law enforcement is legitimately concerned with crime. The strategies it employs, however, should not result in racial damage. Racial targeting and abuse by police are costly enterprises. US taxpayers have footed the bill for hundreds of millions of dollars in police brutality and abuse lawsuits. Many of the nation's cities are in need of better—that is, more responsive and less punitive—police services. The huge sums of money paid out in legal damages should instead be available to protect and serve the people. Police abuse, harassment, and brutality exact a tremendous social, psychic and economic toll on society. As discussed, some of the problematic racially motivated encounters that take place in public spaces do not involve the police. In some instances, citizens are engaging in harassment and racial targeting. These incidents also impose a social and psychic toll, particularly on those most likely to be racially targeted. The issue of disproportionality has blurred many people's ability to see the problem of racial discrimination. The reality of racial targeting should not be dismissed, rejected, or trivialized. The problem is real and undercuts the criminal-legal system's ability to mete out justice.

# 5

## Racial Hoaxes

I am an invisible man. . . . I am a man of substance, of flesh
and bone, fiber and liquids—and I might even be said to
possess a mind. I am invisible, understand simply because
people refuse to see me. . . . When they approach me they
see only my surroundings, themselves, or figments of their
imagination—indeed, everything and anything except me.
—Ralph Ellison, *Invisible Man*

The racial hoax is a classic example of playing the race card. It is a cynical manipulation of our deepest fears about race, violence, and victimization. Racial hoaxes are deeply woven into the sociological and historical landscape, past and present. For centuries Black men were offered up as scapegoats for the real and imagined crimes of Whites. At the beginning of the twentieth century it was not uncommon for Black men to face false allegations of rape. White fear of the Black brute sexually violating the White female was the purported rationale behind the lynch laws. The punishment for these crimes—beatings, prison, being run out of town, and lynchings—all served to uphold White rule.

Today racial hoaxes are less common but no less incendiary. They have been the subject of satire and art exhibits and serve as plotlines for books, movies, and television shows. The continuing harms of the racial hoax are difficult to measure but are nevertheless real. How we treat them is a measure of how we assess and punish racial harms. Very little academic attention has been devoted to racial hoaxes. This chapter defines, identifies, and evaluates racial hoax cases, including the differences between hoax incidents with Black perpetrators and those with White perpetrators. The chapter also looks at the harms done by hoaxes, including the effect on race relations and the appropriate sanctions for these false allegations. The chapter shines a light on the modern era of hoax cases, beginning in the latter part of the twentieth century.

## In Black and White

Racial hoaxes are not new. False allegations of crime against Black men were used to support the broad-scale lynching of Blacks (see chapter 3) and initiate race riots, such as the 1921 Tulsa massacre. The Susan Smith hoax is likely the one that has received the most publicity. In 1994, Susan Smith, a White mother in South Carolina, told police that she had been the victim of a carjacking. She described her assailant as an armed Black male, between twenty and thirty years old. According to Smith, the man drove off with her two sons, ages three years and fourteen months. In the days that followed, Smith appeared on national TV and pled for their lives: "Your momma loves you. . . . Be strong."[1] The press and the public believed her story. Based on Smith's description of the assailant, the police drafted and widely disseminated a sketch of a young Black man. The FBI was brought in, and there was an extensive air and ground manhunt was conducted to find the assailant. Police received calls from all over the country suggesting the whereabouts of the boys. Police stopped, questioned, and detained Black men in the area of the alleged carjacking.

Nine days later we learned that Smith had fabricated the entire story. There was no Black carjacker. She had created the fictional bogeyman to shift attention away from herself. Smith had murdered her two boys. She had placed them in their car seats, driven to a lake, exited the vehicle, released the car's emergency brake, and allowed the car to plunge into the water.

Though Smith's claims strained credulity, the mainstream media and the public still believed her tale—an updated version of the Black-savage-terrorizing-innocent-White-person fantasy. Upon calm reflection, at least two questions should have been given serious consideration: When was the last time you saw a young Black man walking around town with two young White children? Where could this kidnapper go without arousing suspicion? Unbeknownst to the public, early on local police were suspicious of Smith's allegations. Her narrative and timeline were filled with inconsistencies.

In 1989, Charles Stuart told police that he and his wife, Carol, who was seven months pregnant, had been shot and robbed on their way home from a birthing class. According to Stuart, the man was Black and wore a jogging suit. During the attack, Charles Stuart was shot in the stomach and Carol Stuart was shot in the head. Days later she and her unborn child died. Police invaded Mission Hill, a predominantly Black neighborhood in Boston, in search of Carol Stuart's killer. After viewing a police lineup, Charles Stuart picked a Black man named Willie Bennett as the person who looked like the attacker. Based on inconsistencies in Stuart's story and incriminating information obtained from his brother, Matthew Stuart, the police soon shifted their investigation to Charles Stuart. Shortly thereafter, Charles Stuart committed suicide. Police later determined that Stuart had planned the murderous hoax as a scheme to cash in on his wife's insurance policy and continue a relationship with his mistress.

The actions of racial hoax perpetrators have made prophetic the words of Ralph Ellison quoted at the beginning of this chapter. In 1947, when Ellison wrote about the invisibility of the Black experience, he could not have envisioned that the negative image of Blackness would become so pervasive that *imaginary* Black people would be regularly invented as criminals. The Smith and Stuart cases are not aberrations.

In some instances, the hoax perpetrator makes up a crime story that implicates a real person. The New York Central Park incident involving Amy Cooper and Christian Cooper (no relation) provides an example. Amy, a White woman, was walking her dog when she encountered Christian, a Black man, who was bird-watching. Christian informed Amy that they were in section of the park that required pet owners to keep their dogs on leashes. She did not leash her dog, and Christian stated, "You're not going to like what I do," and proceeded to offer dog treats to her pet.[2] He also started videotaping the incident. Amy, who appeared visibly upset, walked quickly toward Christian and asked him to turn off his camera. He refused, and she responded by saying she was going to call the police and tell them she was being threatened by "an African American." Amy called the New York Police Department and told the 911 operator, "There is a man, African American, he has a bicycle helmet and he's recording me and threatening me and my dog." Further embellishing her claims, she stated, "I am being threatened by a man in the Ramble, please send the cops immediately!" The police responded to the call, and after speaking with Amy Cooper and Christian Cooper, they concluded there had been a verbal dispute and no arrest was made.

Later that evening, Christian Cooper's sister posted the video online. Christian Cooper was fortunate that the incident resulted in nothing more than an inconvenience.

## Defining Terms

There are two types of racial hoaxes:

1. When a person fabricates a crime and blames it on another person because of that person's race.
2. When an actual crime has been committed and a person falsely blames someone else because of that other person's race.

The first type of hoax is used as a means to achieve a goal, such as getting attention or getting time off from work. The second is used to cover up the person's involvement in a crime, such as murder or insurance fraud.

Hoax perpetrators are most frequently charged with filing a false police report. In many instances, however, they are not charged with any wrongdoing at all. The prevalence of racial hoaxes suggests that false report statutes do not operate as effective deterrents. Over the years, some states, such as New Jersey, have considered passing legislation to criminalize racial hoaxes. Because hoaxes impose social, psychological, economic, and legal costs on society, the actions of Susan Smith and others should be recognized for what they are: serious criminal offenses, regardless of whether they are used to cover up actual or fictional crimes.

Although a racial hoax can be perpetrated by a person of any race, against a person of any race, the primary focus of this chapter is on cases involving Whites and Blacks. While hoaxes are perpetrated by and against members of other racial groups, rarely have these incidents become national news stories. A few of the hoax cases, though, involve perpetrators or victims of other races.

In the overwhelming majority of incidents where someone falsely accuses another person of a crime, the victims are members of the same race. However, these cases rarely make headlines. Interracial hoaxes involving Blacks and Whites are the most likely to receive media attention. They also exact a high social and economic toll. As the following discussion details, racial hoax incidents add fuel to the ever-simmering fire of US race relations. With this in mind, it is argued that regardless of race, hoax perpetrators should face criminal punishment.

Hoaxes perpetrated by Blacks cause social harm as well. Specifically, they reinforce interracial tensions. Most importantly, they may make allegations of anti-Black violence less credible. The harms posed by these cases are discussed later in the chapter as part of the Jussie Smollett case.

Racial hoaxes perpetrated to fabricate a Black criminal impose a special type of harm. They create a distinct, acute social problem. African Americans in general and African American young men in particular are already saddled with a negative image. In fact, crime and young Black men have become synonymous in the American mind. As noted in earlier chapters, these images have combined to create the *criminalblackman*. Given the pervasiveness of this stereotype, it is not surprising that so many people have manipulated this negative image to avoid facing criminal responsibility.

Racial hoaxes are devised, perpetrated, and successful precisely because they tap into widely held fears. The harm of the racial hoax is not limited to reinforcing deviant, centuries-old images of Blacks. Hoaxes also create these images for new generations of young people. The racial hoax should be recognized as a separate criminal offense, subject to a mandatory prison term, regardless of whether it is used to cover up an actual or fabricated crime.

## Trends and Patterns

Table 5.1 provides case data for 134 hoaxes perpetrated between 1987 and 2020 (end of this chapter). As indicated in the table, the majority of hoaxes involve Whites who falsely accused Blacks of committing a crime. Table 5.2 (end of chapter) provides a breakdown of racial hoaxes involving Blacks and Whites (and in some instances, hoaxes involving members of other racial groups). Hoax cases were located through newspaper sources, including initial searches of LexisNexis, an automated database that stores news articles. Table 5.1 includes information on the race of the hoax perpetrator, the race of the victim, the alleged crime, whether a false report charge (or related charge) was filed against the perpetrator, and the state where the hoax took place. For some cases, information on some of these data points was not available. In addition to the information on hoax cases provided by the tables in this chapter, Appendix B includes a list and summary of each racial hoax case.

The 134 cases included in Table 5.1 represent only a fraction of all racial hoax cases. Most hoaxes are not classified or reported as such. For example, cases in which a newspaper reported on a hoax but did not state the race of the perpetrator or victim could not be included. More importantly, the overwhelming majority of criminal cases are investigated and closed by the police without ever making the news.

Several patterns emerge from the racial hoax cases[1]:

- Approximately 58 percent of all cases involved White-on-Black hoaxes, and one-quarter involved Black-on-White hoaxes.[3]
- Almost 70 percent of hoax cases involve fabricated claims of a crime, not cover-ups for actual crimes.
- Hoaxes were most frequently used to allege assault, murder, or rape.
- Hoax perpetrators were charged with filing a false police report in approximately 55 percent of the cases.
- Hoaxes were perpetrated by people representing all races, classes, ages, and geographic regions.
- Thirteen percent of the cases involved a hoax perpetrated by a college student or college administrator.

## Other Notable Cases

While they do not fit neatly within the definition of a racial hoax, some other hoax cases deserve comment and are included in Table 5.1. In a few incidents, hoax perpetrators cited the 2016 election of Donald Trump as US president as the reason for the hoax. In one, a White woman, Halley Bass, falsely claimed that she was attacked for wearing a pro-Brexit button. The woman said that she was attacked on the street by man who cut her face with a safety pin, and that her attack was due to the increase in hate crimes following Trump's election. In another case, a White Indiana man, George Stang, said that his church had been vandalized with anti-Semitic slurs. Following his admission that he created the hoax, he said that his goal was to "mobilize a movement" in response to Trump's election. In another case, a Muslim college student, Yasmin Seweid, claimed that three men yelled, "Donald Trump," before attacking her in a New York subway. She said the men tried to forcibly remove her hijab and called her a terrorist. The young woman, who was charged with filing a false police report, said she fabricated the crime because she was having problems with her family. These cases and others underscore the fact that hoaxes in general and racial hoaxes in particular reflect the social climate.

### White-on-Black Hoaxes

SORDID DETAILS

In several cases, the hoax was created with great attention to detail, sometimes bordering on a malevolent fantasy:

- A White woman in Pennsylvania reported that she had been attacked by a thirty-something, muscular Black man with a crew cut. She told police that the knife-wielding attacker used the weapon to play a game of tic-tac-toe on her arm. The woman claimed that the same man returned two months later to terrorize her. (Lisa Tanczos)
- A forty-seven-year-old White man told police that he had been robbed at gunpoint by a Black man, with "light-colored hair, 6 to 8 inch braids, a deformed pupil in one eye, acne scars on his cheeks, and one or two missing front teeth." (Paul Veach)
- A White woman reported that while she was at an automated teller machine, she and her two-year-old daughter were approached by a Black man wielding a gun. The woman told police that the man "put a gun to [her] child's head while he laughed." (Maryrose Posner)

These cases show how Whites have visualized the *criminalblackman*. These images, generated by various media and ubiquitous American lore, create a menacing caricature of young Black men. It was not enough for the perpetrators to describe the fictional assailant as Black; they added menacing, demonic-sounding details. Many White-on-Black hoaxes are successful because society buys the much-stated connection between Blackness and crime.

In one hoax incident that stands out from the others, a White Louisiana woman told police that she had been sexually assaulted by a Black man. She said the attacker had a tattoo of a serpent on his arm. A police sketch of the rapist was widely circulated in Baton Rouge. In a bizarre twist, *twenty-eight* other women notified the police that they, too, had been assaulted by the imaginary "serpent man." The high number of copycat victims suggests more than the usual hysteria associated with criminals on the loose. Within days, the alleged victim confessed that she had made up the rape story (Unnamed 1994–2).

## POLICE AND JUDICIAL OFFICIALS

Many of the cases involve hoaxes committed by legal officials themselves. In approximately 10 percent of the cases, the hoax perpetrator was a police officer or officer of the court:

- A White deputy sheriff told police that while he and his wife were out walking, they were accosted by two Black men. Both the sheriff and his wife were shot. His wife died following the attack, and he sustained a flesh wound. It was later discovered that the sheriff had hired a hit man to kill his wife to cash in on her insurance policy. (Thomas DiBartolo)
- A Delaware state trooper reported that she had been shot by a Black teenager. She said her attacker was named "Willy" and described him as a light-skinned Black male, between sixteen and nineteen years old, six feet tall, and weighing 160 to 170 pounds. After a two-month investigation, the trooper admitted she had made up the story to cover up the fact that she had accidentally shot herself in the arm with her service revolver. (Dawn Frakes)
- A New Jersey prosecutor claimed that someone was trying to kill him. He reported that two Black men chased him and shot at his car. He later confessed to making up the attempted-murder story. (Samuel Asbell)
- Two New York City police officers got into a physical fight over who would file a police report in a fire incident to which both men had responded. The altercation left both officers with extensive cuts and bruises. To hide their fight, the officers filed a police report stating that one of them had been assaulted by a Black man. At least six officers were involved in the cover-up. Two weeks later an officer who witnessed the fight told authorities of the hoax. (Thomas Drogan and Louis Papaleo)
- A White court deputy told police that a Black man had attempted to rape her in the hallway of a federal courthouse. Several Black male courthouse

employees were questioned about the attack. After extensive questioning by the FBI, the alleged victim confessed to fabricating the attack. (Lisa Wight)

- A police chief in Biscayne Park, Florida, directed three of his officers to charge innocent Blacks with burglary. Three Blacks were falsely charged, including a sixteen-year-old male. The police chief hatched the false-charge scheme so that he could improve the police department's clearance rate. (Raimundo Atesanio)

## All-Purpose Suspects

A handful of these hoaxes involve insurance scams. In one case, Robert Harris told police that he and his fiancée had been shot and robbed on a quiet Baltimore street. Harris's fiancée died from her gunshot wounds. Harris described the attacker as a Black man who was wearing a camouflage jacket and black and white pants. Based on the mistaken belief that he was the named beneficiary on his fiancée's $250,000 insurance policy, Harris had hired a White hit man to kill his fiancée.

In another murder-for-money case, Jesse Anderson told police that he and his wife had been attacked by Black assailants in a restaurant parking lot. Anderson's wife was stabbed twenty-one times and died following the assault. After a five-day search for the nonexistent Black assailants, Anderson was charged and ultimately convicted of his wife's murder. Police learned that Anderson had called his wife's insurance company one month prior to her murder, and asked whether her policy was in effect. (See also Matthew Gayle in Appendix B.)

Sometimes hoaxes are devised for more mundane reasons. In the case of the "runaway bride," Jennifer Wilbanks created an elaborate tale to avoid her upcoming wedding. Wilbanks, a White woman, disappeared from her Duluth, Georgia, home days before the scheduled ceremony. Family members and friends suspected foul play and notified authorities. A few days later the missing woman called her fiancé and told him that she was in Albuquerque, New Mexico. She said she had been kidnapped by a Hispanic man and White woman and that the couple had sexually assaulted her. She repeated the same tale to law enforcement officers. Then Wilbanks confessed to authorities that she was under stress about her upcoming wedding and that she had purchased a bus ticket in the week prior to her wedding. Wilbanks pled no contest to giving authorities false information. She was sentenced to two years of probation, required to perform 120 hours of community service, and fined $2,250. This case is the most prominent one in which a Hispanic was falsely accused in a hoax incident. It is unclear why Wilbanks added this racial twist to her story; perhaps she believed it would boost her credibility and evoke sympathy.

Perpetrators' reasons for using hoaxes run the gamut, from the mundane to the silly. Excuses include the desire to get time off from work, to win attention from a spouse, to garner sympathy, to make a political statement, and to avoid parental discipline for violating curfew. Here are some of the fabrications that perpetrators used:

- A White man reported that he had been carjacked by a Black man. He told police that he was forced at knifepoint to drive his kidnapper from Philadelphia to Atlantic City. After intense questioning, the man admitted that he had devised the story to avoid further car payments. (Dennis Pittman)
- A nineteen-year-old White woman told police that she had been kidnapped from a mall and raped by an armed Black man. Within two days, she admitted to making up the story as a cover for the fact that she stayed out all night with her boyfriend. (Kelli McGuire)
- A White New Jersey man told police that he saw a Black man running into a wooded area carrying a small White child. Based on his statement, an extensive air and land search was mounted. The next day, the man admitted to making up the story. The story was concocted so that he could get the afternoon off from work. (Michael Shaw)
- A White woman told police that she had been kidnapped from a shopping mall by three Black men. She said she was raped and forced to take drugs. She later confessed that she had made up the story to avoid punishment for staying out past her curfew. (Janet Maxwell)

## Multiple Perpetrators

White-on-Black hoaxes are often perpetrated by more than one offender. Thus, hoaxes cannot be dismissed as the work of loners. These multiple-perpetrator hoaxes have been used to cover up a variety of offenses, including accidental shootings (Adam Baisley, Tonya Gibson, et al.), a work-related scuffle (Thomas Drogan and Louis Papaleo), domestic violence (Tina Gateley and William Karaffa), and a planned crime (Joshua Green, Neva Veitch, and David Craig).

## The Interracial Rape Hoax

Approximately 20 percent of the White-on-Black hoaxes are based on concocted claims of rape by a White woman who said she was assaulted by a Black man (fourteen cases). For many Blacks, particularly those over a certain age, the mention of interracial rape taps into age-old allegations of Black men forcing themselves on innocent White females. Historically, protecting the virtue of White women was placed on a legal pedestal. The fear of Black male sexual assault against White women was the stated impetus behind the lynch laws. Given this backdrop, it is not surprising that so many White women have created Black male rapists as their fictional criminals.

Throughout history, rape has been the most common criminal hoax played on Black men. The case of the Scottsboro Boys is perhaps the best-known example of Black men being used as racial scapegoats. In 1931, Victoria Price and Ruby Bates, two young White women, alleged that they had been assaulted and raped by nine "Negro boys." Following a swift legal process, eight of the Black boys were sentenced to death. The final case resulted in a hung jury. The press portrayed Bates and Price as symbols of southern White womanhood. Eventually, Bates recanted her story.

A racial hoax also triggered the 1923 massacre in Rosewood, Florida. A false claim by a White woman that she had been raped and beaten by a Black man led Whites in the next town to go on a killing rampage and burn down the all-Black town of Rosewood. According to official estimates, 6 Blacks and 2 Whites were killed. Unofficial estimates are that between 40 and 150 Blacks were killed. Seven decades later, in 1994, a court awarded Rosewood family descendants more than $2 million in reparations. In 1921, there was a race riot in Tulsa, Oklahoma. Members of the affluent, thriving Black Greenwood community—also known as the "Black Wall Street"—were attacked by White mobs. The mobs massacred hundreds of people and torched over one thousand homes. The mob violence was spurred by a false claim that a Black man had assaulted a White woman.

## Black-on-White Hoaxes

The thirty Black-on-White hoaxes offer an interesting counterpoint to the White-on-Black hoaxes. Most Blacks who carried out hoaxes created a scenario in which they were victimized because of their race. Most of these were staged as hate crimes. A hate crime was typically used as a cover for an insurance scam (e.g., Tracy Birt, DeWayne Byrdsong, and Persey Harris). Apparently these hoax perpetrators believed that a hate crime would be the most believable offense that a White person could commit against a Black person. The frequency of hate-crime hoaxes underscores the prevailing view: except for hate crimes, most of us have difficulty imagining someone White committing a random act of violence against someone Black.

Black-on-White hate-crime hoaxes contrast sharply with White-on Black racial hoaxes. The latter are typically created as random acts of Black violence against Whites, which matches with the public perception that Blacks run amok committing depraved, unprovoked acts of violence against Whites, while the only Whites who commit violent crimes against Blacks are racial extremists. As is true for White-on-Black hoaxes, the motivations for Black-on-White hoaxes are varied. Some Black-on-White hoaxes are perpetrated as insurance scams, some to make a social statement, and still others are fabricated to evoke sympathy. Oftentimes, these hoaxes are triggered by a combination of factors.

## Tawana Brawley, Duke Lacrosse, and Jussie Smollett

Until the 2019 Jussie Smollett case, the Duke Lacrosse and Tawana Brawley cases were the most well-known hoaxes involving Black perpetrators. In 1987, Brawley, a fifteen-year-old Black girl from Wappingers Falls, New York, told police that she had been abducted and raped by six White male police officers. She also said she was smeared with feces, placed in a plastic bag, and left in a gutter. The story drew national attention. After convening for seven months and hearing from 180 witnesses, the grand jury concluded her claim was false and declined to issue any indictments in the case. The fallout from the case included the disbarment of C. Vernon Mason, one of Brawley's attorneys. As well, a court issued a civil judgment in favor of Stephen Pagones, one of the officers accused of assaulting Brawley. Mason, Al Sharpton, and attorney Alton Maddox were ordered to pay $185,000 for defamation. Although Brawley stands by her original account, the incident has been widely discredited as a hoax.

Two decades later, three members of the Duke University lacrosse team were accused of raping an exotic dancer. Team members hosted a party and hired exotic dancers to provide entertainment. Two dancers, both Black, were hired to perform at the event hosted by the all-White collegiate team. The young women arrived at the house and left a short time later, after hearing some harsh language directed at them by some of the young men.[4] Some of the other partygoers, however, managed to persuade the women to go back inside to finish the show. The dancers returned to the house and finished their performance. After they left, one of them called the police and said that she had been forced into a bathroom and sexually assaulted by three team members. This explosive allegation led to heated and rancorous debates about a multitude of topics—race, socioeconomic status, sex workers, college sports, the South, sexism, White privilege, elite universities, the criminal-legal system, "jungle fever," the credibility of rape victims, elite sports, the media, *and* the Tawana Brawley case.

Many people believed that the students had been set up by a scheming Black woman. Others believed the young woman and felt that her claims were not taken seriously because she was Black and a strip club dancer. Still others felt the case presented an opportunity to address the harms of the "boys will be boys" mentality, regardless of whether a rape took place. The incident also highlighted the squeamishness that many people feel about exotic dancers: that strippers stand barely one rung above prostitutes.

From the beginning, the case had holes in it. For instance, one of the young men who had been identified as an attacker had a credible alibi. A taxicab driver said he had picked up the student from the party and taken him to an automated teller machine. There were also inconsistencies in the young woman's story regarding the timeline, the nature of the attack, the number of people involved, and their physical descriptions. From the beginning of the case, there were questions about the judgment and motives of the district attorney, Mike Nifong. More than one year after the initial allegations were made, the rape charges were dropped. Nifong was disbarred and later declared bankruptcy. No false report charges were filed against the accuser.

In 2019, actor Jussie Smollett filed a crime report with the Chicago Police Department. Smollett said he left his Chicago building at approximately 2 a.m. to go to a nearby Subway sandwich shop. As he walked back, he was assaulted by two White men, one of whom was wearing a Make America Great Again (MAGA) hat. According to Smollett, one of the men recognized him as an actor, and the pair proceeded to hurl anti-Black and anti-gay slurs at him, beat him up, and wrap a noose around Smollett's neck.

During the investigation, police found video of two Black men walking in the same area where Smollett said he was assaulted. These men were questioned by the police and said they knew and worked with Smollett. They reported that Smollett had hired them to stage a racial attack on himself. Following this, the public tide turned against Smollett, who was widely seen as having orchestrated a racial hoax. The prosecutor charged him with sixteen offenses, including filing a false police report. Later, in an unexpected twist, the Cook County prosecutor's office dropped all charges against him. The Chicago Police Department was particularly outraged and sought to have Smollett repay the department $130,000 for the costs of investigating his false claims (police resources, including overtime pay). Other charges were filed, including a claim by Smollett that he was the victim of malicious prosecution. In 2020, a judge dismissed this claim. The case caused a great public uproar about celebrity, race, the LGBTQ community, and justice. Smollett's claims were initially met with support and outrage that he been attacked. However, as more facts came out, support dwindled as many noted inconsistencies and questionable behavior by Smollett (e.g., why was Smollett walking outside in below-freezing weather at 2 a.m., and how likely is it that two White men would have recognized him as a gay, Black actor on the series *Empire*?). As is true for the other high-profile Black perpetrator hoaxes, Smollett has not recanted his story and maintains that he was the victim of a vicious assault.

*The Exonerated Five*

The case of the Exonerated Five, initially known as the "Central Park Five," underscores the fact that random, private citizens are not the only ones who perpetrate hoaxes. In some instances, professionals within the criminal-legal system are responsible for creating false claims. These instances are particularly problematic, given that they involve representatives of the system hired to carry out justice. Further, in these instances, the racial hoax victims are not random individuals but people specifically targeted by police officers or prosecutors. This is true of the young men—Antron McCray, Yusef Salaam, Korey Wise, Kevin Richardson, and Raymond Santana Jr.—at the center of the Exonerated Five case.

In 1989, a White woman was brutally beaten and raped during an evening jog through New York's Central Park. The near-fatal attack was a huge media story, with almost daily calls for the death penalty for the woman's attackers. It was widely reported and believed that a large gang of youths were in the park that evening committing various assaults on joggers, walkers, and bicyclists. "Wilding" was the word used to describe their actions, including the sexual assault on Trisha Meili. Within days of the attack, Donald Trump took out a full-page ad in the *Daily News* calling for the return of the death penalty in New York.

Five young men, ages fourteen to sixteen years old, were arrested and charged with the assault. Following hours and hours of questioning, they confessed. They later recanted. At trial, they were convicted and sentenced to serve between six and thirteen years in prison. In two trials, the five young men were found guilty of various offenses related to the assault and other crimes in Central Park that night. There was no physical evidence linking the young men to the crimes.

In total, the five men served more than forty years behind bars. The men were exonerated in 2002 following DNA testing and a confession by a convicted rapist, Matias Reyes. In 2014 they received a combined settlement of $41 million. The 2019 release of Ava Duvernay's film *When They See Us* details their story, including the actions of the district attorney and the police—who were said to have coerced confessions, overlooked evidence of their innocence, and presumed their guilt. Thus, this case offers another highly problematic instance in which racial hoaxes are used *by the justice system itself* (see also Raimundo Atesanio, Appendix B). Here, the perpetrators were not private citizens, but rather justice system professionals sworn to uphold the rule of law.

## Comparing Harms: Black-on-White versus White-on-Black Racial Hoaxes

Several features distinguish White-on-Black from Black-on-White hoaxes. First, as discussed earlier, Black-on-White hoaxes are almost always drawn as hate crimes. When Whites create imaginary crimes, they are unlikely to use hate crime as a ruse. Second, the White-on-Black hoax causes greater social damage and harm than the Black-on-White hoaxes, primarily because Black-on-White hoaxes are less likely to receive national attention. Third, in hoaxes involving an interracial crime, a White person who claims to have been victimized by a Black person is much more likely to be believed than a Black person who claims to have been victimized by a White person.

### An Aggrieved Community

Overall, the social and legal response to hoaxes differs according to the race of the person alleging that a crime has occurred. For example, Charles Stuart's claim that he had been shot by a Black jogger led to a full-scale police invasion of Boston's Mission Hill. Blacks in Boston, as well as many Blacks nationwide, felt some sense of responsibility for the crimes committed by the fictional Black criminal. Although the police department of Union, South Carolina, handled the Susan Smith case much differently, the town's Black community still felt betrayed by the hoax, as did many other Blacks. The same sense of community betrayal does not exist with Black-on-White hoaxes. There was no "White community" that bore comparable responsibility or group shame in the Tawana Brawley or Sabrina Collins cases. Nor was there a White community that was placed under siege after Brawley and Collins made their allegations.

In the Jesse Anderson, Susan Smith, Miriam Kashani, and Charles Stuart cases, there were calls for an apology to the Black community, suggesting that the response to and perception of racial hoaxes varies according to the race of the perpetrator. The demands for an apology indicate that many Blacks believed the racial hoax had created a communal injury. Although Susan Smith's brother offered an apology to the Black community, Ray Flynn, the mayor of Boston at the time of the Charles Stuart case, declined to issue an apology.

Because Black criminals are perceived as more menacing than White criminals, hoaxes created with a Black villain are treated differently than hoaxes created with a White villain. Greater social harm results when someone White falsely accuses someone Black of a crime than when the reverse occurs. This is not to suggest that no social harm is associated with Black-on-White hoaxes. Black-on-White hoaxes make it easier for Whites to dismiss claims of White racism. This concern was raised during the fallout from the Jussie Smollett case.

Historically, however, White-on-Black hoaxes pose a greater, more harmful social impact. They create and enforce negative racial stereotypes for a new generation of young people. The case of Lucille Magrone offers an example of this effect. Magrone, a White woman living in Upstate New York, sent out letters purportedly written by a Black man. The letters, delivered to neighborhood Whites, threatened them with rape and murder if they did not move from the area: "You white people cannot live here. I will see you dead."5 After Magrone's hoax was unmasked, one of her White neighbors stated,

> Small children in the neighborhood have been introduced to racism that was never there before. Now it is in their minds that black people are bad, that black people are trying to break in—that there's a bogeyman, a black bogeyman out there who is going to get [them].[6]

Another indicator that the criminal stereotypes of Blacks are having an impact on young people is the number of racial hoaxes involving a perpetrator under the age of twenty-one. In several cases, White youths fabricated a crime against someone Black (e.g., Kendra Gillis, Edward O'Brien, and Toby Campbell). In one case, a seven-year-old girl made up an assault charge against a Black man (Unnamed 1994-3).

## Credibility

The public appears to be more willing to believe a White person who claims to have been victimized by someone Black than a Black person who claims to have been victimized by someone White. The Tawana Brawley, Duke Lacrosse, and Jussie Smollett cases are examples of this difference. From the beginning, many people suspected that the Brawley and Duke Lacrosse allegations were fabrications. By contrast, the stories of Susan Smith and Charles Stuart cases were readily believed. The reluctance to believe the Brawley and Duke Lacrosse claims, though, may be partly due to the fact that they involved criminal allegations against protected communities (the police and an elite athletic team). Regarding the Smollett case, early on there were credibility questions as to the likelihood of the incident, given the freezing weather and that he was seen walking with a noose around his neck following the alleged incident.

Additionally, Black-on-White hoaxes more frequently conclude without the perpetrator acknowledging they committed a hoax. In the Brawley case, for instance, the grand jury's refusal to issue an indictment against law enforcement officials caused her claim to be widely considered a hoax. Similarly, in the Duke Lacrosse case, the accuser stands by her story that she was sexually assaulted by members of the team. In the first instance, the case was "closed" based on the findings of an independent judicial body. In the second, as details of the district attorney's case surfaced (including the fact that he never actually interviewed the accuser), many people concluded that the case was a hoax. Likewise, Jussie Smollett still maintains that he was assaulted. Unfortunately, in these cases Blacks and Whites remain largely divided. Many Blacks claimed there was a cover-up, and many Whites claimed there was a hoax.

Another indication of the tension created by these cases is the amount of litigation they spark. Following the Brawley investigation, a $30 million defamation suit was brought against her and her advisers. A default judgment was entered against Brawley, and a few years later, one of her lead attorneys was disbarred. The case has continued to follow the Reverend Al Sharpton, who says that at the time of the allegations he believed Brawley's story, as did many others. He has since worked with numerous families victimized by police brutality and in 2004 ran for president.

## False Report Charges

Table 5.1 shows that hoax perpetrators are not always charged with filing a false report. The seriousness of the offense is not determinative, since some perpetrators charged with murder (e.g., Thomas DiBartolo) faced charges for filing a false report whereas others (e.g., Donald Cherry, Susan Smith) did not. For some prosecutors, it may be that adding a false report charge to a murder case is perceived as excessive. Notably, in many of the cases involving money scams, false report charges were filed (e.g., Sonia James, Daniel Mayo and Philip LaForest, Jaelyn Sealey). In several cases, though, perpetrators faced other criminal charges for their hoax—for example, felony disorderly conduct (Alicia Hardin). One clear trend is that hoax perpetrators are increasingly likely to face false report charges. Another clear trend is that the more recent the case, the greater the likelihood that the perpetrator faced a hoax-related charge.

Equating Black-on-White with White-on-Black hoaxes ignores the different social reaction to these hoaxes. Black men have always been perceived as a physical threat; however, until recently, that threat was portrayed in sexual terms. In the past twenty years, the image of the Black male as rapist has evolved into the image of the Black male as the symbolic pillager of all that is good. The *criminalblackman* stereo-type persists, despite the fact that the majority of people arrested each year are White. The negative perceptions of Black men affect how Blacks and Whites, as individuals and as group members, are affected by racial hoaxes.

White-on-Black hoaxes follow a standard pattern. First, law enforce-ment officials are called into action. They are asked to protect an in-nocent White person from further harm and to apprehend a widely perceived threat, a menacing Black man. Second, the incident arouses sympathy and results in calls for swift and stiff punishment. Third, even after the hoax is uncovered, the image of the *criminalblackman* lingers and becomes more embedded in our collective racial consciousness.

## Other Cases and Patterns

### COLLEGE HOAXES

One of the most striking patterns that has emerged since earlier investigations of racial hoaxes is the number of cases that involve college students or that took place on a university campus. Fifteen of the cases (13 percent) were perpetrated by a college student or administrator. For a variety of reasons, a college campus is fertile ground for hoaxes. First, for some students, college is the first interaction they have had with members of other racial and ethnic groups. Second, for many students, college provides their first exposure to student activism and political dissent. Third, for some students, college may represent their first in-depth exposure to and exploration of sociopolitical issues, including race.

Blacks and Whites have both perpetrated university hoaxes. A number of these hoaxes were designed to "send a message"—that is, to make a social or political statement about an issue of importance to the hoax perpetrator. The following cases are representative:

- A young White female student at the University of Montana told police that she had been robbed by a Black man. She said her attacker took one hundred dollars. She described him as six-feet-three with a dark or Black complexion. After discovering several inconsistencies in her story, police charged her with filing a false police report. (Emily Clark; Josephine Lupus)
- A Black student at Trinity International sent out hate mail to Black and Latino students. The letters threatened violence. As a precautionary response, school officials moved all minority students off-campus to hotels. After two weeks of campus turmoil, Alicia Hardin admitted that she had sent the letters. She wanted to transfer to another school and thought this tactic would make her parents believe that Trinity International was not a safe school for minority students.(Alicia Hardin)
- A White female student at George Washington University reported that another White female had been raped by two Black men with "particularly bad body odor." The perpetrator later claimed that the hoax was staged to "highlight the problems of safety for women . . . [and was] never meant to hurt anyone or racially offend anyone." (Miriam Kashani)

Perhaps the most unusual campus hoax is the one involving Keri Dunn, who in 2004 was a visiting professor at Claremont McKenna College. Dunn, who is White, claimed that she was attacked one evening as she returned to her car. She had just given a lecture on hate crime. Dunn said that her vehicle had been spray-painted with racist and anti-Semitic slurs ("kike whore" and "nigger lover"). A campus uproar followed, and classes were canceled for one day. Officials later concluded that Dunn had staged the hoax herself. She was sentenced to one year in prison and restitution of twenty thousand dollars, the cost of investigating the incident. This case is unusual in that Dunn is White, and she perpetrated a hoax that implicated Whites.

It is noted that the list of hoax cases includes three involving Muslim perpetrators. In all three cases, the fabricated offense was framed as a hate crime. Also, in two of the cases, the person perpetrating the hoax was a minor (Yasmin Seweid, Unnamed 2018–3, and Unnamed 2016).

### HOAXES WITH A TWIST

A number of hoaxes defy easy categorization. Sometimes cases are not discovered to be hoaxes until years or decades later. In one instance, a twenty-year-old racial hoax was uncovered by police. In 1982, Mark Mangelsdorf was involved with a married woman, Melinda Raisch. Raisch, who was part of a religious community and worked at a Bible college, did not want to suffer the stigma of a divorce, so she and Mangelsdorf conspired to kill her husband, David Harmon. The pair murdered Harmon with a crowbar while he lay sleeping. At the time, Raisch blamed the murder on Black intruders into the Harmon home. After police reopened the case in 2001, both Mangelsdorf and Raisch were convicted of second-degree murder in Harmon's death. In 2006, both received sentences of ten to twenty years in prison.

In another twist on the traditional racial hoax, Donald Cherry, a White father of two, told police that his two-year-old son had been killed by Black youths following a traffic dispute. According to Cherry, following the traffic encounter, the youths fired shots at his car after he made an obscene gesture at them. Within one week, Cherry told police that he had been involved not in a traffic dispute but rather in a drug deal gone awry. Cherry had driven across town to purchase crack cocaine. His small children were in the back seat of the vehicle. As it turned out, the suspect, who admitted to firing the shot, is Black. The case is unusual because Cherry attempted to portray himself as an innocent victim of random Black crime, thereby attempting to make the actions committed by the Black youth appear even more sinister.

There were two incidents in which White assailants robbed White victims and demanded that they tell the police that the assailants were Black. In one case, a gang of White thieves robbed a man and threatened to kill his family unless he told police that the robbers were Black. In another case, a White man robbed an elderly couple of $2,850 and told them to blame the crime on a Black man. These cases mirror the rationale behind the racial hoax cases: to play on racial stereotypes and avoid criminal responsibility.

In another case, a nineteen-year-old White man, David Mazziotti, used face paint to disguise his race. The Philadelphia man also hid a pillow under his clothes to make himself appear obese. Mazziotti had created this obese Black man disguise so that he could rob banks. In one South Africa case, a gang of White robbers wore mud masks to disguise their race and trick their victims into believing and reporting that the perpetrators were Blacks. Because Mazziotti was arrested before he could carry out the crime, the case does not classify as a typical racial hoax. However, Mazziotti's perceptions and beliefs about race and crime are identical to those of perpetrators of successful hoaxes.

Based on the uncorroborated testimony of a lone undercover agent, police in Tulia, Texas, arrested more than forty African American residents, approximately 16 percent of the town's Black population. This undercover drug sting operation, by a White officer, resulted in numerous convictions and sentences. An investigation by a special prosecutor revealed that the evidence was unreliable, and all the convictions were voided. By itself, this incident represents more than forty separate racial hoaxes.

In each of these hoaxes, it is clear that the goal was to have someone Black singled out and held responsible for a crime he or she did not commit. These cases, when added to the others, make a compelling argument for publicizing the prevalence and harms of hoaxes. That some people have gone to the extreme of using Blackface to avoid criminal responsibility demonstrates the strength of the perceived link between Blackness and crime.

## Economics of the Racial Hoax

Beyond causing social injury, racial hoaxes exact a financial toll. Untold resources have been wasted on efforts to locate fictional Black criminals. The following comment illuminates the varied harms of racial hoaxes:

> [A racial hoax] accusation affects us all. It terrorizes a community and discriminates against a race of people. And it is the kind of crime that costs taxpayers thousands of dollars to launch massive, futile investigations.[7]

Indeed, the economic consequences of many hoax cases underscore this point. Several hoax incidents triggered massive searches and investigations by police departments and sometimes involved multiple law enforcement agencies. The costs of these cases ran cumulatively into the tens of thousands of dollars. Increasingly hoax perpetrators are being required to pay investigative costs. In one case, a White college student falsely claimed that she had been raped by a Black man. After confessing to the fabrication, she had to repay the police for the costs of investigating her case (Michele Yentes). Several other cases have imposed restitution on hoax perpetrators (Keri Dunn, Sonia James, and Jennifer Wilbanks). The Chicago Police Department presented Jussie Smollett with a bill for $130,000—the amount including costs for overtime paid to police officers investigating the case.

## A Legal Response: The Law and the Logistics

### False Report Statutes

Though they are on the books, false report laws are not always used to punish racial hoax offenders. Just over half of the hoax perpetrators were charged with filing a false police report. False reporting charges are most often filed in cases involving less serious offenses. The fact that false report charges are not uniformly sought renders them an ineffective deterrent against future hoaxes. Further, under most false report laws, a hoax is a misdemeanor offense, which undercuts the law's deterrence value. On the one hand, adding a false report charge to a murder case such as Susan Smith's might appear to be overload. At the other extreme, pursuing a false police-report charge against someone like Miriam Kashani might seem like a waste of the prosecutor's time and resources. The failure to punish racial hoaxes, however, only makes it more likely that they will continue.

## The Law on Hate Crimes

Hate crime statutes can be divided into two types. First, some statutes treat hate crimes as independent criminal offenses. These are referred to as "pure bias" statutes. The Minnesota statute at issue in *R.A.V. v. St. Paul* is an example of this type.[8] The US Supreme Court held that the state's bias-crime law impermissibly criminalized certain forms of hate speech, in violation of the First Amendment.

A second kind of hate-crime statute provides a "penalty enhancement" for crimes motivated by bias. Under these statutes, when the court finds that the offender has committed a crime against a person because of his or her race, it may impose additional penalties. In some states, for example, a person convicted of assault could face one year behind bars, but if the assault was racially motivated, the penalty could be increased to two years. A number of states have adopted the Model Bias Crime provision, drafted by the Anti-Defamation League. The federal government has also enacted penalty-enhancement legislation.

Penalty-enhancement statutes have been upheld by the US Supreme Court. In *Wisconsin v. Mitchell* a Black defendant challenged the state's penalty-enhancement statute.[9] Mitchell, who had been convicted of assaulting a fourteen-year-old White youth, faced an increased prison sentence of five years because the crime was motivated by bias. Finding the state law constitutional, the Supreme Court noted that "bias-inspired conduct" is an appropriate arena for penalty enhancement because it is "thought to inflict greater individual and societal harm."[10] Further, the Court observed, such conduct is likely to provoke "retaliatory crimes, inflict distinct emotional harm on their victims, and incite community unrest."[11] A racial hoax law could be framed as either a pure bias-crime statute or as penalty enhancement. Given that the Supreme Court has upheld bias-crime enhancement, this looks to be the safer constitutional route.

## The Racial Hoax as Crime: Constitutional Concerns

The road to making the racial hoax a crime is, constitutionally speaking, a much smoother road than the one that earlier hate-crime legislation had to travel, primarily because First Amendment concerns do not pose a barrier to making the racial hoax a crime. A long-standing principle of constitutional law is that when speech involves imminent lawless action, it is not accorded First Amendment protection. Thus, one does not have the right to scream, "Fire," in a crowded building.[12]

When one uses a racial hoax to mislead law enforcement, a chain of predictable responses follows. The speech element of the racial hoax ("A Black man harmed me") triggers numerous actions, including the deployment of police officers to particular neighborhoods to locate potential suspects, the creation of "wanted" posters, the dissemination of information about the offense to the media, the distribution of all-points bulletins, and meetings by the police and community groups to discuss what actions should be taken. The person uttering the words of a racial hoax has done more than simply speak. He or she has pointed a finger at a community of people with the goal of thwarting justice. By design, the speech of the racial hoax is actually lawless conduct, which is unprotected by the First Amendment.

It could be argued as well that, given the historically fraught relationship between the African American community and law enforcement, Black-on-White hoaxes, in particular, have the potential to result in violence. Arguably, then, they represent "true threats" that suggest that the hoax perpetrator intends to commit an act of violence against the victim—by triggering police action. In *Virginia v. Black*, the US Supreme Court determined that state legislation that punishes content-based speech is permissible in some instances, particularly for speech with a long and historical connection to violence.

## Proposed Legislation: An Example

Following several high-profile hoax cases, Shirley Turner, a New Jersey state senator, drafted legislation in 1996 to punish racial hoaxes. The proposed law distinguished between a hoax used to cover up an actual crime (false incrimination) and one used to mask a fake crime (fictitious reports), and attaches a harsher penalty to the former offense. Although the False Reports to Law Enforcement Authorities bill was not signed into law, it offers an example and opportunity for discussing how a racial hoax law might be framed:

- *Falsely incriminating another.* A person who knowingly gives or causes to be given false information or a description of a fictitious person to any law enforcement officer with purpose to implicate another because of race, color, religion, sexual orientation, or ethnicity commits a crime of the third degree (punishable by three to five years in prison and/or a fifteen-thousand-dollar fine).
- *Fictitious reports.* A person who files a fictitious report is guilty of a crime of the fourth degree if the person acted with purpose to implicate another because of race, color, religion, sexual orientation, or ethnicity (punishable by eighteen months in prison and/or a ten-thousand-dollar fine).
- *Restitution.* In addition to any other fine, fee, or assessment imposed, any person convicted of an offense under this section is to reimburse the governing body of the municipality for the costs incurred in investigating the false information or the fictitious report.[13]

This proposed law serves as a reference for the following discussion on the ideal components of a racial hoax law.

## The Offender

Arguably the hoaxes that cause the most harm are those perpetrated against Blacks. However, hoaxes perpetrated by Blacks that target Whites can also cause great harm. The following discussion and analysis focuses primarily on the harms associated with anti-Black hoaxes. The damage done by a fabricated claim is so great that there should be no exclusion as to who can be punished. Harm occurs irrespective of whether a hoax perpetrator is White or Black.

Community responses and harms may differ depending on the race of the hoax perpetrator. When a White offender points the finger at a Black person, it acts to further polarize Black and White communities. As a result, Blacks feel more vulnerable to indiscriminate police practices, and Whites feel more vulnerable to crime by Blacks. Conversely, when the hoax perpetrator is Black and the victim is Black, the alleged crime will likely not be taken as seriously. Unless it is a celebrity, police are less likely to respond as quickly to a Black person claiming harm as they would to a White person claiming harm. White-on-Black hoaxes receive much more media attention than Black-on-Black hoaxes, and Black-on-Black hoaxes are less likely to be uncovered because such a fabrication would appear to represent the status quo: the erroneous belief that the majority of crime in the United States involves a Black offender. In fact, Whites make up the majority of the people arrested for crime in any given year. Furthermore, more than 80 percent of all crime is intraracial, involving a victim and offender of the same race. Both Black-on-Black and White-on-Black hoaxes should be punished because they perpetuate the *criminalblackman* stereotype.

Legal scholar Mari Matsuda, in a compelling argument for criminalizing race-based hate speech, contends that only Whites can be offenders. She states that the harm of racist speech is greatest when the speech reinforces a "historically vertical relationship."[14] Likewise, attorney Marc Fleischauer has argued that penalty enhancement should only attach in cases involving a White offender. Without this "White-only" rule, "minorities will be subjected to enhanced penalties at a disproportionate rate compared to Whites because it is the nature of society for the majorities to prosecute minorities more frequently and with more vigor than vice versa."[15] The fact that *Wisconsin v. Mitchell*—the only hate-crime sentencing-enhancement case decided by the US Supreme Court—involved a Black defendant supports Fleischauer's observations.

Although Fleischauer and Matsuda make strong points, the race-of-the-perpetrator / race-of-the-victim line that they draw should not be applied to a racial hoax law. First, unlike the victim of racist hate speech, the victim of a racial hoax is not directly assaulted by the offender. Second, not just one person is harmed by a racial hoax but an entire community. Given the harm done by pointing a false finger at a Black person, anyone of any race who perpetrates a hoax against someone Black should be penalized. The proposed New Jersey legislation correctly makes no distinction based on the race of the perpetrator.

*Targets and Victims*

With regard to who is classified as a victim for the racial hoax, two questions arise. First, should a racial hoax law mandate an identifiable, named victim—a "Willie Bennett requirement"? Willie Bennett is the Black man whom Charles Stuart identified as the person who shot and robbed him and his wife. Since current false report statutes do not require an identifiable victim, there should be no such requirement for a racial hoax law. The goal of false report statutes is to punish intentional efforts to thwart law enforcement. Whether there is an identifiable victim or not, the racial hoax causes harm. A penalty is also justified by the communal harm it causes.

Professor Frederick Lawrence, in a discussion of the breadth of harm caused by hate crimes, states, "The victim suffers for being singled out on the basis of race, and the general community of the target racial group is harmed as well."[16] As applied to the racial hoax, a "victim" who says, "a Black guy did it," has hurled an actionable racial epithet. Given the predictable responses of law enforcement, the hoax is a kind of physical harassment, solely on the basis of race. It is as if Susan Smith and all the other hoax perpetrators called every Black man a "low life," "hoodlum," or "criminal" *because* of his race. The racial hoax exemplifies philosopher Ludwig Wittgenstein's assertion that "words are also deeds."[17]

Fleischauer, in his discussion of Florida's hate-crime statute, argues that it would be constitutional to make minorities the only protected group. He observes that one of the explicit goals of hate-crime legislation is to curb racism and empower minorities. Allowing a racial hoax law to encompass White-on-Black hoaxes *and* Black-on-White hoaxes unfairly accords the two equal weight. Beyond the individual harm that a racial hoax may cause a targeted Black person, it brings harm to Blacks as a group and creates more tension between Blacks and Whites. A look at the hoax cases establishes that the harm of a White-on-Black hoax is not comparable to the harm of either a White-on-White or Black-on-White hoax. The proposed New Jersey legislation is silent with regard to the victim's race, implying that a hoax victim may be of any race.

The equal protection clause of the US Constitution would present the biggest roadblock to legally differentiating a hoax based on the race of the victim. As a general rule, White-on-Black hoaxes result in more harm than Black-on-White hoaxes, and false reporting laws are an adequate penalty for Black-on-White hoaxes. However, as the Smollett case shows, Black-on-White hoaxes can cause great social and economic harm. Further, given the US Supreme Court's race-neutral leanings, the safest route is to draft hoax legislation that would protect a victim of any race. This legal compromise, however, does not provide adequate protection to Blacks as a group.

## Intent

A racial hoax law could be written to require either specific or general intent on the part of the perpetrator. A distinction could be made between whether the perpetrator acted "knowingly" or "purposely." If the requirement is that the perpetrator acted "knowingly," the prosecution would have to show only that the hoax perpetrator was "practically certain" that law enforcement forces would respond and that some harm would occur as a result of the perpetrator's race labeling. If the requirement is that the perpetrator acted "purposely," prosecutors would have to prove that the hoax perpetrator had as a conscious objective causing the particular result: triggering a manhunt *and* harming a specific Black person or Blacks as a group. This higher standard of intent should not be required for a racial hoax law.

The New Jersey legislation appears to impose a general-intent requirement. Under the proposed law, one could be charged with false incrimination on the basis of race, when one "knowingly" gives false information to a police officer with the goal of implicating another person because of that person's race. To avoid the problem of attempting to determine whether the hoax perpetrator intended to cause harm to Blacks as a group or to any particular Black person, specific intent should not be an element of a racial hoax offense. The very fact that a racial hoax has been employed means that existing stereotypes have been reinforced and racial dissension furthered. Legal scholar Charles Lawrence elaborates:

> Traditional notions of intent do not reflect the fact that decisions about racial matters are influenced in large part by factors that can be character-

ized as neither intentional—in the sense that certain outcomes are self-consciously sought—nor unintentional—in the sense that the outcomes are random, fortuitous, and uninfluenced by the decision maker's beliefs, desires, and wishes.[18]

Prosecutors should not be required to establish that a hoax perpetrator is a racist or that he or she intended to mislead law enforcement. As set forth in the proposed New Jersey law, it is sufficient that the perpetrator has blamed someone *because* of his or her race. The reasons behind the racial finger-pointing should be irrelevant.

## Legal Sanctions

Perpetrating a racial hoax should be a felony offense because it is a serious crime and has ramifications beyond any one particular case. Further, a penalty should be imposed that would be likely to deter others from devising hoaxes. A state could decide to impose a criminal fine and prison time. Beyond a prison term, all racial hoax perpetrators should be required to pay restitution. The New Jersey provision requires restitution in the amount of law enforcement costs for wasted resources. Additionally, payment of court costs and restitution to any identifiable victims should be imposed.

## Moral Sanctions: An Apology

In addition to imposing criminal penalties and restitution, the hoax offender should be required to publicly apologize for playing on racial stereotypes. An apology would be one step toward healing a racially divided community. In recent years, some criminal court judges have strongly encouraged offenders (e.g., batterers, drunk drivers, corporate polluters) to apologize. Regardless of whether a hoax case reaches trial, the mayor, police chief, or other official could ask perpetrators to apologize to the community.

Following Susan Smith's confession, there were numerous calls for an apology. Columnist William Raspberry commented, "This may be difficult for non-minorities to accept, but black people do feel specially violated by Susan Smith's lie."[19] At the same time that the Black community is injured, so are other communities of color, and so are Whites. An apology, therefore, is due the entire community.

## Data Collection and Reporting Requirements

In the same way that the law imposes reporting requirements for bias crimes, there should be reporting requirements for racial hoaxes. It is impossible to estimate the annual frequency of racial hoaxes because there is no database for this information. A national repository should be created that tracks information on racial hoaxes, including the race, sex, and age of the offender and victim; the underlying hoax offense; and the estimated cost of investigating the hoax. These data could be compiled as part of the information collected for the Hate Crime Statistics Act.

## The Future of the Racial Hoax

The racial hoax should be subject to criminal penalty. With the exception of the proposed New Jersey legislation, the legal silence on the ravages of the racial hoax is deafening. Our legal analysis makes clear that a racial hoax law is constitutionally permissible. A racial hoax law provides a legal route for addressing this country's racial past as it is played out today in perceptions of crime. As importantly, given that hate crime statutes are similar to antidiscrimination laws, a racial hoax law is a natural and necessary extension of redress for legally recognized racial harms. In sum, a racial hoax law acknowledges American racial history, the power of negative stereotypes based on this history, and the need for legal redress.

Absent a specific legal intervention, people will continue to use hoaxes to play the race card and avoid criminal liability. Without such a law, we are in effect encouraging people to employ racial hoaxes. Enactment of racial hoax legislation would send a message, both functional and symbolic, that the wide-ranging and deleterious impact of racial hoaxes will not be tolerated.

TABLE 5.1. Racial Hoaxes: Summary Data of 134 Cases, 1987–2019

| Name of Hoax Perpetrator | Year | Perpetrator: Race/Sex | Victim: Race/Sex | Alleged Crime | False Report Charge | State |
|---|---|---|---|---|---|---|
| ADAMS, Bradley | 1995 | White/Male | Black/Male | Murder | No | IL |
| ALLMAN, Sarah | 1997 | White/Female | Black/Male | Arson | | CA |
| ANDERSON, Jesse | 1992 | White/Male | Black/Male | Murder | No | WI |
| ANDERSON, Tisha, and LEE, William | 1995 | Black/Female and White/Male | White/Male | Hate crime (vandalism) | Yes | — |
| ANTHONY, Casey | 2008 | White/Female | Hispanic/Female | Kidnapping; Sexual assault | Yes | FL |
| ASBELL, Samuel | 1990 | White/Male | Black/Male | Attempted murder | Yes | NJ |
| ATESANIO, Raimundo | 2014 | Hispanic/Male | Black/Female, Male | Burglary | No | FL |
| AVENT, Anthony | 1994 | Black/Male | White/Male | Assault | No | FL |
| BAISLEY, Adam | 1996 | White/Male | Black/Male | Assault | No | — |
| BASS, Halley | 2017 | White/Female | White/Male | Assault and battery | Yes | MI |
| BIRT, Tracy | 1996 | Black/Male | White/Male | Hate crime (vandalism) | Yes | AR |
| BOLDUC, Daniel | 1995 | White/Male | Black/Male | Vandalism | Yes | CT |
| BRAWLEY, Tawana | 1987 | Black/Female | White/Male | Rape; Hate crime (assault) | No | NY |
| BYRDSONG, DeWayne | 1995 | Black/Male | White/Male | Hate crime (vandalism) | Yes | IA |
| CAMPBELL, Toby | 1995 | White/Male | Black/Male | Robbery | Yes | SC |
| CAVIL, Khalil | 2018 | Black/Male | White/Male | Hate speech | No | TX |
| CHERRY, Donald | 1996 | White/Male | Black/Male | Murder | Yes | TN |
| CLARK, Emily | 2004 | White/Female | Black/Male | Robbery | Yes | — |
| CLEMENTE, Garrick | 1995 | Black/Male | White/Male | Hate crime (vandalism) | No | RI |
| COLLINS, Sabrina | 1990 | Black/Female | White/Male | Hate crime (threats) | No | GA |
| COOPER, Amy | 2020 | White/Female | Black/Male | Threats; Assault | Yes | NY |
| CRANE, Henry | 1995 | White/Male | Black/Male | Carjacking | Yes | — |
| CUTHRELL, Olander | 2013 | Black/Male | White | Arson; Hate crime (vandalism) | — | VA |
| DACRI, Tanya | 1989 | White/Female | Black/Male | Kidnap | Yes | PA |
| DiBARTOLO, Thomas | 1996 | White/Male | Black/Male | Murder | No | WA |
| DIXON-COLE, Sherita | 2018 | Black/Female | White/Male | Sexual assault; Kidnap | No | TX |
| DROGAN, Thomas and PAPALEO, Louis | 1993 | White/Males | Black/Male | Assault | Yes | NY |
| DUKE LACROSSE* | 2006 | Black/Female | White/Male | Rape | No | NC |
| DUNN, Kerri | 2006 | White/Female | White/Male | Hate crime | Yes | CA |

TABLE 5.1. (*cont.*)

| Name of Hoax Perpetrator | Year | Perpetrator: Race/Sex | Victim: Race/Sex | Alleged Crime | False Report Charge | State |
|---|---|---|---|---|---|---|
| DUTZ, Mitchell | 2018 | White/Male | Black/Male | Carjacking; Kidnapping; Robbery | Yes | IL |
| EXONERATED FIVE* | 1989 | White/Female | Black/Males | Rape; Attempted murder | No | NY |
| FRAKES, Dawn | 1995 | White/Female | Black/Male | Assault | Yes | DE |
| GATELEY, Tina and KARAFFA, William | 1993 | White/Male and Female | Black/Male | Attempted robbery; Assault | Yes | PA |
| GAYLE, Matthew | 1995 | White/Male | Black/Male | Murder | No | FL |
| GIBSON, Tony, et al. | 1996 | White/Males, White/Female | Black/Male | Attempted murder; Burglary | No | — |
| GILLIS, Kendra | 1994 | White/Female | Black/Male | Assault | No | NY |
| GREEN, Joshua, et al. | 1994 | White/Males | Black/Male | Robbery | Yes | — |
| HARDIN, Alicia | 2005 | Black/Female | White/Male | Hate crime (racial threats) | No | IL |
| HARMON, Breana | 2017 | White/Female | Black/Males and Females | Kidnap; Sexual assault | Yes | TX |
| HARRIS, Persey, et al. | 1996 | Black/Males and Black/Females | White/Male | Hate crime (assault, verbal threats) | Yes | — |
| HARRIS, Robert | 1996 | White/Male | Black/Male | Murder | No | CA |
| HEBERT, Jeffrey | 1995 | White/Male | Black/Male | Murder | No | — |
| HUENEKE, Brenda | 1995 | White/Female | Black/Male | Robbery | Yes | — |
| HUNTER, Eric | 2018 | White/Male | Black/Males and Females | Assault; Shooting | Yes | VA |
| IRVINE, Frank | 1994 | White/ Male | Black/Male | Assault | Yes | — |
| JACKSON, Angela | 1996 | Black/Male | White/Male | Hate crime (racial threats, slurs) | Yes | MN |
| JAMES, Sonia | 1996 | Black/Female | White/Male | Hate crime (vandalism, racial slurs) | Yes | — |
| JOHNSTON, Kathleen | 1994 | White/Female | Black/Male | Assault; Robbery | No | MD |
| JONES, Heidi | 2010 | White/Female | Hispanic/ Male | Assault; Attempted rape | Yes | NY |
| KASHANI, Miriam | 1990 | White/Female | Black/Male | Rape | No | DC |
| KING, Andrew | 2018 | White/Male | Black | Hate speech; Vandalism | Yes | NY |
| LAMBIRTH, Mark | 1995 | White/Male | Native American/ Male | Kidnapping; Rape | No | NC |

## TABLE 5.1. (cont.)

| Name of Hoax Perpetrator | Year | Perpetrator: Race/Sex | Victim: Race/Sex | Alleged Crime | False Report Charge | State |
|---|---|---|---|---|---|---|
| LEWIS, Mark | 1994 | White/Male | Black/Male | Assault | No | — |
| LIMOS, Marcy | 2003 | White/Female | Black/Male | Rape | Yes | — |
| LITTLE, Marquie | 2017 | Black/Male | White/Male | Vandalism; Racial threats | Yes | MD |
| LOCHTE, Ryan | 2016 | White/Male | Latin American/ Males | Armed robbery | Yes | [Brazil] |
| LUPIS, Josephine | 1994 | White/Female | Black/Male | Robbery | Yes | NY |
| MAGRONE, Lucille | 1990 | White/Female | Black/Male | Assault; Threats | Yes | NY |
| MARTINEZ, Ramon, et al. | 1995 | Hispanic/Males | Black/Male | Assault | Yes | — |
| MAXWELL, Janet | 1993 | White/Female | Black/Males | Kidnapping; Rape | Yes | — |
| MAYO, Daniel , and LAFOREST, Philip | 1997 | White/Males | Black/Male | Hate crime (vandalism, destruction of property) | Yes | — |
| McCOOL, Cecil | 1995 | White/Male | Black/Male | Police misconduct | No | IL |
| McGUIRE, Kelli | 1997 | White/Female | Black/Male | Rape; Kidnap | Yes | FL |
| METCALFE, Milton | 1993 | Black/Male | Black/Male | Hate crime (assault) | No | OH |
| MILAM, Richard | 1994 | White/Male | Black/Male | Murder; robbery | No | IL |
| MILLER, Phillip | 1994 | White/Male | Black/Male | Robbery | Yes | — |
| MITCHELL, DeAntrious | 1996 | Black/Male | White/Male | Assault | Yes | IA |
| NELSON, Nathaniel | 2017 | Black/Male | Black | Vandalism; Arson; Theft | Yes | MO |
| NICOLAS, Richard | 1996 | Black/Male | White/Male | Murder | No | MD |
| O'BRIEN, Edward | 1995 | White/Male | Hispanic/ Male Black/ Male | Murder | No | MA |
| OWENS, Marcus | 2016 | Black/Male | White/ Males | Assault; Racial slurs | No | IA |
| PATTERSON, Brian | 1996 | White/Male | Black/Male | Murder | Yes | — |
| PITTMAN, Dennis | 1996 | White/Male | Black/Male | Carjacking; Kidnapping | No | PA |
| POSNER, Maryrose | 1994 | White/Female | Black/Male | Robbery | Yes | NY |
| PRINCE, Christopher | 1994 | White/Female | Black/Male | Attempted rape; Burglary | No | VA |
| RAM, Kissie | 2019 | Black/Female | White | Racist notes; Hate speech | Yes | IA |
| REED, Loretta | 1997 | White/Female | Black/Male | Carjacking; Abduction | Yes | — |

TABLE 5.1. (*cont.*)

| Name of Hoax Perpetrator | Year | Perpetrator: Race/Sex | Victim: Race/Sex | Alleged Crime | False Report Charge | State |
|---|---|---|---|---|---|---|
| RIMES, Kristen | 2018 | White/Female | Black/Male | Assault | Yes | SC |
| RIPLEY, Patricia | 2020 | White/Female | Black/Male | Carjacking; Abduction | Yes | FL |
| RIVERA, Reggie | 1993 | Black/Male | White/Male | Rape | No | NY |
| ROBB, Katharine | 2001 | White/Female | Black/Male | Rape | Yes | IA |
| ROUTIER, Darlie | 1996 | White/Female | White/Male | Murder | No | TX |
| RUSSELL, Judy | 1988 | White/Female | Middle Eastern/ Male | Assault | Yes | NJ |
| SARABAKHSH, Zhaleh | 1995 | Middle Eastern/ Female | White/Male | Attempted murder | Yes | ND |
| SATTERLY, Ed | 2004 | White/Male | Black/Male | Attempted murder | Yes | — |
| SAULS, Jay | 1997 | White/Male | Black/Male | Assault | Yes | — |
| SCRUGGS, Shawnda | 1996 | Black/Female | White/Male | Hate crime (vandalism, burglary) | — | — |
| SEALEY, Jaelyn | 2000 | Black/Female | White/Male | Hate crime (vandalism, arson) | Yes | NC |
| SEWEID, Yasmin | 2016 | Muslim/Female | White/Males | Hate speech; Assault | Yes | NY |
| SHAVER, Dorne | 2000 | Black/Male | White/Male | Assault | Yes | — |
| SHAW, Michael | 1995 | White/Male | Black/Male | Kidnapping | Yes | — |
| SKIPPER, Carlton | 1997 | Black/Male | Black/Male | Assault; Robbery | — | DC |
| SMITH, Susan | 1994 | White/Female | Black/Male | Carjack; Kidnap | No | SC |
| SMOLLETT, Jussie | 2019 | Black/Male | White/Males | Assault / hate speech | Yes | NY |
| SOLIMAN, Mounir | 1994 | Middle Eastern/ Male | Black/Male | Robbery | Yes | TX |
| STANG, George | 2018 | White/Male | White/ Unknown | Racist graffiti on church | Yes | IN |
| STORRO, Bethany | 2010 | White/Female | Black/ Female | Chemical assault | Yes | WA |
| STUART, Charles | 1989 | White/Male | Black/Male | Murder | No | MA |
| SWEETEN, Bonnie | 2009 | White/Female | Black/Males and Females | Carjacking; Kidnapping | Yes | PA |
| TANCZOS, Lisa | 1995 | White/Female | Black/Male | Assault | Yes | PA |
| TELFAIR, Brian | 2017 | Black/Male | White/Male | Racist threats | Yes | VA |
| TICKNOR, Harry | 1997 | White/Male | Black/Male | Robbery | Yes | — |
| TODD, Ashley | 2008 | White/Female | Black/Male | Armed robbery; Assault | Yes | PA |
| TOURCOTTE, Mary | 2011 | White/Female | Black/Male | Rape; Assault | No | NY |
| TULIA, TEXAS | 1999 | White/Male | Black/Males and Females | Drug sales | Yes | TX |

TABLE 5.1. (*cont.*)

| Name of Hoax Perpetrator | Year | Perpetrator: Race/Sex | Victim: Race/Sex | Alleged Crime | False Report Charge | State |
|---|---|---|---|---|---|---|
| VEACH, Paul | 1995 | White/Male | Black/Male | Kidnapping; Robbery | Yes | IA |
| VEITCH, Neva, and CRAIG, David | 1989 | White/Male and Female | Black/Male | Murder; Kidnapping; Attempted rape | No | GA |
| WAGNER, Candice | 1995 | White/Female | Black/Male | Kidnapping; Rape | Yes | — |
| WIGHT, Lisa | 1996 | White/Female | Black/Male | Attempted rape | No | — |
| WILLIAMS, Dauntarius | 2017 | Black/Male | White/ Unknown | Racist graffiti | No | KS |
| WITT, Joshua | 2017 | White/Male | Black/Male | Assault and battery | Yes | CO |
| YOVINO, Nikki | 2017 | White/Female | Black/Males and Females | Rape; Assault | Yes | CT |
| Unnamed | | White/Female | Black/Male | Kidnapping | — | KY |
| Unnamed 1991 | 1991 | White/Female | Black/Males and Females | Sexual assault; Kidnapping | No | NY |
| Unnamed 1994–1 | 1994 | White/Female | White/Male | Kidnapping; Rape | — | FL |
| Unnamed 1994–2 | 1994 | White/Female | Black/Male | Sexual assault | Yes | LA |
| Unnamed 1994–3 | 1994 | White/Female | Black/Male | Assault | — | ME |
| Unnamed 1994–4 | 1994 | White/Female | Black/Male | Assault | — | NJ |
| Unnamed 1995 | 1995 | White/Male | Black/Males and Females | Assault; Grand theft | — | VA |
| Unnamed 1996–1 | 1996 | White/Female | Black/ Males | Assault | — | FL |
| Unnamed 1996–2 | 1996 | White/Female | Black/Male | Assault; Rape | No | WI |
| Unnamed 2013 | 2013 | White/ Unknown | Black/Male | Theft | No | NY |
| Unnamed 2016 | 2016 | Middle Eastern/ Male | White/Male | Threats | No | MI |
| Unnamed 2017–1 | 2017 | Black/Male | White | Terroristic threats; Cyber harassment | Yes | PA |
| Unnamed 2017–2 | 2017 | Black/Female | White/ Unknown | Vandal-ism; Racist threats | No | MO |
| Unnamed 2017–3 | 2017 | Black/Female | White/ Females | Hate speech; Threats | No | DC |
| Unnamed 2017–4 | 2017 | White/ Unknown | White/ Unknown | Hate speech | No | MN |
| Unnamed 2017–5 | 2017 | Black/Male | White/ Unknown | Racist threats | No | CO |
| Unnamed 2017–6 | 2017 | Black/Female | White/ Unknown | Racist threats | No | MN |

## Table 5.1. (cont.)

| Name of Hoax Perpetrator | Year | Perpetrator: Race/Sex | Victim: Race/Sex | Alleged Crime | False Report Charge | State |
|---|---|---|---|---|---|---|
| Unnamed 2017–7 | 2017 | Black/Male | White/Male | Racist messages; Hate speech | — | CO |
| Unnamed 2018–1 | 2018 | White/Female | Black/Male | Assault; Hate speech | Yes | VA |
| Unnamed 2018–2 | 2018 | White | Black | Violent attacks | No | — |
| Unnamed-2018–3 | 2018 | Middle Eastern/ Female | Black/Male | Hate speech; Assault | Yes | VA |
| Unnamed 2019 | 2019 | White/Female | Black/Male | Robbery | — | MA |

*Name of racial hoax victim
—Information not available

## Table 5.2. Racial Hoaxes Involving Blacks and Whites

| Race | Number of Cases | Overall Percentage |
|---|---|---|
| White Perpetrator / Black Victim | 79 | 58% |
| Black Perpetrator / White Victim | 33 | 25% |
| White Perpetrator / White Victim | 6 | 4% |
| Black Perpetrator / Black Victim | 3 | 2% |
| Other Hoaxes (race unknown) | 13 | 10% |
| **Total** | 134 | |

# 6

## White Crime

No one focuses on White crime or sees it as a problem. In
fact, the very category "White crime" sounds funny, like
some sort of debater's trick.
—Richard Delgado[1]

It has been said that you can tell a lot about how something is valued in
a culture by the number of names, genres, or classifications it has been
given. For instance, the automobile has many names; there are hundreds
of makes and models. The same is true for a variety of things, such as
trees, colors, movies, architecture, books, paint, computers, desserts, and
so forth. Given the perceived prevalence of fear associated with Black
crime, perhaps the various labels for it is not surprising. Sometimes it
is called "Black offending," "Black-on-Black crime," or "Black criminality." Terms such as "urban crime," "inner-city crime," "metropolitan
crime," "big-city crime," and "street crime" are all references to Black
crime. There are also offense-specific markers for Black crime, such as
gang-related offenses, carjackings, and sexual assault crimes. Given the
various synonyms for Black crime, it is no surprise that the criminal that
most Americans "see" when they think of crime is Black. This reality
challenges the popular public fantasy that we are color-blind or that we
don't see race.

Given how crime is labeled and in light of society's emphasis on street
crimes, which Blacks disproportionately commit, it is also no surprise
that Blacks, Latinx, Whites, Native Americans, and Asian Americans
alike visualize crime in Blackface. It would be hard for a person to avoid
seeing crime portrayed in shades of Black and Brown in the media. It
is particularly striking, though, that Whites as a group escape a racialized crime label. Specifically, we do not have language to describe crime
committed by White people that is comparable to the language we use
to describe crime committed by Black people. This would include terms

such as "White crime," "White criminality," or "White-on-White crime." In some instances, crime is racialized in other colors besides Black—for example, references to Latinx or Asian gangs. No other group, however, is as closely linked to crime by language as African Americans.

Although portraying crime in Blackface is widespread within the media, social scientists who study crime also portray it in varied hues of Black. Social scientists rely heavily on terms that spotlight crimes associated with Blacks. At the same time, however, they do not use similar labels to describe the crimes committed by Whites. The work of academics suggests that they are not much better at putting a realistic color on the face of crime than the lay public.

This chapter looks at crime data by race, with an emphasis on White crime. The first section examines the amount of involvement Whites have in the criminal-legal system, as measured by arrest and prison rates. Then we discuss whether social scientists should use terms to highlight offenses by Whites, including "White crime" and "White criminality." The chapter also considers whether the relatively small number of criminologists of color affects the use of racial labels. One downside of the way we currently talk about crime and race is that it supports partial truths. The chapter ends with a detailed discussion of this problem, using James Q. Wilson's "Black crime causes White racism" thesis as an example. The chapter concludes that half facts skew our perception and thereby our understanding of the relationship between race and crime.

## The Study of White Crime

Contrary to popular belief, more Whites are arrested each year than members of other racial groups. As Table 6.1 shows, this is not a new trend, nor is it particularly surprising given that Whites are more than two-thirds of the US population. In fact, from 2015 to 2019 Whites made up at least 69 percent of all arrests each year. These figures are consistent with Uniform Crime Report (UCR) data from prior decades. In 2018, for instance, law enforcement made over eight million arrests. In three offense categories, Whites account for approximately 80 percent of those arrested: DUI (82 percent), liquor law violations (78 percent), and drunkenness (74 percent). For these three crimes, White arrest rates are on par with or above their percentage in the population. The data also show that Whites have high arrest rates for several other offenses, including arson (71 percent), vandalism (68 percent), sex offenses (71 percent), fraud (66 percent), and forgery and counterfeiting (65 percent).[2]

Not only do Whites represent the majority of all those arrested in any given year, they make up a sizeable percentage of the people under the control of the criminal-legal system. In 2018, Whites were approximately 50 percent of the people on probation, on parole, in jail, or in federal prison, and constituted 30 percent of the inmates in state prisons. Often left unsaid is that White criminal representation, though not disproportionate, is quite high. A public discussion about crime and race necessarily means discussing White crime. One outcome of the fact that race has become synonymous with being Black is that White crime is rarely labeled—and rarely discussed.

TABLE 6.1. Black and White Arrests, Percentage Distribution, 2014–2018.

|      | Black | White |
|------|-------|-------|
| 2014 | 28%   | 69%   |
| 2015 | 26%   | 70%   |
| 2016 | 27%   | 69%   |
| 2017 | 27%   | 69%   |
| 2018 | 27%   | 69%   |
| 2019 | 26%   | 69%   |

Source: Bureau of Justice Statistics, Crime in the United States, 2013–2018 (Table 43).

## Public Beliefs about Race and Crime

There is a widespread belief that Blacks disproportionately commit crime and are responsible for the majority of crime. The first belief is true; the second is not. But the second belief—that Blacks commit most crime—is an extension of the first. Though distinct, these perceptions, one fact and one fiction, are jumbled in the public mind. The general public's inaccurate picture of the amount of Black crime is partly media driven, since television in particular focuses to a great extent on street crime. Although each year, two-thirds of the people arrested for street crimes are White, Blacks continue to represent the public face of street crime.

The perception that crime is violent, Black, and male has converged to create the *criminalblackman* (see chapter 1). By itself, this mythical racialized criminal symbol is scary enough. The figure has become even more ominous, however, because we do not have anything with which to compare him. There is no *criminalwhiteman*. There is every reason to believe that if more images of White criminals and White criminality were in the media spotlight, the public image of crime would shift. The damage of the "Blackness = crime" stereotype, however, cannot be undone simply by highlighting White crime. The media and the academic community will also have to expose the *criminalblackman* image as a misrepresentation.

## Invisible Labels

Disproportionately high rates of crime by Blacks cannot be used to explain why we rarely see crime represented in other colors. Our public discussion of race and crime is not so much segregated as it is one-dimensional. Nobel Prize Laureate Toni Morrison keenly observed that the racial presentation of crime reinforces "racial half-truths. . . . Unless you can intelligently use the phrase 'White on White crime,' you can't use the phrase 'Black on Black crime.'"[3] A review of newspaper, law review, and social science research articles indicates that when the topic is race and crime, Blacks are usually the race under discussion.

Whether you look at newspaper articles, legal databases (e.g., Westlaw, LexisNexis), academic journals, or law reviews, there are few instances in which the terms "White crime," "White-on-White crime," or "White criminality" are used. Further, in the rare instances that link Whiteness and crime, the articles typically make note of Black criminality as well. In other words, while "Black crime" is a widely accepted, discussed, and debated phenomenon, the same is not true for "White crime." When discussing race and crime, legal analysts, journalists, and the public have a hard time envisioning and treating White crime as a phenomenon.

The virtual absence of articles on White crime suggests that, in our individual and collective minds, "White" and "crime" simply do not go together. By way of example, decades ago, when I presented an early draft of this chapter at a conference (for the first edition of this book), the moderator introduced me by stating my name, my university affiliation, and the title of my paper, "White-Collar Crime"! He never caught his mistake—that he had *added* the word "collar" to the title of my paper. In my initial remarks, I referenced the moderator's error and suggested that it underscored the racialized ways in which we think and talk about crime. For most of us, White crime is rarely conceptualized as a separate phenomenon, one unhooked from Black crime.

In addition to journalists and law professors, criminologists have largely overlooked White crime. This is not new. Historian Khalil Muhammad documents the attempts by early-twentieth-century White researchers to treat crime committed by Blacks differently than crime committed by Whites. He comments,

> White criminality was society's problem, but black criminality was black people's problem. Such thinking contributed to discriminatory social work approaches and crime fighting policies in black communities, with devastating consequences. . . . Among whites, struggling neighborhoods were considered a cause of crime and a reason to intervene.[4]

The connection between Blackness and criminality has deep roots, including racial designations made by the Uniform Crime Reports in the 1930s.[5]

A review of criminology journals reveals few articles that explicitly use the term "White crime." While criminologists are indeed studying crime committed by Whites, these crimes are not racialized as emblematic of Whiteness or race. For instance, academic articles that focus on the deviance of White adults and White youths largely avoid using terms such as "White criminality" or "White-on-White crime." The failure to label crime by Whites as White crime contrasts sharply with the pervasive label of crime by Blacks as Black crime. In addition to the reluctance to label White crime, researchers use other terms to signal crime committed by Blacks. These terms include "urban center," "inner city," and "street crime." These alternative phrases widen the extent to which Black crime is indicated by social scientists.

The skewed focus of journalists and academics on Black offending may simply mirror society's skewed concern with street crime. By this reasoning, because Blacks are responsible for a disproportionate amount of street crime, they receive a disproportionate amount of attention by academics and the media. Such reasoning, however, rings only partially true. Disproportionate offending by Blacks may explain why research centers on Black crime, but it does not explain why so little research and media attention focus on White street crime. Also, it does not explain why crime by Whites is rarely referred to as "White crime." Finally, a look at the history of race and crime suggests that offenses committed by Blacks have always received extraordinary attention. This was true long before "disproportionality" and "disparity" became part of the public lexicon on crime.

## White Crime: Some Examples

Several areas of research could be labeled "White crime," such as white-collar crime, rural and suburban crime, race-based hate crime, police killings, and mass shootings.

### WHITE-COLLAR CRIME

"White-collar crime," as defined by Edwin Sutherland, is "crime committed by a person of respectability and high social status in the course of his occupation."[6] Bernie Madoff, who created a complex corporate Ponzi scheme with over thirty-five thousand victims, with losses estimated as high as fifty billion dollars, is a notorious contemporary white-collar criminal. Researchers have observed that Whites have disproportionate opportunities to commit high-status offenses because they are more likely to hold high-status jobs. With the exception of fraud and embezzlement, arrest data on white-collar offenses is not included in the UCR. Although white-collar criminality may never produce the same degree of fear as street crime, its impact on society is substantial. Many researchers have observed that white-collar crime is associated with violence and imposes moral damage on society. Researchers Francis Cullen and Michael Benson state, "The costs of white collar crime—the violence it entails, the money it transfers illegally, its damage to the moral fabric—may well outstrip the costs of traditional street crimes."[7] It is estimated that white-collar crime costs ten times as much as street crime. Why there is no annual count of white-collar crimes remains a mystery. Cullen and Benson suggest that white-collar crime is downplayed because criminologists do not view it as real crime:

> Criminologists secretly may believe what . . . politicians are saying [that street crime is more serious than white-collar crime]. At the very least, their raised consciousness does not dispose them to place knowledge about white-collar crime on an equal footing with knowledge about street crime.[8]

These perceptions signal our fears of who the real criminals are. They indicate who we think belongs in prison and reflect our definitions of justice.

## RURAL AND SUBURBAN CRIME (NONURBAN CRIME)

If it is commonplace to hear that Blacks in urban areas offend at a disproportionately high rate, it is also worthwhile to hear reports that Whites who live mostly in rural and suburban areas offend in these communities at rates close to their percentage in the population. In nonmetropolitan, rural areas, Whites constitute a disproportionately high percentage of the arrests for all crimes. UCR data show that for numerous offenses—including arson, auto theft, burglary, embezzlement, larceny, DUI, sex offenses, and vandalism—Whites account for more than 80 percent of the arrests. For Whites who live in suburban areas, their arrest rates are over 70 percent for several offenses, including arson, drunkenness, DUI, and burglary.[9]

## RACE-BASED HATE CRIMES

Crimes motivated by hate could also be placed under the umbrella of "White crime." These offenses range in severity and include murder, rape, assault, vandalism, and intimidation. In 2019, there were more than seven thousand reports of bias incidents. More than one-half of these incidents (57 percent) were motivated by race or ethnic bias. All told, more than two-thirds of race-based hate crimes are against people of color. There is little empirical attention given to the differences between White ethnic groups. To address this gap, some researchers propose conducting studies that compare the successes and failures of the White ethnic groups denoted by the US Census. Political science professor Andrew Hacker has observed, somewhat tongue-in-cheek, that if some researchers can insist on examining Blacks and low achievement, the same can be done with Whites. His research indicates that French-Canadian and Dutch Whites are much less likely to complete college than Russian and Scottish Whites.[10]

## POLICE KILLINGS

The disproportionately high number of police killings of Blacks is another area that could be labeled "White crime." In all but a few instances, these police killings have not led to criminal charges or criminal liability. Most notably, Steve Pantaleo, the New York police officer involved in the 2014 choke-hold killing of Eric Garner, faced neither state murder charges nor federal civil rights charges in the case. The list of police shootings and killings of Blacks under questionable circumstances—including many instances in which the victim was unarmed—is long indeed. Here are a few of the post-2010 cases involving police killings: Ahmaud Arbery, Rayshard Brooks, Andrew Brown, Michael Brown, Philando Castile, Stephon Clark, Samuel DuBose, George Floyd, Mario Gonzalez, Atatiana Jefferson, Botham Jean, Bettie Jones, Corey Jones, Eric Logan, Laquan McDonald, Tamir Rice, Walter Scott, Alton Sterling, Breonna Taylor, and Dante Wright.

In the overwhelming majority of these cases, police officers are not held criminally responsible for these deaths. Almost all of the cases end with the officer not even being charged with a homicide offense because the prosecutor declined to file charges, or if charges were filed, the officer was acquitted. Three recent cases are noteworthy because the police officer involved was held criminally liable for causing a death. In Walter Scott's 2015 case, he was stopped by police for a broken taillight. After he was pulled over, Scott, who was unarmed, ran from his vehicle. A North Charleston, South Carolina, officer, Michael Slager, ran after Scott, caught up with him, and the two struggled. Scott got free, and continued to run away. Slager shot Scott eight times in the back. Following the shooting, Slager placed his taser next to Scott's body. The shooting was captured on video. Slager's state trial for murder resulted in a mistrial. Slager pled guilty to federal charges and was sentenced to twenty years in prison.

In 2015, Corey Jones was stranded on an I-95 off-ramp in South Florida after his car stopped running. As he waited for a tow truck to arrive, police officer Nouman Raja drove up to Jones. Raja was in an unmarked vehicle and in plain clothes. He did not identify himself as an officer when he approached Jones. Jones, who believed he was being robbed, pulled out a handgun that had been lawfully purchased. Raja then shot him several times. Jones died on the scene. Raja was fired after the shooting. In 2019, Raja was found guilty of manslaughter and attempted murder.

The shooting death of Justine Damond provides a sharp contrast to what happens in most cases involving police shooting deaths. In 2015, Damond, a White woman, called 911 in Minneapolis to report a sexual assault. When officers arrived, Damond approached their vehicle. She was shot by officer Mohamed Noor. He was fired from the department and charged with murder. A jury later convicted him of third-degree murder. It is reasonable to ask whether the case outcome was influenced by the racial makeup of the victim and the officer. Here the victim was White and the officer was a Black Somali American. Notably, although the majority of police shootings are by White officers, in two recent and rare cases in which an officer has been held criminally responsible for homicide, the officers were not White.

Given this history, it is particularly noteworthy that the police killing of George Floyd led to criminal charges and criminal convictions against Derek Chauvin. Chauvin, who held his knee on Floyd's neck for more than nine minutes, was convicted of his murder and manslaughter. The other officers with Chauvin—Thomas Lane, J. Alexander Kueng, and Tou Thao—were charged with aiding and abetting second-degree murder. The charges against the officers were increased following widespread outrage and criticism of the initial criminal charges. All four officers were fired from the Minneapolis Police Department.

### THE NEED FOR DATA

To date, the US government does not gather official statistics on police killings. That task has been left to nongovernmental entities. The *Washington Post*, for instance, tracks data on police killings, including information on victims and officers (e.g., race, gender, age, type of weapon involved). Table 6.2 provides a look at data from 2015 to 2019:

TABLE 6.2. Police Killings by Race of Victim, 2015–2019.

| | 2015 | 2016 | 2017 | 2018 | 2019 |
|---|---|---|---|---|---|
| White | 497 [50%] | 465 [48%] | 459 [46%] | 452 [45%] | 403 [40%] |
| Black | 258 [26%] | 234 [24%] | 223 [22%] | 229 [23%] | 250 [25%] |
| Hispanic | 172 [17%] | 160 [16%] | 179 [18%] | 164 [16%] | 162 [16%] |
| **Total** | 994 | 962 | 986 | 992 | 999 |

Note: Number [Overall percentage]
Source: *Washington Post*, Fatal Force website.

Several findings stand out from the data. First, of the three racial groups—White, Black, and Hispanic—Blacks are the only group disproportionately overrepresented as victims of police killings. Second, the numbers have been consistent over the period from 2015 to 2018. This is particularly remarkable given the public's rising awareness of the prevalence of police killings, due largely to videos viewed across social media, and steps taken by some law enforcement agencies, including the rise in use of body cameras and implicit bias training. Third, the fact that there are nearly one thousand police killings each year means that, on average, approximately nineteen are committed each week. The absence of official data gathering by the federal government only compounds the belief that ending these deaths is a low priority.

### Opioids, Crack Cocaine, and Race: A Note

Much has been made of the difference in media attention and the legal responses to crack cocaine, compared with the opioid epidemic. Media portrayals of opioid use are more likely show users in a humane light, as victims who fell prey to a lethal drug—and thus deserve treatment within a public health framework rather than a criminal punishment framework.[11] The prevailing images of opioid users stand in stark contrast to the widespread images of crack cocaine users in the 1990s as out-of-control and dangerous. The current opioid epidemic has been largely cast as a White problem. The data support this racial characterization. In 2015, for instance, Whites made up 90 percent of the thirty-three thousand opioid overdose deaths.[12] This number of deaths reflects a *quadrupling* in the number of deaths since 1999. Notably, while rates of opioid use are higher for Whites, rates of death have been steeply rising for Blacks. A look at how race, opioid use, and related criminal offending intersect is helpful in evaluating how views of race shape perceptions of criminality. Arguably, opioid addiction is labeled "White crime" and is subject to less harsh sanctions within the judicial system.

## Mass Shootings

Studies consistently show that the typical profile of a mass shooter in the United States is a White male. A study that looked at 121 mass shootings that took place between 1982 and March, 2021 found that 54 percent were committed by White men,[13] which is particularly significant when we consider that White men make up approximately 34 percent of the total US population. While overall, mass shootings are a small percentage of the annual homicide number, they induce fear and thus maintain a stronghold on American imagination because they occur in places people regularly frequent. For instance, in recent years, mass shootings have taken place at an elementary school in Newtown, Connecticut (twenty-six people killed); a nightclub in Orlando, Florida (forty-nine people killed); a church in Charleston, South Carolina (nine people killed); a country music concert in Las Vegas, Nevada (fifty-eight people killed); a night spot in Dayton, Ohio (nine people killed); and a Walmart in El Paso, Texas (twenty-two people killed). The impact and harm caused by mass shootings extend beyond those who are killed. The harmed include the injured and the family members of the victims.

## Labeling Race

Race and criminal law are inextricably linked, and therefore the phenomenon of Black crime cannot be discussed without a discussion of the phenomenon of White crime. If Black crime is labeled, then White crime should be given a label. Racial labels could be imposed for all crime. As discussed earlier, crime in rural areas could be labeled White crime. In this way, "rural" crime would be used to denote race in the same way that "urban crime" or "street crime" is used to signal African American offending.

Another option, eliminating labels altogether, is unrealistic since they are already widely used. Further, if race labels were discouraged, some researchers and journalists might rely more frequently on code words, which would not solve the underlying problem.

Perhaps the biggest concern with using racial labels, however, is the implication that something about crime is race specific. Without a comparable language that defines and analyzes White crime, the implicit message is that Blackness somehow "explains" criminality. Thus, the label of "Black crime" may cause some people to conclude, improperly, that Black people are genetically predisposed to commit crime. That race is a social rather than biological reality unmasks the fallacy of racial determinism. Further, due to the history of colonialism and slavery and mixed-race liaisons, many Blacks are only Black because we still employ the one-drop rule. It has been estimated that 75 percent of Black people have some White ancestry.[14]

## Black Protectionism

Black protectionism is one of the consequences of having a society that does not see White criminality but clearly sees, criminalizes, and harshly punishes offending by Blacks. The term describes what happens when the reputation, past history, or behavior of a high-profile African American is called into question. Historically, the Black community's reaction has been protective, almost maternal. The Black community's support places a fortress around its fallen hero. Once allegations are made, African Americans ask questions and offer explanations. The questions include: (1) Did he commit the offense? (2) Even if he did, was he set up? (3) Would he risk his professional reputation to commit this offense? (4) Are White people who are accused of committing this offense given the same level of scrutiny? (5) Is this accusation part of a government conspiracy to destroy the Black race? This five-part analysis stands in sharp contrast to the typical sole trigger question for Whites: Did he commit the offense? Black protectionism has surfaced in many cases involving high-profile African Americans, including Clarence Thomas, Mike Tyson, O. J. Simpson, Bill Cosby, and Michael Jackson.[15] The availability and degree of Black protectionism has declined over the years, partly because of social media platforms that allow Black community members to offer opinions, insights, and conclusions that differ from those of Black elected leaders or appointed spokespersons for the Black community.[16] Black protectionism has been one of the Black community's responses to being burdened with the Black crime label. Protectionism operates as a kind of community coping mechanism, one that insists that successful Blacks accused of wrongdoing cannot be summarily "cancelled." Black protectionism and other community coping strategies are important to understanding how the Black community perceives and interacts with law enforcement.

## Who Studies Race and Crime?

It is reasonable to believe that the people who study crime determine which aspects of crime are placed under the microscope. The race of those engaged in criminological study impacts which aspects of crime are deemed important and worthwhile for analysis. Thus, it is noteworthy that approximately two-thirds of the people who receive doctorates in criminology are White, approximately 10 percent Black, 9 percent Latino, and 7 percent Asian.[17] Criminologists are not the only academics who analyze race and crime issues. Social scientists in various fields—most notably sociology, but also psychology, economics, political science, and anthropology—do as well. That said, the small number of Blacks in criminology, the behavioral science that focuses predominantly on street crime, is problematic in view of the disproportionate rates of Black arrest, conviction, and incarceration. Studies indicate that to some degree a researcher's race is correlated with his or her ideology and areas of research interest. If so, the racial makeup of the profession is relevant. A look at journalism and law, two other arenas that affect research and public discussion on the criminal-legal system, also reveal a pattern of Black underrepresentation. In the US, 5 percent of the attorneys[18] and journalists[19] are Black. An increase in the number of Black criminologists might hasten the development of useful theories to explain Black overinvolvement in crime and shift some of the focus from Black crime to White crime.

## Fearful, Angry White People: The "Black Crime Causes White Fear" Thesis

Whites and Blacks oftentimes see and experience the world quite differently. Unfortunately, as noted earlier, we know relatively little about how other groups of color view racialized incidents because the media is fixated on the Black-White dichotomy. Racism is the thread that unites and reinforces these group-based views. Whites are much less likely to believe that racism still exists than are African Americans.

The din coming from both racial camps is at times deafening. Let us, however, examine one theory about White racism, James Q. Wilson's thesis that "Black crime causes White racism." Wilson's theory continues to pervade discussions of how race matters in our understanding of crime. Given this, it is worth a detailed critique.

In 1992, Wilson, a political scientist, wrote an editorial that argued that if Blacks would stop committing so much crime, there would not be so much White racism. His thesis, developed in subsequent writings, is that White racism and White fear of Black and Latino men are justified because Black and Latino men have high rates of crime.[20] It is fear, Wilson contends, not racism that accounts for the negative perceptions that White people have of Black and Latino men. In fact, Wilson states, "fear can produce behavior that is indistinguishable from racism."[21] His tacit conclusion is that the current level of White racism is acceptable, so long as it coexists with the current level of Black and Latino crime. At first read, Wilson's argument sounds vaguely tenable, or at least difficult to dismiss. A careful consideration of his underlying premise, however, indicates that his thesis raises more questions than it answers.

At its core, Wilson's thesis argues the following one-directional relationship:

Black crime rates → White racism

Two major assumptions underlie Wilson's hypothesis. First, the Black crime rate is the primary source of White racism. Second, solving the Black crime problem rests almost entirely with the Black community.

## White Fear and White Racism

According to Wilson, "The best way to reduce racism real or imagined is to reduce the black crime rate to equal the white crime rate."[22] It is not clear what Wilson means by "imagined." He points out that Black men offend at a rate six to eight times greater than the rate for Whites.

Accordingly, it is reasonable to expect that White racism will persist until Blacks and Whites offend at an equal rate. Awaiting such a drop in the Black crime rate is neither the best nor the quickest way to reduce White racism. Ignoring the interconnection between crime, poverty, and education, Wilson exhorts Blacks to rise above their circumstances before they can ask for a reduction in White racism. This is a tall order.

Not only does Wilson imply that the Black crime rate is the sole source of White racism; he also places the onus of eradicating White racism on Blacks. Even if the Black crime rate were reduced to equal the White crime rate, how would this affect the *amount* of White racism? Is Wilson suggesting that if Black and White crime rates were equal, or nearly proportionate, that White racism would disappear completely? Drop by one-half? Wilson implies that White racism will wither away or decline substantially if the rate of Black crime were equal to the rate of White crime. Wilson provides neither theoretical nor empirical support for this sweeping assertion. In fact, he could not, as no such data are available.

Wilson also offers an incomplete analysis of the role of fear. His hypothesis suggests that fear is a one-dimensional variable. White fear, however, has at least four related, though distinct, components: the fear of crime, the fear of losing jobs, the fear of cultural demise, and the fear of Black revolt. Wilson overlooks the fact that the generalized White fear of Black crime encompasses these other fears.

Studies show that the closer Whites live to Blacks, the more fearful they are of crime. This fear is justified since Whites who live near Blacks also face the greatest threat of victimization by Blacks. Although levels of neighborhood integration may explain why Whites who live in urban areas are fearful of Black crime, it does not justify the general, nationwide White fear of Black people, particularly of Black men. Most Whites do not live close to Blacks, which is not surprising, given that Blacks are a relatively small percentage of the US population (13 percent). Furthermore, given the fact that more than 80 percent of all crime is *intra*racial, White fear of Black crime is inexplicably high. In part, Whites' discomfort about race relations informs their attitudes toward crime.[23]

Sometimes Whites point to Blacks' own fear of crime to justify their attitudes beliefs about race and crime. Comments made by civil rights activist Jesse Jackson offers a case in point. Jackson said he is sad about the disproportionate rate of Black criminal offending. He said that when he walks down the street at night he is actually relieved to discover that the person coming toward him is White.[24] Following his remarks, several White commentators pointed to Jackson's comments as "proof" that White fear of Black crime is justified. However, this argument overlooks the fact that, statistically speaking, the greatest crime threat to Jesse Jackson *is* another Black man. On the other hand, the greatest crime threat to someone White is another White person, because most crime is intraracial (see Appendix A, Table A.5). At least Jackson's fears are factually based.

The fear of victimization at the hand of a Black criminal has led some researchers to study the link between abortion and crime. Professors John Donohue and Stephen Levitt note that abortion is most common for poor, minority women and find that "legalized abortion can account for about half of the observed decline in crime in the United States between 1991 and 1997."[25] This research prompted the former secretary of education William Bennett to say, "If you wanted to reduce crime . . . you could abort every black baby in this country, and your crime rate would go down."[26]

There is an economic component to White fear of Blacks. This fear is commonly couched in terms of affirmative action. Many stories have been written about "qualified" White people who lost out on jobs, government contracts, or university admissions to "unqualified" Black people. Many Whites believe that Blacks—and, similarly, Latinx and recent immigrants—pose a serious threat to their economic well-being. Affirmative action is perceived as a threat by many Whites, who fear losing their privileged status. Although many Whites have legitimate fears about the state of the economy, blaming Blacks for downsizing and global economic decline misses the mark. Andrew Hacker observes that Whiteness has been devalued, and "for the first time in this country's history, [Whites have been] made to feel they no longer come first."[27] The media's response to this fear has created more heat than light. It has failed to report the obvious: it is statistically impossible for Blacks, who constitute less than one-sixth of the population, to take most of the jobs, government contracts, and college, graduate, and professional school admissions spots.

Another type of fear that Whites have of Blacks is cultural. Some Whites view Black culture as the antithesis of American culture. This fear manifests itself when Black culture crosses over into White culture, such as in music, clothing, hairstyles, speech patterns, and posture. Loud cries of cultural decline are heard when White youths mimic and adopt aspects of Black culture (e.g., music preferences, interracial dating, slang, and speech patterns). Specifically, calls for school dress codes, record-label warnings, standard English, and music morality are sounded when Black culture and other cultures of color contaminate Whites. The creation of moral panics to marginalize a racial or ethnic group from the mainstream is not new.

Other fears include losing majority status and the possibility of Black revolt. The fear that Blacks along with other people of color would become the majority race and in turn use their power to pay Whites back for centuries of slavery was expressed as early as the year 1751.[28] More than two hundred years later, conservative pundit William F. Buckley commented that many Whites favor abortion to ensure that Blacks do not overpopulate the country.[29] Referring to the fear of "racial revenge," Andrew Hacker states, "There is a fear in White America of this second nation, this Black nation. There is fear of rebellion."[30] Some people have speculated that this fear drives popular support for abolishing welfare and affirmative action.

As the foregoing discussion makes clear, most of the fears that Whites have of Blacks are not rational. Wilson's dichotomous treatment of White fear obscures its dimensions and its irrationality. For Wilson, White fear is a typical, therefore justifiable, response to Black crime. Wilson's analysis glosses over the fact that although it may be common-place for Whites to fear Blacks, it is not necessarily reasonable. Fear is not always a rational emotion; however, to use fear to justify racism, which Wilson does, the fear must be grounded in reality. A great deal of White fear—of crime, of economic loss, of cultural demise—has been a knee-jerk response to media stories. By all indicators, Wilson is correct when he says that Whites are fearful of Blacks, yet his analysis assumes that White fear is logical. Why does this matter? Whether or not White fear is justified, whether White fear is used to cloak prejudice and hate has *everything* to do with determining the relationship between White racism and Black crime. A generalized, empirically insupportable White fear of Black crime cannot be used to excuse White racism.

The problem with allowing White fear to justify White racism is driven home when we consider Blacks' fears of Whites. Although rarely acknowledged publicly, many Blacks, as well as members of other minority groups, are fearful of Whites. They are fearful of becoming victims of a hate crime. There is also a more general fear of White violence and assault—against the poor, against urban dwellers, and against the disenfranchised generally, such as within the criminal-legal system. Black fear of Whites may stem from the fact that while there has been racial progress, White people remain at the helm of almost every American institution. The office of the president, Congress, the Supreme Court, and the private sector, including media business owners, show White faces almost exclusively. Black fears of White power and its abuses, however, do not justify Black racism against Whites. Are Blacks "excused" from being racist because they fear Whites? Wilson says no. Wilson characterizes Black outrage at the verdict in the LAPD trial involving the beating of Rodney King as "appalling racist bigotry." How is it that Wilson allows Whites to leap blindly from fear to racism, yet this same leap is impermissible for Blacks? Wilson's "White-only" fear-racism link speaks volumes.

### White Racism or Black Crime Rates: Which Came First?

Wilson offers little historical support for his assumption that high Black crime rates trigger White racism. Considering the fact that Whites kidnapped Africans and brought them to this country in chains, it would be a safe bet that White racism existed centuries before disproportionate rates of Black crime. For proof of this supposition, one need only review the slave codes and Black codes for blatant examples of White racism enshrined into early American criminal law. Wilson's thesis conveniently ignores this history.

Derrick Bell provides an interesting counterpoint to Wilson's thesis. In his book *And We Are Not Saved*, Bell considers what would happen if Black crime magically disappeared. Bell describes a hypothetical scenario in which magic stones have been discovered. Once ingested, the stones eliminate all desire to engage in crime. The stones, whose power only works for Blacks, are distributed throughout the country. However, now that "Blacks had forsaken crime and begun fighting it, the doors of opportunity, long closed to them because of their 'criminal tendencies,' were not opened more than a crack."[31] The fact that there was no longer a crime excuse did not reduce the barriers to racial equality. Bell's conclusion is much closer to reality than Wilson's suggestion that White racism surfaced only in response to high Black crime rates.

### Whose Fault Is It Anyway?

Wilson draws an interesting configuration. He assigns Whites a passive role in the Black-crime/White-racism dynamic. Simply put, he blames Blacks for White racism. Wilson has asserted that Blacks unfairly use racism as an excuse for criminal activity. According to Wilson, racism that is "imagined" by Blacks will disappear if the Black crime rate declines. Wilson never tells us what "imagined" racism is. The reader is left to surmise that this is racism that only exists in the minds of Blacks. How is it that a reduction in the Black crime rate will cause a reduction in imagined racism? Wilson does not tell us this either. Rather than holding Whites accountable for their racism, Wilson allows them to claim victim status: they are victimized by Black crime. Wilson allows the blame for White racism to be placed entirely on Black shoulders. Yet he charges that Blacks unfairly place all the blame for the Black crime rate on Whites. This smacks of a double standard.

Another troublesome aspect of Wilson's argument is that it encourages us to think along racially segregated tracks about crime and other societal problems. His argument is that Blacks are responsible for Black crime and that White racism is part of the larger racial finger-pointing that persists. None of this, however, reduces the crime rate or diminishes racial divisions. The net result is that Blacks blame Whites for their lack of progress, and Whites blame Blacks for all social ills. As detailed in the first part of this chapter, the overemphasis on Black crime makes it difficult to see that "race and crime" is not synonymous with "Blacks and crime." More must be done to present the public with an accurate racial picture of crime, including White crime.

One of the biggest roadblocks to an informed discussion about crime and race is the perpetuation of half-facts. Half-facts are statements or propositions about crime that are discussed in a vacuum, divorced from their context. Wilson's discussion of the relationship between White racism and Black crime exemplifies this phenomenon.

## Conclusion

This chapter argues that crime has many colors. The language of crime matters and affects how we see crime. Specifically, it influences how we define offenses and which ones deserve sanction by the criminal law. If we agree that it is acceptable to label crime by race for Blacks, the same should be true for other racial groups. Otherwise, a message is sent that something about Black crime is unique—different and more loathsome—than crime committed by Whites, Asian Americans, Native Peoples, Latinx, or members of other racial groups.

7

## Race and Crime Literacy

[Critical Race Theory] . . . is a sickness that cannot be allowed to continue . . . please report any sightings so we can
quickly extinguish!
—@realDonaldTrump, September 5, 2020

When I was in graduate school studying criminology, "race" seemed to
be shorthand for "African Americans." Most of the assigned material—
books, research articles, and government reports—cast Blacks either as
offenders or as victims of crime, primarily at the hands of Black offenders. Much of the readings focused on or highlighted "Black crime" (cases
involving a Black offender) and "Black-on-Black" offending (cases
involving Black victims and Black offenders), with an analysis of various theoretical explanations for crime. At the same time, however, there
was no discussion of the causes of "White crime" or "White-on-White
crime," or any acknowledgment of any such phenomenon (see chapter
6). Adding insult to injury, very little of the research we read about had
been conducted by academics of color. For example, we never studied
or discussed *The Philadelphia Negro*, W. E. B. Du Bois's seminal work—
considered by many scholars to be the ancestor of the famed Chicago
School of sociology (see discussion in chapter 1).[1] Sociologist Monroe
Work's research was another glaring omission from the curriculum. Further, there was very little discussion of systemic discrimination or other
factors that would explain, or at least contextualize, disproportionately
high rates of Black offending. Along with many of my fellow students,
I was left with the unstated yet unmistakable impression that crime
and Blackness go hand in hand. Had I not known better, I might have
accepted the conclusion, promoted by some criminologists, that there is
a link—a genetic one—between Blackness and criminality.

When I was in my first year of law school, one of my professors
declared, "Poor people are programmed to default." He made this

statement as we discussed the well-known case of *Williams v. Walker-Thomas Furniture*.[2] The case involved a Black woman named Ora Lee Williams who lived in Washington, DC. She had signed a contract to purchase furniture. Under the installment terms of the agreement the store could demand payment in full at any time. When Williams fell behind on her monthly bill, the store sued her to recover the amount due and the furniture. The appeals court, finding the contract language "unconscionable," voided the installment contract. My professor took great issue with this decision. During the lecture, he made no mention of race or the intersection of race, class, and gender. Though race was not explicitly referenced, the lecture and discussion hinted at Williams's race. The professor did not address segregation, redlining, poverty, or employment discrimination against Blacks, some of which would have given the case some historical and contextual perspective. As presented, the analysis of the case drew a bold line connecting poverty with Blackness and Blackness with deviance.

Both of these academic experiences took place while I was in my twenties. At that time, I had neither the knowledge nor the language—in history, law, or sociological research—to debate or rebut the half-truths that were being presented as facts. Even if I had, it is unlikely that I would have challenged a professor on the facts as presented.

Unfortunately, my educational experiences are not unique. In academia, issues of race are often ignored, dismissed as irrelevant, or used as code for "Black." When race is equated with "Black" or "people of color," this connection allows Whites and Whiteness to go unchallenged or unanalyzed in discussions of how race, crime, and law intersect. Chapter 6 provides a more detailed look at "White crime" and argues that if we focus on some racial groups' involvement in crime, we must focus on all racial groups' involvement in crime. A narrow focus on "Black crime" sends an inaccurate message that mostly Blacks are involved in the criminal-legal system. Further, there is ample research to refute this assumption. As well, the failure to expand "race and crime" to include all racial groups sends a message that something about Blackness is tied to criminality. In turn this provides tacit support for theories of genetics and biology (and race).

I believe that much of the racial silence I witnessed was due to benign neglect. For the most part, professors teach what they themselves learned in their undergraduate, graduate, and professional programs. If they were not required to read scholarship that addresses and contextualizes race, racism, and this country's history, they would not have a comprehensive understanding of the foundational relationship between race, crime, and law. No matter the rationales for the largely inadequate analysis of race in our educational institutions, the harm impacts all of us, not just students, faculty, and researchers of color.

Where and how do we begin to make changes? Are students to blame for appearing to know so little about the historical relationship between race and crime? Professors often bemoan the "ignorance" of students. We are told that they cannot find the continents on a world map, that they do not know the text of the preamble to the US Constitution, or that they do not read books, have few analytical skills, and so on. While these are legitimate concerns, they are the wrong place to focus. The people who teach should be the primary focal point. We should not let educators off the hook. Again, whatever gaps in knowledge educators have are passed along to their students. It is not only that their gaps in knowledge will mean that areas of intellectual knowledge are not taught and learned, it is also that the failure to teach these areas sends a direct message to students that they are unimportant, not part of the sociological canon, and not essential to becoming a criminologist, ethnographer, or sociologist who studies crime.

The failure to integrate race broadly across the criminology curriculum means that students who are interested in learning about criminology and race will have to learn it on their own. In fact, that is what many of us had to do, whether through choice of dissertation topic, research focus, or in selecting which courses we would teach. We created our own versions of independent studies on race. The goal of this chapter is to create an interruption to a status quo criminology education that minimizes or does not fully articulate race in its theoretical teaching of crime and criminality. This brings us to the focus of the chapter: the need for race and crime literacy, using a framework of sociological literacy.

## Sociological Literacy

Anthropologist Judith Shapiro uses the term "sociological illiteracy" to describe the lack of knowledge most students have regarding historical issues of race, gender, and class. She observes that many of us are focused on our immediate and personal experiences and are unable (or unwilling) to see how they are shaped by social and historical forces. Shapiro notes that this inability to engage in critical analysis reflects a lack of what sociologist C. Wright Mills called "the sociological imagination." Shapiro states,

> When people are ignorant about quantum mechanics or medieval literature, they are generally aware of their ignorance, readily admit it, and understand that the remedy for their ignorance is serious and systematic study. When, however, the subject is how societies operate, or why people behave the way they do, the situation is different. Confusing their folk beliefs with knowledge, people typically don't realize their ignorance.[3]

Shapiro's conception of sociological literacy offers a helpful framework for reformulating E. D. Hirsch Jr.'s examination of cultural literacy. His book *Cultural Literacy: What Every American Needs to Know* argues there is an identifiable set of historical, contemporary, and social facts that culturally knowledgeable Americans should be informed about. To this end, his book includes an index of more than five thousand names, phrases, dates, and concepts considered by Hirsch to be "essential." Some scholars argued that his thesis was elitist since his list reflected dominant ideologies and mainstream gazes on race, class, and gender and was devoid of the philosophies, scholarship, events, and art of people of color.

## Building Race and Crime Literacy

Using the goals identified by Shapiro and the framework offered by Hirsch, this section offers a race and crime literacy index. This index of seminal laws, cases, incidents, and people highlights the broad, deep, and historical ways that race works and showcases race and crime as an important area of intellectual research engagement. The list is not complete. It is offered as an invitation to readers to consider and identify what other items should be included.

This list serves to help build a healthy, complex language around race and crime. For instance, many contemporary conversations about race and racist language could be characterized as superficial. For instance, if a White sportscaster, believing her microphone is off, uses the word "nigger," she will be roundly criticized and likely fired. This is all well and good. However, firing people who use racial slurs does not solve the problem of systemic racism (or perhaps more accurately, systems of racism). It is not that these issues are not important—they are—it is that addressing them only solves the tip of the racial iceberg. The Race and Crime Literacy Index is an attempt to expand the understanding of the language of race and crime. The breadth of the list shows how racist slurs are not one-offs but are deeply tied to centuries-old laws and well-embedded practices and policies. Sundown towns, restrictive covenants, and redlining (see chapter 3) are examples of laws and practices that affirmed the social and political second-class status accorded African Americans.

The following list of terms can be considered components of this sociological literacy. The list identifies terms, names, and concepts that focus on African Americans and Whites, and is intended to be illustrative, not exhaustive. It can be used to generate and encourage more detailed discussions and curricula on race. Of course, familiarity with and knowledge about some of these terms will vary from individual to individual. Readers will have a passing familiarity with many of the entries, such as well-known African Americans Harriet Tubman, Martin Luther King. Jr., and Rosa Parks. However, it is likely that most names, concepts and cases will likely be unfamiliar.

## Race and Crime Literacy Index

| | |
|---|---|
| Affirmative action | Black Lives Matter |
| *An American Dilemma* (book) | Black Muslims |
| Arbery, Ahmaud | *Black Panther* (movie) |
| Attica prison | Black Panthers |
| *Bakke v. U.C. Regents* | Blake, Jacob |
| *Batson v. Kentucky* | Bland, Sandra |
| *Bell Curve, The* (book) | Bloody Sunday |
| *Birth of a Nation* (movie) | Brawley, Tawana |
| Black codes | Brown, Michael |
| Blackface | *Brown v. Board of Education* |

This index is offered as a possible starting place for foundational knowledge on the United States' history of race, law, crime, and justice. Without question the list is incomplete. Many, many other names, incidents, cases, theories, practices, and principles are equal parts of this history. The central goal of the index is to acknowledge the rich base of historical and contemporary racial realities and to encourage readers to dig into this vast history. The breadth of the items on the list makes clear that the interplay between race and crime impacts a wide range of areas. The workings of the criminal-legal system are connected to the workings of the educational system, which are tethered to the political system, which themselves are tied to the economic system, and those are tied to health care. The broad base of items on the Race and Crime Literacy list shows the connective racial threads between these various operating systems.

## A Forward Lurch

George Floyd's killing in 2020 exposed the deep racial divide in interest in and knowledge about policing and race in the United States. His killing was viewed by millions of people on social media platforms and mainstream outlets. For African Americans, Floyd's death was one in a long line of police killings of Black men and women (including the killings earlier that year of Ahmaud Arbery and Breonna Taylor). For many Whites, however, Floyd's killing was a wake-up call. There were palpable expressions of concern and desire to understand how and why a Black man could be killed in broad daylight by a White police officer, who kneeled on his neck for nearly nine minutes, while other officers watched, along with bystanders, one of whom taped the incident. Public awareness of America's history of anti-Black racism took a big leap to center stage in the news. Books on race rose to the top of best-seller lists. Discussions on police violence, White privilege, and racism, many awkward and wrenching, took place in public and in private. During this time, massive groups of youths—largely non-Black—took to the streets in large cities and small towns around the country. Around the globe, in Japan, Australia, China, South Africa, Italy, Canada, Kenya, and the United Kingdom, protesters of myriad races and cultures held up signs with images of George Floyd and "Black Lives Matter" posters. They gathered to protest and proclaim that Black life is valuable.

In the wake of Floyd's killing, new words, concepts, phrases, and incidents entered the public domain. Overnight it seemed, business owners, politicians, newscasters, university administrators, celebrities, and protesters were making references to "systemic racism"—a term that would more typically have been used in a college classroom or a gathering of progressives—along with other topics, such as Juneteenth, police funding, and abolitionism. All of this indicated that a seismic shift in the public's racial consciousness was under way.

## Language as a Bridge

As noted earlier, we do not have a well-developed, cohesive, nuanced language on race and crime. What we seem to have are a series of terms that act as signifiers and themes. For instance, phrases such as, "affirmative action," "reverse racism," "Second Amendment," and "I'm color-blind, I don't see race," evoke one type of conversation—while terms such as, "racism," "police violence," "White supremacy," "systemic racism," and "Black Lives Matter," bring forth a different conversation. The post-Floyd social moment in the United States began to yield deeper discussions of how racism has historically worked to minimize Black progress. These signifiers are used as shorthand for larger themes and issues involving race. Ideally, the value of the Race and Crime Literacy index is to force the "national conversation on race" to move beyond individual people, cases, and incidents to see how past practices continue to manifest themselves in contemporary social, legal, and political practices.

The goal of the list is to push for a deeper examination of race and crime and to question the application of one-stop solutions—such as body cameras for police officers—for complex social problems. In its totality, the index argues for taking bold steps to address race-related harms and histories. This would include understanding how systemic racism works to maintain entrenched levels of racial disparity, and what steps can be taken to address the problem. Ensuring that more people are knowledgeable about race and crime is important to building a more informed citizenry. Adequate and workable long-term solutions to long-standing social problems are not possible without a broader historical base of knowledge. This is particularly important for those who teach in areas that overlap with racial issues, particularly those tied to crime and justice. This is true for educators at all levels, including secondary, post-secondary, graduate, or professional. As noted earlier, educators have the power to impact how students, who are future professors and future criminal-legal professionals, see, interpret, and analyze race—and ultimately, what structural changes they see as necessary to address racial discrimination and inequity in the criminal-legal system.

## Working Myths

The discussion in this chapter makes a case for why a Race and Crime literacy project is necessary. However, getting widespread buy-in is another matter. For instance, for educators, integrating the substance of the index would require broad changes in curriculum and pedagogy. This would take a lot of work and a long-term commitment. Further, there is our collective allure of myths and history as previously told. To a large extent, we are happy with our race and crime myths; they work for us.[4] Myths are easy to perpetuate, and they do not require us to think critically, just reflexively. And most importantly, they signal our membership in the group of believers. We are all in the gang of myths.

We repeat what we have heard, pass it along, and believe we have done no harm. In this large-scale version of the children's game of telephone, what is ultimately repeated as fact is a caricature of any initial truth. Mythmaking makes it easier for us to collectively treat Blackness and Brownness as signifiers of criminality, deviance, and general unworthiness. The bottom line is that, as a society, we have a set of deeply held racial myths. However, we struggle with how and when to discuss them, and what terms to use. It is not surprising that myths rule. Let us consider two examples. The first discusses the Implicit Association Test, and the second involves racial representations and interpretations of good and bad.

## The Implicit Association Test

The Implicit Association Test (IAT) is a popular psychological test that measures the degree to which someone has a preference for a particular racial group. One version of the test evaluates one's preferences for Blacks and Whites. In his best-selling book *Blink*, Malcolm Gladwell, who identifies as Black, notes that he was startled to discover that his IAT score indicated a preference for Whites. The online test presents a series of photographs and words on the screen, and the test taker is required to categorize them as Black, White, good, or bad. My results were less remarkable than Gladwell's. Each time I have taken the test, my score indicated, "Little to no automatic preference between Black and White people." The majority of all IAT test takers, however, indicate a "strong" or "moderate" automatic preference for Whites. These findings may simply reflect the race of the test taker or may tell us something more: that when given a choice, people, regardless of race, prefer Whites over African Americans.

## Doll Tests

The famous doll study conducted by psychologists Kenneth and Mamie Clark was designed to evaluate the psychological impact of racial segregation on Black children. Their doll test used plastic, diapered dolls who were identical, except for skin color. Black children between the ages of three and nine were shown the dolls and asked questions about their racial preferences and perceptions. They were instructed, "Show me the doll that you like best" and "Show me the doll that looks 'bad.'" Black children in the North and the South, when asked to choose the doll that looked most like them, selected the White doll.

The majority of the children chose the White doll as the one they liked best and chose the Brown doll as the one that looked "bad." The Clarks, whose research was cited by the US Supreme Court in *Brown v. Board of Education*, concluded that "segregation of white and colored children in public schools has a detrimental effect upon the colored children."[5] The Supreme Court outlawed segregation in public schools as a violation of the Fourteenth Amendment's equal protection clause. Although Justice Earl Warren's opinion did not reference it, the court was aware of social science evidence showing that racially segregated schools also cause harm to White children.[6]

In a stunning replication of the doll test, in 2007, Kiri Davis interviewed preschool-age Black kids.[7] Davis, who conducted her study when she was only sixteen years old, wanted to find out whether anything had changed in the fifty years since the Clarks did their study. After placing a White doll and Black doll on a table, Davis asked each child to point to the doll that they liked the most and asked them which doll they looked the most like. She found, as the Clarks had, that the Black children greatly preferred the White dolls over the Black ones. The seven-minute film of the interviews painfully affirms the Clarks' findings and demonstrates how very young children have already learned to associate images of Blackness with something bad and Whiteness with something good.

These are only two of the many examples of how Blackness is perceived. The results of the doll study are particularly troubling since they involve the impressions of young children. As has been discussed throughout this book, racial portrayals have been fairly consistent in presenting Black skin as deviant, as criminal, or as an "other" curiosity. Without question, across media, contemporary portrayals of Blackness are much more nuanced and diverse than in the past. There remains, however, a steadfast link between Black skin and deviance, particularly as tied to policing. The underlying narrative following police shootings and killings of Blacks is consistent. It points to the victim's role in his or her own harm and then makes reference to "bad apples" or outliers to explain the harm.

## Teaching Lessons

The Race and Crime Literacy Index can be used to create both individual and system-level changes. Educators can integrate some of the topic areas into curriculum offerings—in high school, college, professional, and graduate programs. The index provides an opportunity to more fully integrate these issues across the primary and secondary curriculum. It is time to require that young people are introduced to a broader story of US racial history. Early on, the chapter noted that professors often complain about huge gaps in student knowledge. It is time for an expansion of how race and history are taught to young people. It is particularly important to integrate racial history into the K–12 curriculum; creating opportunities for meaningful student interactions across races and increasing teacher diversity would be meaningful ways to combat racism.[8]

The breadth of the items listed on the index makes the point that issues of race and justice extend well beyond the criminal-legal system. The devastation of the COVID-19 pandemic offers a clear case of how race and justice intersect with other sociopolitical issues. Not only does the pandemic present an opportunity to talk broadly about race—such as observing that it has had a grossly disparate impact on African Americans and members of the Latinx community—the coronavirus has had an impact on numerous sociopolitical and socio-legal issues. Here are some topic areas relating to the COVID-19 pandemic that involve issues of race, racial disparity, and justice:

- Availability of testing for coronavirus
- Availability of personal protective equipment (PPE) for medical workers and other front-line employees
- Access to hospital bed space
- Access to health care
- Selection of medical subjects for testing potential coronavirus vaccines
- Constitutionality of holding prisoners in jails and prisons following outbreaks of the virus
- The impact of low wages and high exposure to the virus on the essential workforce
- Access to mental health care
- Impact of online K–12 education for students without laptops or Wi-Fi access
- Selection of small businesses that were awarded COVID-19 stimulus checks
- Tax implications of the stimulus checks
- Impact of COVID-19 on voting

- Availability of moratoriums on rent for families unable to pay for housing
- Constitutional challenges to business or government mandates to wear masks
- Criminal actions against citizens attacking store workers who require masks
- Connection of coronavirus to number of domestic violence cases

The above issues tie directly to topics included in the Race and Crime Literacy Index. The index provides a framework and foundation for understanding how race and crime operate in the United States. Its sociopolitical and historical grounding is key to analyzing how and why the coronavirus has had such a grossly disparate impact on African Americans and Latinx community members. This history includes a look at the relationship between Blacks and the medical community (e.g., Tuskegee syphilis experiment, eugenics), fights for desegregation (e.g., *Brown v. Board of Education, Shelly v. Kraemer*), systems of punishment and surveillance (e.g., prison industrial complex, slave patrols, COINTELPRO), and voting rights (e.g., Fifteenth Amendment, Voting Rights Act).

## Conclusion

This chapter makes the case that we need to actively cultivate specific literacy on race and crime. Hopefully the list serves multiple purposes: to demonstrate the breadth of people, laws, cases, incidents, and books that are integral to the US history of race and crime; to provide a starting point for individuals interested in expanding their knowledge base; to work as an entrée for educators seeking to delve further into this country's racial history; to show the connective threads between the actions of state institutions (e.g., courts, prisons, schools, businesses, political organizations) and how these institutions treat African Americans and reveal systems of racialized treatment; to sharpen critical analytical tools, which are necessary to identify and contextualize race; and to support and hopefully encourage more people to learn about and engage in the detailed study of African American life and the criminal-legal system.

# 8

## The Soul Savers

To address the fundamental injustice, cruelty, brutality, and inhumanity of slavery in the United States and the 13 American colonies between 1619 and 1865 and to establish a commission to study and consider a national apology and proposal for reparations for the institution of slavery, its subsequent de jure and de facto racial and economic discrimination against African-Americans, and the impact of these forces on living African-Americans, to make recommendations to the Congress on appropriate remedies, and for other purposes.
—Commission to Study and Develop Reparation Proposals for African-Americans Act, H.R. 40 (January 3, 2017)

## Introduction

Storytelling has always played a role in movements for racial and socio-legal justice. Stories help educate, illuminate, and motivate new approaches to racial understanding. Sometimes the stories are based on actual events. Sometimes the stories are fictional. In either form, these narratives can help us see, interpret, and reflect upon racial conditions. Further, they can strengthen and challenge our perceptions of how race matters today and how race relations will work in the future.

One of the most incisive and provocative stories related to law, race, and justice is Professor Derrick Bell's parable "Space Traders," in his book *Faces at the Bottom of the Well*. Professor Bell, one of the founding members of Critical Race Theory, wrote the apocalyptic tale to instigate discussions about America's deeply rooted entanglements with race and racism. "The Soul Savers" is offered as both a tribute to Professor Bell and an attempt to follow in his narrative footsteps by raising and pondering new and old frameworks about race and law. The tale, a parable, incorporates a range of issues—police violence, economic justice, mass incarceration, reparations, artificial intelligence, and immigration—that have been discussed explicitly or implicitly throughout this book. Using Professor Bell's narrative storytelling as a backlight, "The Soul Savers" asks readers to consider the outer limits of our contemporary racial experiment: What constitutes humane treatment, and how will we know it when we see it? In particular, "The Soul Savers" parable pushes for a cold analysis of where we are on the continuum of racial progress and whether racial advances over time indicate substantive advances or something less promising.[1]

## The Call

On June 19, 2047, the call was made. The drums were heard by anyone subject to the one-drop rule.[2] The beating drums meant it was time to go underground. That was best. They were over fifteen million people strong. When they heard the drum calls, they knew it was their summons. Each family had been assigned a safe space: a restaurant, a hotel, a car, an abandoned building, a store, a trailer, an office. Some were lucky enough to get a room in a house.

Black people began to disappear themselves. The masses began traveling to their assigned safe spaces, in the secret, prearranged order. They took what they could carry. Electronic devices were not allowed. Most bags held clothing, toiletries, and a few small cherished items, such as old photographs, jewelry, and books. They didn't know when or if they would return.

Some Black people who questioned the wisdom of the call to go underground left the country. Some escaped on foot and some drove, rode buses, or took planes to lands north of New York and Washington, south of Florida, and west of California. The average Black person could not afford to escape from the United States. Most Black people were still trying to make a dollar out of fifteen cents.[3] Travel costs for one person, let alone an entire family, sounded like a cruel proposition. Like those New Orleanians in the Ninth Ward who were instructed to evacuate in advance of Hurricane Katrina,[4] how could you afford to leave when you barely had enough money to stay?

## Missing Black People

Whites quickly realized that something was amiss. Once they discovered that Black people had gone AWOL, all hell broke loose. For weeks, headline news stories on TV, social media, and what remained of print media asked, "Where did they go?" and "Why would they leave?" Some White people wondered aloud whether this was an elaborate hoax by Black people to avoid paying their rent, gas, or tax bills. Some who were angry demanded to know, "Who gave them permission to leave?" Others said, "Good riddance." Many of the news reports, which focused on the low unemployment rates for Blacks and the increasing number of multiracial families,[5] concluded that there was no pleasing Black people. The country had already done so much to support and uplift African Americans. After all, in previous decades, Congress had apologized for US chattel slavery, which lasted from the early 1600s to the mid-1800s, and lynchings.[6] Furthermore in the 1970s, Congress had implemented some affirmative action programs and in the early decades of the twenty-first century, some states had removed Confederate statues.[7]

Other groups of color were concerned about the millions of missing Black people. Some members of the Latinx community tried to imagine what fate had befallen Black Americans and whether their absence was voluntary. Indigenous community members speculated about whether Black people had been kidnapped en masse. Asian Americans, along with members of other racial and ethnic groups contemplated which group would be next to disappear.

## Life and Times

Black people went underground as a last resort. The past three decades had made it clear that no matter what they did, their race would be used as a prison to incarcerate them.[8] It didn't make a difference how successful or how hardworking they had been, or how much they had sought to lift themselves up by their bootstraps. Their Blackness had been treated as a scarlet letter: race defined their place in education, politics, health care, housing, economics, and law.

Scary things were happening. There had been so many killings. Black bodies were piling up. Every day, there were stories about dead Black people. Reports came from states ranging from Florida to Washington and from California to New Hampshire. The bodies offered no evidence that would lead to the killer or killers. Bodies were discovered mostly in rural areas, miles from interstate highways. Speculation was that the killings happened in the dark of night, in areas where neighbors were few and far between. Social media was flooded with photographs and videos of the dead.[9] Sometimes the posts showed one body, sometimes two bodies, sometimes three. Every so often, an entire family. There were hundreds of websites that posted graphic photos of the Black dead. As well, a continuous stream of photos appeared across social media. There had been more than ten thousand dead Black bodies in one year, and little hope that the death curve would flatten anytime soon.

No one bothered to call the police. With a nod from the country's head legal eagle, the Attorney General, the police—local, state, and federal—had long ago stopped aiding people who raised doubts about racial profiling, fairness, and police legitimacy.[10] Early on, the US Justice Department investigated some of the killings. However, without eyewitnesses, solid leads, physical evidence, or apparent motives, the Attorney General said the Justice Department would pause all investigations of Black deaths until more information was available.

Scary things were also happening in the criminal-legal system. What had been known for nearly a century as the "criminal justice system" was now called the "criminal-legal system." There was no longer any pretense that "justice" lay at the heart of the system. Everyone knew that the three-part system of policing, courts, and corrections worked to systematically target and capture Black people. Next to the military, the criminal-legal system had become the country's largest employer. Incarceration rates had more than doubled. The prison explosion was propelled by more arrests, more convictions, and more sentences, mostly of Black people.

Judges, prosecutors, and public defenders had huge caseloads. Trial court judges in large metropolitan areas, where most of the defendants were Black and Latinx, were especially busy. To handle the overload, courts relied on computer algorithms to manage their dockets.[11] Intricate formulas were used to determine whether a person would be released on bail before his court date. Various factors were weighed, including whether the defendant had any prior offenses, a low credit score, a juvenile record, a high school diploma, or any probation violations. The formula also included the accused person's zip code and the median neighborhood property value. The calculations kept many innocent people in jail before trial and meant they would face longer sentences if they were found guilty. Because there were so many cases, big-city judges had less than sixty seconds to read, review, and resolve each case. There was no time for questions or considerations of nuance.[12] Judges read the electronic case display, looked quickly for the algorithmic ranking, and issued their pronouncement: "Trial date set for Case No. 4664," and every so often, "Case dismissed!"[13]

Record numbers of African Americans were being sent off to prison. In previous decades, Black people accounted for about 32 percent of the people behind bars or under the control of the criminal-legal system.[14] Now 75 percent of the people in jail, prison, parole, or on probation were Black. This meant that every Black man faced a high probability that he would be incarcerated at least once during his lifetime.

Most of the people found guilty in the criminal-legal system had dark brown skin. Those Black people who appeared to have the least amount of White ancestry were the ones most likely to be sent to prison. Earlier in the century, scholars who had studied this issue had predicted exactly this: Darker-skinned Black people are more likely to be convicted of crimes and are more likely to receive lengthier sentences than lighter-skinned Black people.[15]

The steep rise in incarceration was met by a steep rise in prison construction. In their bids to win state and federal prison construction contracts, contractors promised pleasant-looking carceral spaces. For instance, one successful bid promised a massive oval-shaped structure, with an eggshell-white façade, brushed steel lighting, yellow-brick floors, earth-tone colored furniture, and state-of-the-art recreation facilities. It also promised plenty of space so that each inmate would have her own private "cellular unit."

The prison industrial complex had completely altered urban spaces. Urban areas had transformed into outsized, acres-long bus depots. These cement parks were filled with people standing in long, winding lines, awaiting buses to take them to visit loved ones held in prisons in outlying rural areas. They were going to visit mothers, fathers, brothers, sisters, aunts, cousins, in-laws, ex-laws, children, and grandchildren. The bus riders were mostly people who could not afford automobiles, insurance, gas, or tolls. The massive prison expansion had led to never-before-seen declines in Black unemployment and never-before-seen increases in Black incarceration.

Scary things were also happening in the heartland. Most White people were opposed to having a majority-minority country.[16] Some took action. One group of White people initiated a midwestern exodus. More than ten million White people had moved from liberal blue states to conservative red ones. The move had been gradual—never more than five hundred people at any one time. Conservative churches and some big businesses encouraged and sponsored these migration efforts. By the time the mainstream news caught wind of this midwestern phenomenon, millions of White people had already settled into their new states. They called themselves "Redliners" and their activities "redlining." Once they had arrived in their new home states, found lodging and work, the Redliners got involved in local, state, and national politics. Their political activity bore rich political fruit. Red states with the greatest number of Redliners were declared "super red." For this achievement, the Twenty-Eighth Amendment was passed, which rewarded these states with increased electoral votes.

## The President and the Electorate

The President-for-Life paced about the Oval Office. He had to figure out how to handle this latest Black problem. He had been in power for more than three decades. The Twenty-Second Amendment of the US Constitution, which imposed a two-term limit for US presidents, had been superseded by the Twenty-Ninth Amendment. The amendment abolished term limits. The President-for-Life, now a centenarian, would rule the country until his last breath . He had been watching the news about the mounting count of Black bodies, but that wasn't his biggest problem. When Black people across the country stopped showing up for work at their mostly low-wage, service-industry jobs, *that* posed a big problem for the economy. And the economy was his problem.

The President-for-Life was known as the "All-American Economy" president. He was a builder! He had finally been able to make good on the campaign promise that propelled him to his first electoral victory in 2016, building a Southern border wall to prevent immigrants from entering the United States. He did it by doing what he had always done. Building buildings. He created a construction boom. The blueprints detailed hundreds of miles of tall structures, all along the US' Southern corridor. The white brick buildings were designed so that they only had windows and doors on the sides facing north, facing America.

Day-to-day operations were run by his grandchildren and great-grandchildren. Workers were promised job security, health insurance, housing, and most important, a living wage. Workers who had been edged out of every other economic boom hoped this one would be their golden ticket to good times. Anyone driving along even a short stretch of the US southern border would see people of all racial backgrounds on the construction sites—Latinx, Asian, African American, Indigenous, and White: a diverse coalition of people working collectively to build structures that would keep a diverse group of people out of the country.

"This Black magic trick is going to mess things up for me," the President-for-Life mumbled to himself, as he looked out the window. The media was in overdrive reporting stories about the missing Black people. He had to put a stop to this. All this talk of dead Black people might shut down his massive "America Wins" construction projects. The Black runaways had already cost him his Black construction workers. *Poof!* Now they'd gone missing along with many other workers of color. With Black workers gone, and other workers of color, when people drove along the border, they saw White workers building white buildings to keep Brown people out of the United States. The President-for-Life shook his head, knowing that these were not good optics.

The President-for-Life called a meeting with respected members of the executive, judicial and legislative branches. A high-ranking member of the House of Representatives said the Black absence might be the best thing that had ever happened since the founding of the country. The Senate majority leader chimed in, "If we do this thing right, we won't take a hit at all. The Black people will return and we'll get back to business as usual." Others disagreed. The Chief Justice of the Supreme Court said that the situation created a "negative look" for America, "Something must be done or else there will be a tsunami of lawsuits." The secretary of state lamented that the disappearance would hurt international relations, particularly with the continent of Africa.

For the next few weeks, top government officials focused on the twenty-first century's "Negro Problem." They held meetings, brought in trusted advisers, queried their diversity liaisons, floated trial balloons, and scoured nonfiction books by Black authors on subjects including economics, politics, sociology, philosophy, and crime. They sought advice from people who had worked with Black people in corporate America and people who had worked with internationally known Black entertainers, and they sought insight from key congresspersons, governors, mayors, and other politicos. After reading all the books, reviewing all the data, evaluating all the discussions, and engaging in some hand-wringing, the White House concluded that the best move was simply to wait Black people out. Eventually they would have to come back.

Another month went by. Black people remained underground.

## The Offer

Black people had been absent for almost three months. International allies and enemies alike had been very critical of the United States. The Swedish prime minister asked in his weekly address, "Is it wise for us to maintain trade relations with the United States if it cannot account for 14 percent of its population?" China's president said, "All deals are off!" until Black citizens have returned. Presidents of several African countries asked whether the disappearance had been orchestrated by American intelligence agencies. The European Union and the United Nations each said they would take up the issue of the "Missing Black Americans" at their upcoming meetings. Most countries remained silent, waiting to see what would happen next.

In the United States, non-Black members of groups at the margins of society worried that they, too, might disappear. The elderly, the poor, the disabled, the incarcerated, and religious minorities knew their fate was tied to the fate of the missing Black people. These groups held rallies and teach-ins and began door-to-door canvassing to let the world know these are perilous times and what actions they should take.

As weeks passed, the President-for-Life realized that doing nothing was not going to work. He had to take action, maybe even do something radical. He called an emergency cabinet meeting. The President-for-Life, his officials, and their aides stayed locked away in the White House War Room for ninety-seven hours straight. Finally, they emerged with a document and a plan. After the White House Counsel's Office had given approval, the President-for-Life gave a national address. He sat behind his desk in the Oval Office the following morning. On his desk, there was a print-out of his remarks. He read the remarks from the teleprompter:

African Americans are the backbone of the United States. As early as 1619, Blacks were forcibly brought to this land in chains from the continent of Africa. The Middle Passage was used to transport millions of Blacks to this soil. They were forced to provide generations of unpaid, backbreaking, and soul-crushing labor. Blacks have endured an unfortunate and unfair time on this land. They have been subject to the triple winds of slavery, Jim Crow, and mass incarceration—each one deeply anchored in actions taken by the executive, legislative, and judicial branches of the United States government.

Today our African American brothers and sisters have voluntarily disappeared. We do not know where they've gone, but we want them to come back home. African Americans are highly valued members of American society. Their contributions to the workforce and their cultural contributions are sorely missed. The US government is well aware that many African Americans have faced challenging times with employment, education, and the criminal-legal system. Few members of this group have been able to rise above their circumstances.

The African American absence has had a direct impact on the US political and social economies. Millions have abandoned their jobs and left without a trace. There are now more jobs available than people. If Blacks do not immediately return, we will have to restructure our immigration policies to get the economy back up and running. Beyond the country's shores, the Black disappearance has caused our allies and enemies grave concerns.

The time has come to provide reasonable fiscal recompense for the generations of pain and suffering Blacks have been subjected to.[17]

With this promissory note, the US government promises to pay each Black person, as defined below, $1.2 million. Acceptance of the money includes an irrevocable promise to stay in the United States until age sixty-five or death, whichever comes first.

Per this offer, a Black person is a person with two Black parents—that is, parents who self-identify as African American and who are known (or if deceased, were known) to be African Americans within their community.

We welcome your positive response by Monday, October 14, 2047.

I know I speak for the nation when I say, please come home. We miss you and we need you! May God bless the United States of America.

After he was finished reading, the President-for-Life stared straight into the teleprompter. A single tear slid down his cheek and onto his papers. His staff immediately posted the statement and proposal on the President-for-Life's website and his official Twitter account.

## *The World Reacts*

Word of the Offer traveled like wildfire through the Black underground. Black people were stunned. No one was sure what to do. They had three weeks to decide. From their safe spaces, Black people would hear the US debate their worth and their fate.

When Black Americans committed to going underground, they gave the Council of Elders authority to decide if, when, and under what circumstances they would return. The Council got to work immediately.

Social media exploded. Virtual town halls, tweet storms, Instagram stories, emails, Zoom meetings, texts, and Facebook posts rose to peak levels. Online petitions for and against the Offer were circulated. News programs had a field day dissecting the Offer. At any given moment, some news program was debating some aspect of the reparations proposal:

* Whether such a large federal payout for reparations is feasible
* Whether the government should offer less or more money
* Whether the White House has the executive authority to make the offer without input from voters

* Whether Black people could be forced to return
* Whether Black people should be punished for leaving and whether any punishment would violate the UN Human Rights Charter[18]
* Whether Black people should be allowed to receive reparations payments and then allowed to leave the country
* Whether the President's Offer was reverse racism since White people are not allowed to receive reparations
* Whether it is fair to require a racial litmus test (two Black parents) to receive reparations
* Whether Black people should be allowed to return since they had left without good reason

Around the country, large and small groups of White allies gathered to discuss the Offer. Many expressed support for reparations. However, some concluded that it wouldn't be fair to give money to any Black people who were middle or upper class. One of them said, "Class matters more than race. What about Oprah Winfrey? Should she get reparations?" Another responded, "White people sitting around talking about what Black people are entitled to is the perfect example of White privilege!" Most White allies agreed that they should try to support whatever Black people thought was best.[19]

White supremacist groups held marches in every state. They announced a three-point plan, which demanded that the US government (1) Withdraw the Reparations Offer to Black people; (2) Provide reparations to White people, $500,000 for each one; and (3) Remove the President-for-Life and replace him with the highest-ranking Redliner. If their demands were not met, they threatened to expatriate or start a twenty-first-century civil war.[20]

Indigenous peoples, Latinx, and other groups of color had become vocal about the US Reparations Offer. Thousands gathered for a rally on the National Mall, in front of the Smithsonian's National Museum of African American History and Culture. People of all ages, races, genders, nationalities, abilities, and religions waved flags and held up signs:

"Our Brothers and Sisters Deserve Reparations"
"Reparations for Genocide against Black People and Native Americans"

There were chants: "B-B-B! Bring Blacks Back!" Far from the Mall, people held pop-up rallies in front of shopping malls, at major intersections, and along the interstate—that is, until the police arrived and ticketed people for loitering and holding rallies without a permit.

The international community closely watched the goings-on in the United States. Most leaders avoided making public statements. Several reached out to the US President-for-Life and privately offered him advice. Many concluded that the United States was now dealing with a fiscal matter, not a racial issue. Some countries, including Australia, worried that if the United States gave such a large reparations amount to Black people, they might be forced to do the same for Aboriginals in their own country. Most awaited the outcome to see how it would affect their trade, military, and business relationships.

### The Council of Elders Debates the Offer

The Council of Elders was responsible for making the final call, whether Black people would accept or decline the Offer. The Elders were a group of 270 Black women and men over the age of sixty-five. They were from all parts of the country—rural areas, big cities, and small towns—and represented all parts of the African diaspora. The Council included a mix of religious affiliations, as well as agnostics and atheists. The group reflected a range of skin tones, body sizes, sexual orientations, hairstyles, and educational attainment. The Council had gone underground as a group, sharing the same lodging space. They had been discussing, critiquing, arguing, yelling, and crying about the Offer around-the-clock since the President-for-Life's announcement. Their discussions always came back to the same question that Chief Elder Sage had posed as they began their deliberations: "Are reparations enough?"

Some Elders thought the reparations amount was low. After all, Elder Righteous said, the money they were offered was "a drop in the bucket. We should demand more. We should each receive a million dollars for every year we've been on this earth!" Several of the Elders nodded in agreement with Elder Righteous.

Elder Elijah jumped up and said, "No, no! We must take the money and return home. Lord knows we need it. Many in our community have been away from our families and we need to go home. The offer will allow us to make a fresh start. We'll be the twenty-first century's Black pioneers." Some Elders clapped in agreement with Elder Elijah. Elder Elijah used the same three words, in a different order, to answer Chief Elder Sage's question: "Reparations are enough."

Elder Clarity asked whether they should make a counteroffer. Reparations should be given to anyone who was identified as Black on a government document. "They're trying to divide us, and we can't let that happen," Elder Clarity stated. "Reparations shouldn't come with the condition that we stay on US soil until we're sixty-five years old. Hell, we're free people. Under the UN Declaration of Human Rights, we have a right to leave any country, even this one!"[21]

Another Elder cautioned that Black people should steer clear of the Offer. As bad as things had been for Black people, it would be even worse if they received reparations. "White folks will make our lives a living hell. We'll have to hide out again! We can't expect Whites to negotiate a humane outcome for Black life."

Elder Sage asked everyone to write a list of what they would do with $1.2 million. Elder Leader read her list:

1. Get reliable transportation, so I don't have to take the bus.
2. Buy a house for me and my brother's family.
3. Purchase burial insurance.
4. Season tickets to see the Los Angeles Lakers.
5. New dress for church.

Elder Leader continued, "By the time I pay the taxes, that's about all I can get. That's fine with me, though." Another Elder responded, "Me too. We need a boost to level the playing field. Face the facts. We have negative wealth in our community." Elder Leader stood up and said, "I agree with Elder Elijah."

Elder Ross-Bell stood up and asked, "When has the US government ever given Black folks anything?" She continued, "Is this really an offer? Or is it a threat in sheep's clothing?" The room got quiet. Elder Ross-Bell asked another question: "What if we accept their offer, move back, and then they come up with some reason not to keep their word and pay us? They could say that the government is bankrupt or that the Federal Reserve won't honor the government payout. By then, they'll have figured out how to keep us here, for free. Our vote should be 'Hell, no!'" Elder Ross-Bell's words had stirred up everyone. Elder Elijah looked sad.

As the final week approached, the media fascination with the Reparations Offer came to an abrupt halt. An eerie quiet hung over the country. No one wanted to do anything that would upset Black folks or enrage White folks. Social media was mum on the Offer, and the talking heads declined to further speculate about what Black people should do. Poll takers stopped conducting surveys asking White people if they wanted Black people to return to US society. Whites who didn't want the US government to pay reparations to Black people were unsure whether to speak out or be quiet. The same was true for White allies who supported the Reparations Offer. Not knowing what to do, everyone did nothing.

## The African American Vote

The day had come. It was October 10, 2047, time for the Elders to vote. They would take a secret vote. Would they accept the Reparations Offer made by the US government? The Elder Council would make the call. They voted, and the vote was unanimous. The vote count was double-checked and triple-checked. It was time for the three representatives to deliver the decision.

Chief Elder Sage along with Elder Clarity and Elder Ross-Bell drove from Anacostia in Southeast Washington, DC, over the bridge to the White House. When they arrived on the South Lawn, they were greeted by the President-for-Life and other cabinet members. Chief Elder Sage introduced herself and Elders Clarity and Ross-Bell. She then handed the envelope with the vote tally and a letter to the President. As the President-for-Life opened the letter, the Elders said, "Thank you," and made their exit. The reparations vote would usher in a new chapter of African American life in America.

# ACKNOWLEDGMENTS

Thank you to the New York University Press for providing me with the opportunity to revisit and present an updated volume of The Color of Crime. I had a wonderful team of students who provided stellar research assistance—Georry Desruisseaux, Courtney Diaz, and Chelsea Johnson. A special thank you to my colleagues Professor Nancy Dowd, Dr. Patricia Hilliard-Nunn, and Dr. Zoharah Simmons for their comments on an early draft of "The Soul Savers" (chapter 8). Sadly Dr. Hilliard-Nunn passed in 2020.

Last, thank you to the anonymous peer reviewers who provided rigorous, essential insights and suggestions.

## APPENDIX A

*Data Snapshots on Race and Crime*

The data below illuminates and contextualizes the material discussed throughout the text.

TABLE A.1. US Population by Racial Groups, 2019.

|  | Number | Percentage |
|---|---|---|
| *Total Population* | 327 million | 100% |
| White (Non-Hispanic) | 196.2 million | 60% |
| Black | 42.5 million | 13% |
| Latino/Hispanic | 59 million | 18% |
| Asian and Pacific Islander | 19.6 million | 6% |
| American Indian / Alaskan Native | 3.3 million | 1% |
| Two or more races | 9.8 million | 3% |

Source: https://www.census.gov/quickfacts/fact/table/US/IPE120218.

These data provide the base rates for estimating whether a particular racial group is overrepresented or underrepresented in the justice system.

TABLE A.2. Correctional Population and Control Rates by Race (2013-2015).

|  | State Prison[a] | Federal Prison[b] | Jail[c] | Probation[d] | Parole[e] | Total |
|---|---|---|---|---|---|---|
| Total | 1.3 million | 151,732 | 750,000[f] | 3.7 million | 870,000 | 6.8 million |
| White (Non-Hispanic) | 436,000 [33%] | 41,833[g] [27%] | 360,000 [48%] | 2.1 million [54%] | 391,500 [45%] | 3.3 million [48%] |
| Black | 475,000 [36%] | 58,490 [38%] | 255,000 [34%] | 1.1 million [31%] | 330,600 [38%] | 2.2 million [32%] |
| Hispanic | 336,000 [26%] | 45,553 [30%] | 112,500 [15%] | 481,000 [13%] | 130,500 [15%] | 1.1 million [16%] |

## TABLE A.2. (*cont.*)

| | State Prison[a] | Federal Prison[b] | Jail[c] | Probation[d] | Parole[e] | Total |
|---|---|---|---|---|---|---|
| Asian American | * | 2,273 [1.5%] | 75,000 [1%] | 370,000 [1%] | 87,000 [1%] | 535,000 [1%] |
| Native American | * | 3,583 [2.4%] | 90,000 [1.2%] | 370,000 [1%] | 87,000 [1%] | 551,000 [1%] |

Note: Based on availability, this table includes data for years 2013, 2014, or 2015. Numbers and percentages are rounded up.

a Jennifer Bronson and E. Ann Carson, "Prisoners in 2017," Bureau of Justice Statistics, NCJ 252156 (Table 3), 2019, www.bjs.gov.

b Federal Bureau of Prisons, "Inmate Ethnicity," updated May 8, 20201, www.bop.gov.

c Todd Minton and Zhen Zeng, "Jail Inmates in 2015," Bureau of Justice Statistics, NCJ 250394, Table 3, p. 4, www.bjs.gov, 2016.

d Erinn J. Herberman and Thomas P. Bonczar, "Probation and Parole in the United States, 2013," Appendix Table 3, 2015.

e Herberman and. Bonczar, "Probation and Parole in the United States, 2013," Appendix Table 6.

f This figure includes fifteen hundred people identified as mixed-race.

* Reliable prison statistics for Asian Americans and Native Americans are not available.

g The Bureau of Prisons calculates race separately from ethnicity. To compute the number of Hispanics as a racial category, the percentage of Hispanics under the ethnicity calculation was deducted from the White percentage under race.

## TABLE A.3. Arrest Data by Race and Type of Offense, 2018.

| | White | Black | Asian American | American Indian / Alaskan Native | Native Hawaiian / Pacific Islander |
|---|---|---|---|---|---|
| Violent Offenses | 59% | 37% | 1.6% | 2% | 0.4% |
| Property Offenses | 67% | 30% | 1.1% | 1.7% | 0.2% |
| Total | 69% | 27% | 1.2% | 2.1% | 0.2% |

Source: Federal Bureau of Investigation, Uniform Crime Reports, "Arrests by Race and Ethnicity, 2018," Table 43, https://ucr.fbi.gov.

These data are based on the more than 7.7 million arrests in 2018. Under the UCR "Hispanic or Latino" is catalogued as an ethnicity, not a race. For 2018, Latinos constituted 19 percent of overall arrests, 25 percent of arrests for violent offenses, and 16 percent of arrests for property crimes.

## TABLE A.4A. Homicide Cases by Race of Victim and Offender, 2018.

| *White Victims* | 3,315 cases |
|---|---|
| White Victim / White Offender | 2,677 cases |
| White Victim / Black Offender | 514 cases |

**TABLE A.4B. Homicide Cases by Race of Victim and Offender, 2018.**

| *Black Victims* | 2,925 cases |
|---|---|
| Black Victim / Black Offender | 2,600 cases |
| Black Victim / White Offender | 234 cases |

Source: Federal Bureau of Investigation, Uniform Crime Reports, Crime in the United States, 2018, "Expanded Homicide Data, Table 6," https://ucr.fbi.gov.

The overwhelming majority of homicides involve an offender and victim of the same race. For cases involving White victims and White offenders, the figure is 80 percent and for cases involving Black victims and Black offenders, the figure is 89 percent.

**TABLE A.5. Rape, Robbery, and Assault, Percentages by Race of Victim and Offender (2018).**

|  | White Offender | Black Offender | Hispanic Offender | Asian Offender |
|---|---|---|---|---|
| White Victim | 62% | 15% | 10% | 2.2% |
| Black Victim | 10% | 70% | 8% | * |
| Hispanic Victim | 28% | 15% | 45% | * |
| Asian Victim | 24% | 27% | 7% | 24% |

* Discrepancies due to missing data and rounding.
Source: Rachel Morgan and Barbara Oudekerk, "Criminal Victimization, 2018," Bureau of Justice Statistics, September 2019, NCJ 253043, Table 14, www.bjs.gov.

These data show that for Whites and Blacks, the majority of these offenses are intraracial. The data for Hispanics and Asians are exceptions to the general finding that crime is intraracial. Data on American Indians show that 90 percent of their criminal victimization is due to interracial offending.[1]

**TABLE A.6A. Lifetime Likelihood of Serving Time in Prison, by Race, 2001.**

|  | Total |
|---|---|
| *White* | 3.4% |
| Men | 5.9% |
| Women | 0.9% |

TABLE A.6B. Lifetime Likelihood of Serving Time in Prison, by Race, 2001.

|  | Total |
| --- | --- |
| *Black* | 18.6% |
| Men | 32.2% |
| Women | 5.6% |

TABLE A.6C. Lifetime Likelihood of Serving Time in Prison, by Race, 2001.

|  | Total |
| --- | --- |
| *Hispanic* | 10% |
| Men | 17.2% |
| Women | 2.2% |

Source: Tomas P. Bonczar, "Prevalence of Imprisonment in the US Population, 1974–2001," Bureau of Justice Statistics, 2003, Table 9, p. 9. These are the most recent data available.

Nearly one-third of all Black men will spend part of their lives behind bars (32.2 percent). This compares with a 5.9 percent rate for White men. Typically, incarceration rates are much lower for women than men. The rate for Black women (5.6 percent) is almost as high as the rate for White men. The lifetime likelihood rates for Hispanics falls between Whites and Blacks and are at or below their percentage in the overall population.[2]

TABLE A.7. Victimization Rates for Native Americans (2017).

|  | American Indian / Alaska Native | Non-Hispanic White |
| --- | --- | --- |
| Any Lifetime Violence | 84% | 71% |
| Sexual Violence | 56% | 50% |
| Physical Violence by Partner | 55% | 34% |
| Stalking | 49% | 27% |

Source: Nancy Rodriguez, Andre Rosay, Carrie Bettinger-Lopez, Joye Frost, and Bea Hanson, "Violence Against American Indian and Alaskan Native Women and Men—2010 Findings from the National Intimate Partner Sexual Violence Survey," Office of Justice Programs, 2016, www.ojp.gov.

These data show that, compared with other racial groups, American Indians are much more likely to be crime victims, particularly for crimes involving stalking and partner violence.

*Racial Hoax Cases*

## CASE SUMMARIES OF 134 (1987–2020)

*Bradley Adams*

In 1995, Molly Sullivan was killed. Her fiancé, Bradley Adams, was arrested five months after the murder. Adams told police that a group of Black men was responsible for Sullivan's death. He later admitted that Sullivan, who suffered from a degenerative muscle disease, died after he sat on her chest. Adams was convicted of murder and sentenced to seventy years in prison.

*Stevie Allman*

In 1997, Stevie Allman's home was torched. It was believed that Allman, an antidrug activist in Oakland, California, had been targeted because of her efforts to shut down drug dealers. Allman was White, and the suspected arsonists were believed to be Black. The case received widespread publicity. Governor Pete Wilson posted a $50,000 reward, neighbors raised close to $5,000, and the nation's drug czar expressed concern. Four months later, it was discovered that Allman's sister Sarah had killed her, placed her body in a freezer, and firebombed the home to cover up the murder. Police believe the sister had assumed Stevie's identity and planned to cash in on her insurance policy.

*Jesse Anderson*

In 1992, Jesse Anderson, a White man, told the police that he and his wife had been attacked in a restaurant parking lot in suburban Milwaukee. Anderson said two Black men stabbed him and his wife. His wife, who suffered twenty-one stabs to her chest, died following the attack. Anderson received superficial wounds. Following a weeklong search for the fictional criminals, Anderson was arrested and charged with murder. He had planned the murder hoax to get his wife's $250,000 insurance policy. Anderson was convicted of first-degree murder. In 1994, Anderson was murdered in prison along with serial killer Jeffrey Dahmer, causing some people to speculate that he was killed because of the racial upheaval caused by his hoax.

### Tisha Anderson and William Lee

In 1995, Tisha Anderson, a Black woman, and her White boyfriend, William Lee, told police they had received death threats and that their apartment had been defaced with racial slurs. It was subsequently determined that Anderson and Lee had staged the hate crime to get out of their apartment lease.

### Casey Anthony

In 2008, in Orlando, Florida, a toddler disappeared from her home. Six months later, she was found stuffed in a bag, a short distance from her home. The toddler's mother did not report her disappearance for over a month and said she had left her daughter with her Hispanic babysitter, who also disappeared—inferring that the babysitter had kidnapped the toddler. It was later determined there was no Hispanic babysitter. Anthony was charged with giving false statements to law enforcement, child neglect, and obstruction of a criminal investigation.

### Samuel Asbell

In 1990, Samuel Asbell, a White New Jersey prosecutor, told police that he had been involved in a car chase with two Black men. Asbell, who reported that the chase had reached speeds up to one hundred miles per hour, said that the assailants had fired at his car with an automatic rifle. After a police investigation established that the incident could not have happened the way Asbell described it, Asbell admitted that he had shot at his own car. He later said that he had been under stress and checked himself into a psychiatric clinic. Asbell pled guilty to filing a false police report, and his license to practice law was suspended for two years.

*Raimundo Atesanio*

In 2014, police chief Raimundo Atesanio of Biscayne Park, Florida, instructed his officers to arrest innocent Black people for crimes. Atesanio encouraged officers to pin unsolved crimes on innocent minorities and arrest them for the crimes. In two of the cases, Black men were wrongfully accused of burglary. Following an investigation, Atesanio and others were charged with violating federal civil rights, in a lawsuit filed by those who had been wrongfully arrested.

*Anthony Avent*

In 1994, Anthony Avent, a player for the Orlando Magic, told police that he had been stabbed by three White men on an Orlando street. Avent, who is Black, sustained injuries requiring thirty stitches. He later recanted his tale, telling police that he made up the story to hide the fact that he had an altercation with a friend. Avent was fined $3,000 by the basketball team.

*Adam Baisley*

In 1996, Adam Baisley and three other White teenagers decided to cut school and have a party. At the party, a gun was passed around. It accidentally discharged, and a bullet hit one of the boys in the cheek. They told the police that a Black man, wearing a dark sweatshirt and carrying a semiautomatic handgun, had committed the crime. The boys later admitted that they had lied.

*Halley Bass*

In 2017, Halley Bass told police that she had been attacked on a street in Ann Arbor, Michigan. She said it was because she wore a pin that expressed support for Brexit. Bass said a White stranger cut her face with a safety pin. She said her attack was one of the hate crimes following Donald Trump's election. Days later, she admitted to scratching her own face during a mental health episode. She was convicted of filing a false report and sentenced to a year of probation.

*Tracy Birt*

In 1996, Tracy Birt, a Black man, admitted to vandalizing a judge's chambers. Birt, who had worked at the courthouse, used red paint to write racial epithets and symbols in the Little Rock, Arkansas, courthouse. He was charged and convicted of criminal mischief.

### Daniel Bolduc

In 1995, Daniel Bolduc, a White police officer from Hartford, Connecticut, filed a police report wherein he stated that three Black men had smashed the windshield of a police vehicle. When it was determined that the report was fabricated, Bolduc was suspended for one day and placed on sick leave, pending psychological testing.

### Tawana Brawley

In 1987, Tawana Brawley told police that she had been kidnapped and raped by six White men. Brawley, a Black fifteen-year-old from Wappinger Falls, New York, said that the men were law enforcement officers who wore badges. She said she was smeared with feces, placed in a plastic bag, and left in a gutter. The grand jury charged with investigating the case found no basis for issuing criminal indictments. Over the years, Brawley has stood by her initial claims. Today, however, the case is widely believed to have been a hoax.

### Dwayne Byrdsong

In 1995, Dwayne Byrdsong, of Coraville, Iowa, fabricated a hate crime. Byrdsong painted racial slurs on his Mercedes-Benz, including "Go Back to Africa" and "KKK." The Black community mobilized to collect funds for Byrdsong, a minister. He was convicted of filing a false police report.

### Toby Campbell

In 1995, Toby Campbell, a White store clerk in South Carolina, told police he had been robbed at knifepoint by two Black men. He said the men stole a dozen cartons of cigarettes. He provided detailed descriptions of the men, including that one man wore earrings in the shape of a marijuana leaf and a bull. Campbell later admitted that he had stolen the cigarettes.

### Khalil Cavil

In 2018, Khalil Cavil, a twenty-year-old Black waiter in Odessa, Texas, posted a picture on Facebook. The photo showed a restaurant bill for

$108, with no tip added. Instead, on the tip line were the words "We don't tip terrorists." Cavil said this was on the bill from one of the tables he had served that evening. In response, the restaurant banned the customer. When it was later determined that Cavil made up the story, he was terminated.

## Donald Cherry

In 1996, Donald Cherry told police that, following a traffic dispute, Black youths shot and killed his two-year-old son, who was seated in the back of his car. Cherry later admitted that he had gone to purchase drugs and that, while there, he had a dispute with the dealer over payment. When Cherry attempted to leave without paying for the drugs, the dealer shot into his vehicle, killing the boy. Cherry was convicted of reckless aggravated assault and reckless endangerment. He was sentenced to five years in prison.

## Emily Clark

In 2004, Emily Clark, a young White female who was a student at the University of Montana, told police that she was a robbery victim. She said her attacker, who was six-feet-three with a dark complexion, had grabbed $100 from her as she approached her dormitory. After interviewing Clark's friends, the police found inconsistencies with her account. She was charged with filing a false police report.

## Garrick Clemente

In 1996, Garrick Clemente, a Black man, gave a neighbor $400 to paint a racial slur on his apartment door. Clemente's plan was to fake a hate crime. The motive for the hoax is unclear.

## Sabrina Collins

In 1990, Sabrina Collins, a Black freshman at Emory University, told police that she had received a death threat and that someone had scrawled racial slurs on her dormitory walls. Weeks later Collins admitted that she had written the death threat and scrawled the slurs. Her claims of racial harassment led to protests by students and civil rights leaders in Atlanta.

*Amy Cooper*

In 2020, while Amy Cooper, a White woman, was walking her dog in New York's Central Park, she encountered Christian Cooper, a Black man, who was bird-watching. He asked her to place her dog on its leash, as the park signs required. She refused, and Christian responded by offering her dog treats and recording the incident. Amy called the police and said she was being threatened by an African American man and asked the police for help. The police arrived, and after talking to both parties, they determined the dispute had ended.

*Henry Crane*

On New Year's Eve in 1995, Henry Crane notified police that he had been carjacked at gunpoint, by three Black men. After hearing a police broadcast about the incident, another police officer spotted the car and pulled it over. The woman driving the car told police that she and Crane had just had sex at a hotel. Crane fabricated the hoax to avoid having his wife learn that he had been with another woman.

*Olander Cuthrell*

In 2013, Olander Cuthrell, a music minister in Virginia, told authorities that he had been the victim of a racially motivated attack. Cuthrell, who is Black, said that someone had spray-painted his home with racial slurs and torched his house and car. Following the investigation, Cuthrell admitted that he had devised the hoax because he was in debt and faced eviction. He was sentenced to two years in prison.

*Tanya Dacri*

In 1989, Tanya Dacri, a White woman from Philadelphia, reported to the police that her two-month-old son had been kidnapped from her in a mall parking lot. According to her report, two Black men took the infant. Police later learned that Dacri and her husband fabricated the story after murdering and dismembering the child and throwing his remains in a river. The child's crying upset the parents. Dacri is serving a life sentence for murder.

### Thomas DiBartolo

In 1996, Thomas DiBartolo, a sheriff, told officials that he and his wife had been shot by two armed Black gunmen who tried to rob them. DiBartolo sustained a flesh wound, and his wife died following the attack. Early on, police were suspicious of the story and did not release a sketch of the suspects. Three months after his wife died, DiBartolo was charged with and ultimately convicted of first-degree murder. At trial, there was evidence that he carried out the murder to avoid a costly divorce and get his wife's life insurance money. One woman testified that she had sex with him on the day of his wife's funeral. DiBartolo was sentenced to twenty-six years in prison and fined $11,000 in restitution.

### Sherita Dixon-Cole

In 2018, police pulled over Sherita Dixon-Cole for driving while under the influence. She claimed that she was sexually assaulted by the White officers. These claims spread over social media, with many people coming to her defense and calling for justice. Soon after, body camera footage of the stop was released. It showed that Dixon-Cole was pulled over, asked to take a sobriety test, and was arrested and taken to jail. False report charges were not filed against Dixon-Cole, who said she never claimed that she had been sexually assaulted by police officers.

### Thomas Drogan and Louis Papaleo

In 1993, two New York City police officers, Thomas Drogan and Louis Papaleo, got into a physical fight at the police station. The officers fought over who would file a report on a car fire to which both had responded earlier in the day. The fight left both officers with extensive cuts and bruises. To cover up their altercation, they invented a story that a Black man assaulted them. They described him as wearing a blue jacket and sneakers. The hoax was ultimately revealed by a fellow police officer who saw the officers' fight. Officer Drogan was fired, and Officer Papaleo was suspended for sixty days and put on probation for a year.

### Duke Lacrosse Team Case (Hoax Victim)

In 2006, members of the Duke University men's lacrosse team held a party. Two strippers were hired as part of the entertainment. Following the party, one of the women said that she had been raped by members of the lacrosse team. This allegation, brought by a Black woman against the all-White athletic team, led to a firestorm of controversy and media attention. Over several months the prosecution's case began to fall apart. There were questions about the victim's credibility and incompatible DNA evidence. A new district attorney took over the case, and the charges were dropped. The initial prosecutor, Mike Nifong, was charged with several ethics violations and disbarred.

*Kerri Dunn*
In 2004, Kerri Dunn was a visiting psychology professor at Claremont McKenna College. One evening, following a lecture she had given on hate crimes, Dunn returned to her car to discover that it had been vandalized. The vehicle had been spray-painted with racist and anti-Semitic slurs ("kike whore" and "nigger lover"), the tires had been slashed, and the windows broken. McKenna, who is White, notified authorities, who classified the case as a hate crime. Antiracism protests were held and the college was shut down for one day. After talking with witnesses, police and prosecutors concluded that Dunn staged the hoax herself. She was convicted of filing a false police report and insurance fraud. She was sentenced to one year in prison and $20,000 in restitution.

*Mitchell Dutz*
In 2018, Mitchell Dutz told police that he had been carjacked by three Black men who drove away in his car with his thirteen-month-old infant in the backseat. As a result of Dutz's story, an Amber Alert was issued in Farmington, Illinois. It was later determined that Dutz concocted the story to cover up a drug deal gone bad. He pled guilty to vehicle burglary and disorderly conduct.

*Exonerated Five / Central Park Five*
In 1989, while on an evening jog in Central Park, Trisha Meili was violently assaulted and raped. The attack on Meili, a White woman, by a group of Black boys was a huge media story. The attackers were said to be part of a large group of boys who were in the park "wildin'"—assaulting joggers, walkers, and bicyclists. Five youths, between the ages of fourteen and sixteen, were arrested and charged with the attack, and following long hours of questioning, they confessed. There was no

physical evidence linking them to the crimes. Each youth was convicted of various crimes related to the assault on Meili, and in total the five served more than forty years in prison. Over a decade later, a convicted rapist confessed to the attack on Meili. His claims were supported by DNA testing. Investigations into the case revealed a range of questionable behavior by police and prosecutors, including coerced confessions and inattention to crucial evidence that would have led to not guilty verdicts. In 2002, the five men were exonerated and later received a $41 million settlement.

*Dawn Frakes*
In 1995, Dawn Frakes, a White state trooper, told police that she had been shot by a Black teenager. In fact, Frakes had accidentally shot herself in the arm. Officer Frakes gave police a detailed description of her attacker, saying that he went by the name "Willy." Frakes was suspended after it was determined that her story was a hoax.

*Tina Gateley and William Karaffa*
In 1993, Tina Gateley and her boyfriend, William Karaffa, both White, claimed that Black youths had beaten up Gateley and taken her purse. Gateley was hospitalized for three days with broken ribs and other injuries. The pair told their story on local television and urged neighbors to demand police make arrests in the case. Police investigators determined that the story was fabricated to cover up an incident of domestic violence. Karaffa had beaten up Gateley.

*Matthew Gayle*
In 1995, Matthew Gayle told police that his wife had been killed by a Black man wearing baggy pants and a red and white sweatshirt. According to Gayle, his wife was shot as the couple drove through an Orlando neighborhood. It was later determined that Gayle had paid a hit man $10,000 to kill his wife. He concocted the hoax to collect on his wife's $150,000 insurance policy. Gayle was sentenced to life in prison.

*Tonya Gibson, Tynnush Bush, Clayton Henley, William Gibson, and Gary Snyder*

In 1996, five White friends agreed on a racial hoax scheme. They decided to blame an accidental shooting on a fictional Black man. The men informed police that a Black man had broken into their apartment and fired shots, hitting one of them. Based on their description of the attacker, police questioned and arrested John Harris, a Black man. Harris was taken to the scene of the shooting and positively identified as the armed assailant. After police told the men that their friend who had been hospitalized after the shooting would survive and that Harris had a solid alibi, they admitted to making up the story.

*Kendra Gillis*

In 1994, Kendra Gillis, a White student at the State University of New York–Albany, reported that she had been attacked by a Black man wielding a knife. After police questioned her about inconsistencies in her story, she admitted that she had fabricated the story. She had created the tale to protect her father, David Gillis, who had physically abused her. Gillis apologized for the false accusation. No false report charges were filed against her.

*Joshua Green, Daniel Pratt, and Michael Crowley*

In 1994, three White men reported that they had been robbed of $35,000 at the car wash where they worked. They told police that the assailant was a gun-toting Black man. Less than a week later, the police discovered that the story was part of a plan the three men had devised to steal from the car wash. All three men were arrested for larceny. Green and Crowley were also charged with filing a false report.

*Alicia Hardin*

In 2005, Alicia Hardin was a nineteen-year-old college student. Hardin, who is Black, used campus mail to send threatening, racist messages to other minority students. As a precaution, the university evacuated all minority students from the campus dormitories. Hardin devised the ruse to convince her parents that Trinity, her college, was not safe, hoping that they would then let her transfer to another university. She pled guilty to felony disorderly conduct and was sentenced to two years' probation, two hundred hours of community service, and $2,000 in restitution.

## Breana Harmon

In 2017, nineteen-year-old Breana Harmon claimed that she was kidnapped and sexually assaulted by three Black men. Two weeks later, she admitted she had made up the assault story following a fight she had with her fiancé. Following convictions for tampering with physical evidence and filing false reports, Harmon was sentenced to eight years probation and $8,000 in restitution.

## Persey Harris, Ann Vigil, and Caryn Harris

In 1996, Persey Harris, a Black man, was sentenced to fifteen days in jail for filing a false police report. Harris and his cohorts told police that a restaurant owner had threatened them with a four-foot stick and shouted racial epithets at them. Harris later admitted that he had planned to use the fabricated incident to file a civil suit.

## Robert Harris

In 1996, Robert Harris, a White man, claimed that he and his fiancée had been shot and robbed on a quiet Baltimore street. Harris said that the assailant was an armed Black man, wearing a camouflage jacket and black and white pants. Harris's fiancée died from her gunshot wounds. Within three days, Harris confessed that he had hired a hit man to rob the pair and kill his fiancée. Harris was motivated by the mistaken belief that he was the beneficiary of his fiancée's $250,000 insurance policy.

## Jeffrey Hebert

In August 1995, Jeffrey Hebert told police that three Black men had broken into his home, assaulted everyone there, and set the house on fire. Hebert, who is White, was the only survivor. He told police that, following the attack, the Black assailants ran into the woods nearby. Police became suspicious when they discovered contradictions in Hebert's story. Police also observed that the wounds on Hebert's wrists were consistent with a suicide attempt. Hebert, who pled guilty to murder and arson, was sentenced to two life terms behind bars.

*Brenda Hueneke*
In 1995, Brenda Hueneke told police that a Black man had robbed her at knifepoint. She later admitted to making up the story. Hueneke was charged with filing a false police report.

*Frank Irvine*
In 1994, Frank Irvine, a White police officer, told police that he had been attacked by a Black customer at a convenience store. A videotape of the North Miami, Florida, incident indicated that Irvine had assaulted the customer. Irvine resigned his post and pled no contest to misdemeanor battery and filing a false report. He received one year of probation.

*Angela Jackson*
In 1996, Angela Jackson, a twenty-seven-year-old Black woman, sent herself packages containing damaged goods and scrawled with racial slurs. To draw attention to and enhance the legitimacy of her insurance scam, Jackson also sent defaced mail packages to several Black officials, including Jesse Jackson (no relation). Jackson, a law student, blamed United Parcel Service for the racist hate mail and sought $150,000 compensation. Police traced the packages to Jackson, and she was charged and convicted of mail and wire fraud. She was sentenced to five years in federal prison.

*Sonia James*
In 1996, Sonia James told police that her home had been vandalized and defaced with racial slurs. James claimed that intruders had destroyed her furniture, clothing, and personal belongings. Community residents took up her cause and raised more than $5,000 for her. James later told police that she had fabricated the scheme to get money from her home insurance policy. James was sentenced to nine months in jail and ordered to pay $26,000 in restitution.

*Kathleen Johnston*
In 1994, Kathleen Johnston stated that she had been assaulted and robbed at the high school where she worked. The Maryland woman said that two Black males had attacked her. Two months later, she admitted

that her wounds were self-inflicted and recanted her story. Johnston later resigned from her teaching position.

## Eric Jones

In 2018, Eric Jones told police that he had been approached by two Black men outside of a motel in Spotsylvania, Virginia, and that one of the men shot him. The police located the gun used in the shooting in Jones's motel room. They later determined that Jones had shot himself and blamed it on two imaginary Black men.

## Heidi Jones

In 2010, Heidi Jones, a White meteorologist in New York, claimed that she had been attacked by the same Hispanic man twice, once outside her apartment and earlier in Central Park. She said he grabbed her from behind, dragged her into a wooded area, and attempted to rape her. Weeks later she admitted she had fabricated the stories to garner sympathy.

## Miriam Kashani

In 1990, Miriam Kashani, a student at George Washington University, reported that another White female student had been raped by two young Black men, with "particularly bad body odor." The day after press reports about the crime, Kashani admitted that she had made up the story. She said her goal was to "highlight the problems of safety for women."

## Andrew King

In February 2018, Andrew King, a Jewish man, reported that his home had been vandalized with spray painted swastikas and hate messages. A month later he admitted that he had fabricated the hate crimes. His sentence was three years of probation.

## Mark Lambirth

In 1995, Mark Lambirth, a White man, claimed that an American Indian man had forced him at gunpoint to drive from North Carolina to Colorado. Lambirth reported that in Colorado the car got stuck in the snow in a remote area. He also told police that his kidnapper then burned the car and made him walk up a mountain. After investigating the story, police concluded that it was a hoax. Among other things, police found only one set of foot tracks in the snow where Lambirth was allegedly taken.

### Mark Lewis
In 1993, Mark Lewis, a police officer in Lake Worth, Florida, filed a report stating that he had been hit on the head with a wrench. Lewis said that his attacker was a Black man. After investigating the case, police officials concluded that the incident was a hoax that Lewis had staged to garner sympathy for a recent demotion.

### Marcy Limos
A White woman from Reno, Nevada, Marcy Limos, told police that she had been raped by two Black men. According to Limos, while on her way to meet her husband for dinner, she was approached by the men. She said the men dragged her and her one-year-old daughter into an SUV and took them to a park, where Limos was sexually assaulted, and then she was allowed to go free. Limos later admitted that she had fabricated the tale to hide her drug problem from her husband. She was charged with filing a false report.

### Marquie Little
In 2017, Marquie Little, a Black sailor, said his rack and bed had been covered in trash and racial slurs. He posted pictures of the vandalism and said he was not surprised by the treatment he received. An investigation revealed inconsistencies in Little's story and determined that he concocted the incident. He was later charged with making false statements, destruction of government property, and disorderly conduct.

### Ryan Lochte
During the 2016 Summer Olympics in Rio de Janeiro, Brazil, Ryan Lochte, a member of the US swimming team, told people that he and his teammates had been robbed at gunpoint at a gas station. Security footage, however, showed Lochte and fellow team members vandalizing the gas station bathroom. They fabricated the robbery to cover up their vandalism. Rio police charged Lochte with filing a false robbery report.

*Josephine Lupus*

In 1994, Josephine Lupus, a college student at State College at Old West-bury in New York, told police that she had been robbed by a Black man. The 21-year-old White woman said that the attacker had slashed her face and stabbed her in the stomach as she walked to her car following an evening class. Lupus went on television and displayed her injuries. Lupus, who later confessed to making up the whole story, was charged with filing a false police report. The district attorney refused a plea bargain because "he felt strongly about the aspect of trying to blame a Black man."

*Lucille Magrone*

In 1990, White residents in Islip Terrace, New York, began receiving death threats. The letters, allegedly written by a Black man, threatened them with rape, robbery, and murder. One letter threatened, "You people are all dead in 24 hours." White residents became fearful: some purchased dogs, some slept with baseball bats at their bedside, and some believed that they saw intruders in their yard. Five months after the first threatening letter had appeared, Lucille Magrone, a forty-eight-year-old White woman, admitted to writing the letters. She said that the incident was the result of stress she suffered from an assault, months earlier, by a Black man.

*Ramon Martinez, Luis Mendez, and Joseph Degros*

In 1996, Ramon Martinez, an eighteen-year-old from Manchester, New Hampshire, told authorities that he had been shot in the foot. He said that a Black man had shot him after a traffic dispute on a highway. Martinez's story was corroborated by Luis Mendez and Joseph Degros, who said that they were with Martinez and witnessed the assault. Martinez later admitted that he had accidentally shot himself. The men were charged with filing a false police report.

*Janet Maxwell*

In 1993, Janet Maxwell, a twenty-six-year-old White woman, claimed that three Black men had abducted her at gunpoint from a shopping mall. Maxwell told police that she was driven around in her car for ten hours, forced to take drugs, then raped. Police later determined that

Maxwell made up the story so that her parents would not be angry with her for staying out all night. Maxwell was charged with filing a false police report.

### Daniel Mayo and Philip LaForest

In 1997, two White teenagers, Daniel Mayo and Philip LaForest, told police that they had discovered hate graffiti on the walls of a building they were patrolling. The messages included, "KILL WHITY" and "KILL SECURITY." Both Mayo and LaForest, who confessed to spray-painting the messages, were security guards in a Worcester, Massachusetts, apartment complex for elderly residents. The men hoped that the incident would generate publicity and result in a pay raise. They were charged with destruction of property, making a false police report, and intimidation based on race, color, religion, or national origin.

### Cecil McCool

In 1995, Cecil McCool, a White man, accused two Black police officers of leaving his friend, Richard Will, another White man, stranded in a dangerous Chicago neighborhood. Will was later found beaten and burned to death. In fact, McCool and Will were driving through the neighborhood to purchase drugs when police pulled McCool over for a traffic violation. Police took McCool into custody because he had an outstanding warrant. They directed Will to a pay phone three blocks away. Instead Will walked to a crack house, where he was later killed. McCool later admitted that he and Will had been trying to buy drugs and that they had never asked police officers for assistance.

### Kelli McGuire

In July 1997, nineteen-year-old Kelli Maguire told police that she had been abducted and raped by a Black man. She said she had been forced from a shopping mall and assaulted by an armed gunman. Based on McGuire's description, the Fort Lauderdale police released a sketch of the attacker. Within two days, Maguire admitted to making up the story as a cover for staying out all night with her boyfriend.

## Milton Metcalfe

In 1993, Milton Metcalfe, a Black man from Cincinnati, reported that he and his girlfriend had been abducted and held at knifepoint. Metcalfe said that the crime had occurred after he had offered a ride to two Black men. After 911 records revealed that Metcalfe was not at the location that was indicated in his police report, he was charged with and later convicted of filing a false report. Metcalfe spent one night in jail, and his thirty-day jail sentence was suspended.

## Richard Milam

In 1994, Richard Milam told police that his wife had been murdered and that he had been stabbed. According to Milam, a masked Black man attacked and robbed the couple outside a restaurant. Police became suspicious of Milam's story when they discovered that his wife's death made him the beneficiary of a large insurance settlement. Nearly two years after the murder, police located a coworker of Milam's who said Milam had offered him money to kill his wife. Police took Milam into custody, whereupon he confessed to the murder.

## Phillip Miller

In 1994, Phillip Miller, a White convenience store clerk, reported that he had been a crime victim. The North Carolina man said that two Black men had come into the store and robbed him at gunpoint. A week later, Miller was charged with stealing money and filing a false report.

## DeAntrious Mitchell

In 1996, DeAntrious Mitchell was a Black computer science student at Iowa State University and also worked as a security guard. He told police that while making his rounds one evening, he was attacked by eight White men. He said that the men also shouted racial epithets at him. It was later determined that Mitchell fabricated the attack. He was charged with making a false police report.

## Nathaniel Nelson

In 2017, there were reports that a church in Kansas City had been vandalized with racist graffiti and set on fire. The church's insurance company paid over $300,000 in damages to the property. Nathaniel Nelson, a

Black man who worked at the church, later admitted that he had vandalized the property to cover up his theft of church funds. A video recording provided police with crucial evidence of Nelson's culpability. One video showed Nelson spray-painting the outside of the building. He pled guilty to arson in federal court.

### Richard Nicolas

In 1996, Richard Nicolas, a Black man, claimed that while driving on a rural Maryland road with his two-year-old daughter, he was rammed from behind by another car. The driver of that car, a White man with long hair, pulled alongside Nicolas's car and fired a shot that killed his daughter. Nicolas was subsequently charged and convicted of first-degree murder. Months prior to his daughter's death, he had taken out a $15,000 insurance policy in her name, listing himself as the sole beneficiary.

### Edward O'Brien

In 1995, Edward O'Brien, a White teenager, reported that he had been robbed and knifed by two men. He said that one of his attackers was Black and the other was Hispanic. A police investigation indicated that O'Brien had sustained the cuts while murdering his neighbor, whom he had stabbed more than sixty times.

### Marcus Owens

In 2018, Marcus Owens, a Black student at the University of Iowa, told police that he had been attacked by three White men. The men, according to Owens, hurled racial slurs at him. It was later determined that Owens made up the story after being involved in an alcohol-related fight at a bar. He later apologized.

### Brian Patterson

In 1996, a White man told police that he had seen a Black man throw a White person off a bridge. Police searched the area and the river but did not locate a body. Patterson eventually told police that he had fabricated the story.

## Dennis Pittman

In 1996, Dennis Pittman, a White man, told police that he had been car-jacked. He said that a Black assailant pointed a knife at him and forced him to drive from Philadelphia to Atlantic City. The carjacker then left in his car. Shortly after the incident, Pittman admitted that he had made up the story so that he would no longer have to make car payments.

## Maryrose Posner

In 1994, Maryrose Posner told police that she was robbed at an auto-mated teller machine. Posner said that she was with her two-year-old daughter when she was accosted by a Black man. According to Posner, the man held a gun to her daughter's head, laughed, and demanded that she withdraw $200 from her account. After police questioning, Posner admitted that she had used the ploy to get attention from her husband and to cover up the fact that she had purchased an expensive shirt for her father. Days later she said that the police had coerced her into sign-ing a confession and stood by her original story. Posner was charged with filing a false report.

## Christopher Prince (Racial Hoax Victim's Name)

In 1994, a twelve-year-old White girl from Virginia told police that a Black man had broken into her family's home and attempted to rape her. The girl identified her attacker as Christopher Prince, a twenty-one-year-old Black man. Prince, who was arrested, charged with, and convicted of burglary and attempted rape, was sentenced to a twelve-year prison term. After the girl recanted, Prince was released, having served fifteen months in prison. In 1995, Prince was pardoned by the governor, and in 1997, the Virginia Senate voted unanimously to award him $45,000 for wrongful imprisonment. A short time later this award was deemed "illegal," and no other compensation was given to Prince.

## Kissie Ram

In 2018, Kissie Ram, a student at Drake University, admitted writing fake racist notes. The notes, which were placed under the door of some stu-dent dorm rooms, including Ram's, caused a stir on campus. Ram, who is Indian American, was charged with filing a false police report and was sentenced to pay restitution and perform community service hours.

*Loretta Reed*

In 1997, Loretta Reed, a twenty-eight-year-old White woman, told police that she had been carjacked by a Black man. Reed told Sarasota, Florida, police that the man had grabbed her hair and forced her onto the ground. Later she said she made up the story to "protect herself." Reed had given a man her car in exchange for drugs.

*Kristen Rimes*

In 2018, Kristen Rimes told police that she had been accosted in a Walmart parking lot. Rimes said that a Black man wearing a hoodie yanked her out of her car, hit her in the face, and tried to pull down her pants. She claimed that the only reason the attacker was not successful was the arrival of an angel who interrupted the attack. Rimes later posted stories about the incident on social media. It was later determined that Rimes had made up the story.

*Patricia Ripley*

In June 2020, Patricia Ripley told police that her nine-year-old autistic son had been kidnapped by two Black men, who also stole her car. Ripley, who is White, said the men had forced her car off the road. She later confessed to drowning her son in a canal. Her attempt earlier in the day had failed. She was charged with first-degree murder, attempted murder, kidnapping, aggravated child abuse, and filing a false police report.

*Reggie Rivera (Racial Hoax Victim's Name)*

In 1993, four New York livery-van drivers and a mechanic, all of whom were Black, accused a White police officer, Reggie Rivera, of raping them. A two-year police investigation found that the men, some of whom worked in the unlicensed van trade business, made the false allegations as part of a plot to get Rivera fired because he had been ticketing unlicensed van drivers.

*Katharine Robb*

In 2001, Katharine Robb, a White Iowa State University student, claimed that she had been kidnapped and sexually assaulted by four Black men. She said that she was abducted from a campus bus stop by an armed man and then assaulted by the other men. Days later Robb admitted to fabricating the story. Members of the campus community, including Blacks and victims of sexual assault, expressed outrage at Robb's tale. Robb was charged with filing a false police report.

## Darlie Routier

In 1996, Darlie Routier, a White mother of three, told police that a White man, wearing dark clothes and a baseball cap, broke into her home. According to Routier, the attacker stabbed her and two of her sleeping children. Routier received superficial stab wounds in the assault. In 1997, Routier was convicted of capital murder in the death of her youngest child.

## Judy Russell

In 1988, Judy Russell, a White federal prosecutor in New Jersey, reported that she had received death threats from two alleged terrorists who faced extradition to India. She later admitted that she had written and sent the letters to herself. Her actions were part of a scheme to further incriminate the men at their extradition hearing, a case that Russell was prosecuting. In 1989, Russell was acquitted of obstruction of justice charges, based on her insanity plea. The court recommended psychological counseling for Russell because tests indicated that she had multiple personality disorder.

## Zhaleh Sarabakhsh

In 1995, Zhaleh Sarabakhsh claimed that she had been bound, slashed, and left to die in a fire at her family's restaurant in Fargo, North Dakota. Sarabakhsh was found outside the restaurant, bound and with a swastika carved into her abdomen. News of the assault erupted in protests by community members, who denounced the act as a hate crime. Police determined that the wounds were self-inflicted and that she had staged the hate crime herself. She faced several charges, including arson and filing a false police report.

## Ed Satterly

In 2004, a process server for juvenile court shot himself and blamed a fictitious Black man. Ed Satterly of Louisville told police that a man had approached and shot him as he sat in his car reviewing paperwork.

Satterly said that the man had blue and white beads in his braided hair. Police discovered a bullet lodged in the bulletproof vest that Satterly was wearing. After police received information from the crime lab that the bullet matched the gun found in Satterly's trunk, he admitted that he had shot himself and fabricated the entire story.

## Jay Sauls

In 1997, Jay Sauls, a parking-lot security guard, told police that he had been beaten and robbed. He said he was attacked after walking in on two people having sex in a stairwell. Sauls said that he was then assaulted by the man, whom he described as a Black male, five-feet-ten. Several police officers spent hours searching for the fictional Black male attacker. Two weeks following the alleged attack, Sauls admitted making up the story. He was charged with filing a false police report.

## Shawnda Scruggs

In 1996, Shawnda Scruggs, a Sunday school teacher, told police that her home had been vandalized and burglarized. Racial slurs were painted on her walls. She said she would pray for the thieves and turn the other cheek. The thirty-two-year-old Black woman filed an insurance claim for more than $50,000. Her story began to fall apart after inconsistencies were discovered. One of her neighbors reported seeing her china cabinet empty days earlier, and her most expensive possessions were not spray-painted.

## Jaelyn Sealey

In 2000, Jaelyn Sealey told police that her car had been burned and her driveway scrawled with "Go home nigger." The Huntersville, North Carolina, case sparked an outpouring of support for Sealey: more than three hundred people attended a rally in support of her and her family. Sealey later admitted that she torched her vehicle to collect insurance money. She pled guilty to making false statements to police investigators and to mail and wire fraud. Sealey was sentenced to six months in prison, two years' probation, and required to pay $5,000 in restitution.

## Yasmin Seweid

In 2016, Yasmin Seweid, a young Muslim woman, claimed that three men screaming "Donald Trump" attacked her on the subway in Manhattan. She told the police that they tried to pull off her hijab and called her a terrorist. She recanted her story soon after and said that she made it up because of problems she was having with her family. She was charged with filing a false report, as well as obstructing governmental administration.

## Dorne Shaver

In 2000, Dorne Shaver told police that several White men had attacked him and shouted racial slurs at him while he was selling magazines and books door-to-door in DuPage County, Illinois. Shaver was charged with felony disorderly conduct for filing a false police report.

## Michael Shaw

In 1995, Michael Shaw, a White man from Maple Shade, New Jersey, reported that a White toddler had been kidnapped by a Black man. According to Shaw, the young girl's mouth had been bound with duct tape. The police quickly mounted an extensive air and land search for the child. One day later, Shaw admitted that the story was false. Police believe he came up with the tale to get the afternoon off from work. Shaw was charged with making a false report to the police.

## Carlton Skipper

In 1997, Carlton Skipper, a retired Washington, DC, police officer who is Black, told police that he had been assaulted and robbed by two armed Black men. The officer said that he was accosted during his morning run. He was forced to remove his clothing and thrown down an embankment. It was later determined that Skipper may have fabricated the story to cover up a failed suicide attempt.

## Susan Smith

In 1994, Susan Smith, a White woman, told police that a Black man carjacked her and drove off with her two young sons. Nine days after massive federal and state searches had been launched, Smith confessed to drowning her two boys in a South Carolina lake. Smith was depressed over a recent breakup with a boyfriend who did not want to raise children. Smith was convicted of murder and sentenced to life in prison. She will be eligible for parole in 2025.

### Jussie Smollett

In 2019, actor Jussie Smollett filed a report with the Chicago Police Department. He said that on a late-night return from Subway, he was assaulted by two White men, one of whom was wearing a MAGA (Make America Great Again) hat. According to Smollett, one of the men recognized him, and the men shouted anti-Black and anti-gay slurs, beat him up, and wrapped a noose around his neck.

Two men, who were seen on video in the area of Smollett's alleged assault, were questioned by the police. The men, both of whom were Black (and brothers), knew and worked with Smollett. They reported that Smollett hired them to stage a racial attack on himself. By this point, it was widely believed that Smollett had fabricated a hoax. The prosecutor charged him with sixteen offenses, including filing a false police report. Later, in an unexpected twist, the Cook County prosecutor's office dropped all charges. The Chicago Police Department was outraged and sought to have Smollett repay the department $130,000, for the costs of investigating his false claims. The case caused a great public uproar about celebrity, race, and justice. As is true for the other high-profile Black perpetrator hoaxes, Smollett has not recanted his story and maintains that he was the victim of a vicious assault.

### Mounir Soliman

In 1994, Mounir Soliman, a convenience store manager, claimed that two Black men had robbed him of $10,000 while he was taking the money to the bank. The description that Soliman gave police was used to draw a composite sketch. The Texas man ultimately confessed that he had taken the money. He was charged with filing a false report.

### George Nathaniel Stang

In 2018, in Bean Blossom, Indiana, swastikas and the words "Heil Trump" were spray-painted on the outside of an Episcopal church. Authorities said that the church organist, who was Black, was responsible for the racist graffiti. George Stang said he wanted to "mobilize a movement" after the election of Donald Trump. Stang was charged with criminal mischief.

### Bethany Storro

In 2010, Bethany Storro, a White woman, claimed that a Black woman approached her on the street and asked, "Hey, pretty girl, do you want a drink of this?" According to Storro, the woman then poured acid on her face. The acid left severe burns on Storro's face. Police launched an extensive search for this alleged attacker. A fund set up for donations to cover her medical expenses raised $800. Police in Vancouver, Oregon, spent hundreds of hours investigating Storro's claims. She later admitted her story was a lie, spent a year in a mental health facility, and pled guilty to second-degree theft for using the money people donated for her medical costs.

### Charles Stuart

In 1989, Charles Stuart told police that he and his pregnant wife had been shot by a Black jogger on their way home after a birthing class. Stuart's wife and the unborn child died as a result of the gunshot wounds. Stuart identified a Black man from a police lineup as the criminal. The Boston case made national and international headlines. Police ransacked Mission Hill, a predominantly Black neighborhood, in search of the murderer. Matthew, Stuart's brother, informed police that Charles had concocted the hoax as a murderous scheme to collect his wife's insurance money. When Stuart learned that the police were going to question him as a murder suspect, he committed suicide.

### Bonnie Sweeten

In 2009, Bonnie Sweeten called police to say that she and her nine-year-old daughter had been carjacked and abducted near Philadelphia, Pennsylvania, by two Black men. In fact, at the time, Sweeten was using a coworker's name to travel to Disney World with her daughter. She fabricated the carjacking and abduction story to cover up her fraud and theft schemes. Prosecutors estimated that Sweeten stole more than $1 million to support a lavish lifestyle, including payment for in vitro fertilization. Sweeten was charged with filing a false police report, grand theft, and identity theft. She was sentenced to eight years in federal prison.

*Lisa Tanczos*

In September 1995, Lisa Tanczos told police that she had been assaulted by a gun- and knife-wielding man. Tanczos, a thirty-year-old White woman, described her attacker as a muscular Black man in his late thirties. The Allentown, Pennsylvania, woman claimed the assailant scratched her with the knife and used it to play a game of tic-tac-toe on her arm. Two months later, Tanczos said that the same man attacked her at her home and again cut her with a knife. DNA evidence was used to show that Tanczos had fabricated the hoax (DNA was taken from the envelope of a card allegedly sent by the attacker to Tanczos's boss). Tanczos was sentenced to 350 hours of community service at a local Black church.

*Brian Telfair*

In 2016, a city attorney reported that he had received threatening racist calls from an "unknown redneck caller." According to Telfair, the calls targeted him and two other city officials. Telfair later said he made the phone call to himself in order to "preserve the institution of the city," as well as to relieve some of the pressure he felt as a city attorney. As a result of his hoax, the Virginia State Bar suspended Telfair's law license for ninety days. He was also convicted of filing a false police report.

*Harry Ticknor*

In 1997, Harry Ticknor told police that he had been robbed at a gas station by an armed Black man. Ticknor, who is White, later confessed to making up the story. He did not want his girlfriend to find out that he had lost sixty-seven dollars. He was charged with filing a false police report.

*Ashley Todd*

In 2008, Ashley Todd told police that she had been robbed at knifepoint and assaulted while using an automated teller machine. Todd, who is White, said the perpetrator was a six-feet-four Black man. According to Todd, the man carved a letter "B" onto her cheek. Todd, a volunteer for the John McCain presidential campaign, claimed that she was targeted because she had a McCain sticker on her car. It was later determined that Todd fabricated the story. She was charged with filing a false report.

## Tulia, Texas

In 1999, more than forty African Americans were arrested in Tulia, Texas. They were arrested based on the word of a lone undercover agent who said that they were all involved in the drug trade. Many of the charges resulted in convictions and lengthy sentences. An investigation by a special prosecutor determined that the evidence in these cases was not reliable, and all the convictions were voided.

## Mary Turcotte

In 2011, Sister Mary Turcotte, a nun, claimed to have been choked and raped by a Black man in her Brooklyn, New York, neighborhood. She said the man was six-feet-four and 250 pounds. Police released a sketch of the alleged assailant. Following additional questioning, Turcotte admitted that she had made up the rape hoax to cover up her sexual liaison with a bodega worker.

## Paul Veach

In 1995, Paul Veach, a forty-seven-year-old White man from Des Moines, claimed that he had been robbed at gunpoint by a Black man with "light-colored hair in six to eight-inch braids, a deformed pupil in one eye, acne scars on his cheeks, and one or two missing front teeth." Veach said he was forced to drive around for six hours before being put out of his car. A police investigation revealed that Veach had made several ATM transactions at a local horse track. Veach subsequently admitted that he made up the story to hide $390 in gambling losses.

## Neva Veitch and David Craig

In 1989, Billy Joe Veitch, a White man, was brutally murdered. His wife, Neva, told police that she and her husband had been kidnapped by two Black men, who killed her husband and tried to rape her. It was believed that Neva and her husband were targeted by Blacks because they were both KKK members. Neva Veitch told her story at numerous Klan rallies. Two years later, David Craig, Veitch's lover (also a Klansman), confessed to police that he and Neva had killed her husband. The lovers had hoped to cash in on Billy Joe Veitch's insurance. Both were tried for murder. Craig, who was found guilty, committed suicide in prison.

### Candice Wagner

In 1995, Candice Wagner, a twenty-four-year-old White woman, reported that she had been kidnapped at gunpoint from a shopping mall parking lot. Her attacker, described as a "short, slender Black man with a bad complexion," forced her to drive to an isolated area, where he raped her. Wagner told police that she escaped by kicking her attacker in the groin and driving to a friend's home, from which she called the police. After police told her that parts of her story were inconsistent, she admitted that her story was false.

### Lisa Wight

In 1996, Lisa Wight told police that a Black man had attempted to rape her. Wight, a White woman employed as a courthouse deputy, claimed that she had been assaulted in a hallway of the federal courthouse where she worked. After intense questioning by the FBI, Wight admitted that she made up the story. Wight was forced to resign her post.

### Jennifer Wilbanks

Jennifer Wilbanks, also known as the "Runaway Bride," was engaged to be married to John Mason in Duluth, Georgia. Days before their 2005 wedding, Wilbanks disappeared. Her disappearance was a big news story. Mason and Wilbanks were expecting six hundred guests at their nuptials. Three days later, Wilbanks called her fiancé from Albuquerque, New Mexico, claiming that she had been kidnapped and sexually assaulted by a couple, a Hispanic man and a White woman. Wilbanks repeated the same claims to law enforcement officials. A short time later Wilbanks admitted that she had made up the tale because she was under great stress—her pending nuptials. One week prior to the ceremony, Wilbanks purchased a bus ticket to travel west to Las Vegas and then Albuquerque. Wilbanks pled no contest to giving false information to the police. She was sentenced to two years' probation, 120 hours of community service, and $2,250 for restitution.

### Dauntarius Williams

In 2017, a Black student at Kansas State University, told authorities that racial slurs had been painted on his car. The student, Dauntarius Williams, later admitted that he had painted the racist graffiti on his car.

Williams said it was a Halloween prank that got out of control. He apologized and expressed regret for his actions, and did not face criminal charges.

## Joshua Witt

In 2017, a White man named Joshua Witt reported that he had been stabbed in the parking lot of a fast-food restaurant. Witt, a navy veteran, said that he was getting out of his car when a Black man approached him and asked him if he was a neo-Nazi. According to Witt, the man then tried to stab him. Witt posted details of the incident on social media. Following a review of camera footage for the gas station, police determined that Witt had made up the story. They also learned that Witt had purchased a small knife prior to the alleged incident. Witt admitted to law enforcement that he had cut himself with the knife. He was charged with false reporting of a crime.

## Michele Yentes

In 1990, Michele Yentes claimed that she had been raped on the campus of Ohio State University. Yentes, who is White, told police that her assailant was Black. Police spent hours investigating her claim. Yentes later admitted that she had fabricated the rape. Yentes was charged with filing a false police report and fined $15,000.

## Solomon Youshei

In 1995, Solomon Youshei, a jewelry store owner, told police that he was robbed of $500,000 in jewelry and $2,700 in cash. Youshei said that the robbers were two well-dressed Black men wearing white gloves. Police determined that Youshei and his brother made up the story as part of an insurance scheme.

## Nikki Yovino

In 2017, a Long Island, New York, woman named Nikki Yovino told authorities that while she was at a university football party, she was accosted and sexually assaulted by two members of the team. The young men said that they had consensual sex with Yovino. Three months later, Yovino admitted to making up the rape claims so that a potential suitor would not know she voluntarily had sex with the two men. She was sentenced to one year in prison for filing a false report.

*UNNAMED RACIAL HOAXES, ALPHABETICAL BY STATE OR OTHER AFFILIATION*

*Unnamed, Colorado*
In 2017, a Black student at the Air Force Academy said he had been the target of racist messages. The threatening messages, which were sent to several Black students—included one that said, "Go home, nigger,"—were written on the message boards in dorms at the Air Force Academy prep school. It was widely believed at the time that this was a racial attack, and the academy's superintendent stated that this type of language was horrible and not acceptable at the school. It was later determined that one of the Black men was in fact the perpetrator.

*Unnamed, Florida-1*
In 1994, a White high school student claimed that a White man with long hair wearing a Metallica T-shirt kidnapped her at gunpoint outside of a library at the University of South Florida. According to the woman, the man took her to a remote area and sexually assaulted her. Two days later, the young woman recanted her story. At the time of the alleged offense, the girl was at the home of her boyfriend, whom her parents had forbidden her to see.

*Unnamed, Florida-2*
In 1996, a White Florida woman claimed that she was the victim of a sexual assault. She told police that two Black men followed her into her home and slashed her with a steak knife. It was later determined that the story was a hoax.

*Unnamed, Kentucky*
A Louisville girl told police that she had been kidnapped. The fifteen-year-old girl said that a Black man wearing dark clothing and a hooded sweatshirt had tried to force her from her bus stop early one morning. She said that the man grabbed and pulled her and that she was only able to free herself by kicking him in the groin. School officials issued warnings throughout the county. Police gave chase to a Black man who was

seen in the area. Later the same day, police determined that the girl's story was a hoax.

### Unnamed, Louisiana

In 1994, a White woman in Baton Rouge told police that she had been sexually assaulted by a Black man who had a tattoo of a serpent on his arm. Police released a composite sketch of the "serpent man." As many as twenty-eight other women reported that they had seen or had been attacked by the pictured assailant. When the woman admitted to making up the story, police had already fingered a suspect whom they planned to arrest.

### Unnamed, Maine

In 1994, a seven-year-old White girl told police that she had been assaulted by a Black man while she walked across a parking lot with two friends. Her friends corroborated her story. After initiating a statewide search for the assailant, the police discovered that the girls had made up the story of the attack.

### Unnamed, Maryland

In 2017, a threatening message was sent to students at a high school. The messages, supposedly sent from the KKK, said, "We're planning an attack tomorrow." After investigating the threat, the school was able to identify the owner of the sender's account, a fourteen-year-old Black student. She received a juvenile citation for causing the disruption of school activities.

### Unnamed, Massachusetts

In 2016, a Black man in Malden, Massachusetts, filed a police report stating that he had been the victim of racial threats. He said that, after exiting a city bus, he was approached and harassed by two White men. He said the men threatened to lynch him and proclaimed that this is "Trump country now." After prioritizing the case and re-interviewing the alleged victim, the police said the story had been completely fabricated. The man later said that he wanted to "raise awareness about things that are going on around the country."

*Unnamed, Michigan*

In 2016, in Ann Arbor, a Muslim student at the University of Michigan told police that she had been approached by a stranger who threatened to burn her if she did not remove her hijab. After an investigation, the police discounted the story as a hoax.

*Unnamed, Minnesota-1*

In 2017, several racist notes were left on the windshields of Black students at St. Olaf's College. The notes prompted school officials to cancel classes, and students and faculty staged sit-ins in support of Black students. It was later determined that the note had been fabricated to highlight concerns about the racial climate on campus.

*Unnamed, Minnesota-2*

In 2017, a string of anti-Semitic graffiti was found in a high school bathroom in Minnesota. The graffiti included messages such as "Hail the Ku Klux Klan" and a swastika symbol. The incident was reported to have been staged by a non-White member of the school's community.

*Unnamed, Missouri*

In 2017, at a high school in Missouri, graffiti with racially charged phrases like "White lives matter" and the "nigger," were written on a mirror in the girls' bathroom. The graffiti prompted the community at large to organize against racism. A non-White student admitted to posting the graffiti.

*Unnamed, New Jersey*

In 1994, a young White woman reported that she and her seventy-one-year-old mother-in-law had been attacked by a Black male intruder. The police investigation revealed that the woman had been in a fight with another woman and had come up with the story as a cover-up.

*Unnamed, New York*

In 2013, Trayon Christian went shopping at Barney's in New York City and purchased a $349 belt. An employee called the authorities because he did not believe the Black teen could afford such an expensive belt. He assumed the youth had stolen someone else's debit card. When the youth left the store, he was detained by two police officers who took him to the station and questioned him for two hours. Following this, the teen was allowed to leave with his belt, his debit card, and an apology from the police. Barneys later apologized.

*Unnamed, Pennsylvania*
In 2017, several racially threatening messages were posted at West Chester East High School in Philadelphia. The threats appeared on September 11 and were directly targeted at Black, Hispanic, and White students. The messages said that everyone who showed up to school would die. Students were threatened individually by name, and also by racial group, leading to the belief that the attacks were racially motivated. The threats turned out to originate from a Instagram page created by a Black student at the school. The student was charged with terroristic threats, harassment, and cyber harassment.

*Unnamed, Virginia-1*
In 1995, a White man claimed that two Black men had cut him with his own knife and then stolen his van at a traffic light in Fairfax County. The man later admitted that he had parked the van and cut himself with his knife.

*Unnamed, Virginia-*
In 2018, a thirteen-year-old girl reported that a strange Black man approached her, cursed at her, grabbed her arm, showed her a knife, and called her a terrorist. Then the man removed her headscarf and covered her mouth so that she would not scream. Because of the nature of the crime, this was being looked at as a hate crime. Upon further investigation, it was discovered that no such interaction occurred, and the girl had made it up. The girl was charged with knowingly filing a false police report.

*Unnamed, Wisconsin*

In 1996, a White woman in Madison told police that a Black man had dragged her off the sidewalk and raped her. She later admitted that the story was a fabrication. She was not charged with filing a false report.

*Unnamed (State Unknown)*

In 2018, after the release of the movie *Black Panther*, some internet sites falsely reported that Blacks were attacking Whites at showings of the movie. Fake stories of assaults were posted on numerous websites.

# NOTES

## INTRODUCTION

1   Derrick Bryson Taylor, "For Black Men, Fear That Masks Will Invite Racial Profiling," *New York Times*, April 14, 2020, www.nytimes.com; see also Leah Christiani, Christopher Clark, Steven Greene, Marc J. Hetherington, and Emily Wager, "Masks and Racial Stereotypes in a Pandemic: The Case for Surgical Masks," June 29, 2020, https://ssrn.com or http://dx.doi.org (study finds that young Black men who wear a bandana or homemade cloth mask are perceived as more threatening by non-Blacks than when they wear a surgical mask or no mask at all).

2   Nelson Mandela, *A Prisoner in the Garden* (New York: Viking, 2005), 9.

## 1. DEFINITIONS, STATISTICS, AND ISSUES

1   F. James Davis, *Who Is Black? One Nation's Definition* (University Park: Penn State University Press, 1991), 121.

2   Various reports trace the history of race and the US Census. See, e.g., Pew Research Center, "What Census Calls Us: A Historical Timeline, 1790–2000," 2020, www.pewsocialtrends.org.

3   Ibid. Chart includes report for first Census based on data from sixteen states: Vermont, New Hampshire, Maine, Massachusetts, Rhode Island, Connecticut, New York, New Jersey, Pennsylvania, Delaware, Maryland, Virginia, Kentucky, North Carolina, South Carolina, and Georgia (at the time the Census data was published, it did not include statistics from the Northwestern Territory).

4   US Department of the Interior, "Ninth Census, United States, 1870: Instructions to Assistant Marshals," 1870, 10.

5   Questions about ethnicity did not appear until the 1970 Census.

6   US Department of Commerce, "Fourteenth Census of the United States: Instructions to Enumerators," 1920, 27, /www.census.gov .

7   US Department of Commerce, "Sixteenth Census of the United States: Abridged Instructions to Enumerators," 1940, 7. www.census.gov .

8   US Department of Commerce, "Sixteenth Census of the United States: Abridged Instructions to Enumerators," 1940, www.census.gov .

9   The White House, Office of Management and Budget, "Revisions to the Standards for the Classification of Federal Data on Race and Ethnicity," 1997, https://obamawhitehouse.archives.gov.

10 Michael Omi, "Racial Identity and the State: The Dilemmas of Classification," *Law and Inequality* 15, no. 1 (1997): 7–23, quote at 15.

11 Jennifer Kim, Nicholas Jones, and Sarah Konya, "2020 Census Content Updates" US Census Bureau, 2016, www.census.gov.

12 Gregory Korte, "White House Wants to Add New Racial Category for Middle Eastern People," *USA Today*, September 30, 2016, www.usatoday.com.

13 261 US 204 (1923).

14 Ibid., at 214–215.

15 Kent Demaret, "Raised White, A Louisiana Belle Challenges Race Records That Call Her Colored," *People Magazine*, December 6, 1982, http://people.com.

16 Omi, "Racial Identity and the State," 7.

17 Gregory Jaynes, "Suit on Race Recalls Lines Drawn under Slavery," *New York Times*, September 30, 1982, www.nytimes.com.

18 *Doe v. Department of Health and Human Resources*, 479 US (1986) (see p. 1002). The Louisiana law at issue in the *Phipps* case was the last state statute to include a numerical equation for race. It was repealed in 1983. See Frances Frank Marcus, "Louisiana Repeals Black Blood Law," *New York Times*, July 6, 1983.

19 Nicholas K. Geranios, "Rachel Dolezal Struggles after Racial Identification Scandal," Associated Press, March 24, 2017.

20 Rachel Dolezal, *In Full Color: Finding My Place in a Black and White World* (Dallas: BenBella Books, 2017).

21 Michael Yellow Bird, "What We Want to Be Called: Indigenous Peoples' Perspectives on Racial and Ethnic Identity Labels," *American Indian Quarterly* 23, no. 2 (Spring 1999): 1–21, www.jstor.org.

22 Paul Taylor, Mark Hugo Lopez, Jessica Martinez, and Gabriel Velasco, "Identity, Pan-Ethnicity and Race," Pew Research Center, 2012, www.pewhispanic.org.

23 D'Vera Cohn, "American Indian and White, but Not 'Multiracial,'" Pew Research Center, June 11, 2015, www.pewresearch.org.

24 Pew Research Center, "The Rise of Asian Americans," 2013, www.pewsocialtrends.org.

25 Jeffrey M. Jones, "US Blacks, Hispanics Have No Preferences on Group Labels," Gallup Politics, July 26, 2013, www.gallup.com.

26 Stephen Jay Gould, *The Mismeasure of Man* (New York: W. W. Norton, 1981). Gould asks, "Did the introduction of inductive science add legitimate data to change or strengthen a nascent argument for racial ranking? Or did a priori commitment to ranking fashion the 'scientific' questions asked and even the data gathered to support a foreordained conclusion?" (63).

27 See, e.g., William Tucker, *The Funding of Scientific Racism: Wickliffe Draper and the Pioneer Fund* (Urbana: University of Illinois Press, 2007).

28 Gould, *Mismeasure of Man*, 39n27.

29 Ibid., 40.

30 Ibid., 54–56.

31 W. E. B. Du Bois, *The Philadelphia Negro* (Philadelphia: University of Pennsylvania Press, 1899).

32 Khalil Muhammad. *The Condemnation of Blackness: Race, Crime, and the Making of Modern Urban America* (Cambridge, MA: Harvard University Press, 2010).

33 E.g., Bernard W. Bell, Emily R. Grosholz, and James B. Stewart, eds., *W. E. B. Du Bois on Race and Culture: Philosophy, Politics, and Poetics* (New York: Routledge, 1986); Pierre Saint-Arnaud, *African American Pioneers of Sociology: A Critical History*, trans. Peter Feldstein (Toronto: University of Toronto Press, 1996).

34 Shaun L. Gabbidon, *W. E. B. Du Bois on Crime and Justice: Laying the Foundations of Sociological Criminology* (New York: Routledge, 2007).

35 Aldon Morris, *The Scholar Denied: W. E. B. Du Bois and the Birth of Modern Sociology* (Oakland: University of California Press, 2015), 129. Morris states that Du Bois "rejected a sociology that did not incorporate human agency at the core of its conceptualizations because he saw human behavior as characterized by an element of chance" (76).

36 Ibid., 3.

37 Elijah Anderson, introduction to *The Philadelphia Negro*, centennial ed. (Philadelphia: University of Pennsylvania Press, 1996), ix–xxxvi.

38 Morris, *Scholar Denied*, 2–3.

39 Ibid., 4–5, 136–144. See also Gabbidon, *W. E. B. Du Bois on Crime and Justice*, 78–79.

40 "Black criminology" is an approach that a growing number of criminologists have promoted. It centers on the belief that understanding Black offending and victimization requires a detailed consideration of the unique racial history of Blacks in the United States. Black criminology utilizes an intersectional framework that views race as a predominant factor in how Blacks fare across the social spectrum—e.g., economics, education, employment, and housing. In turn, these factors impact the degree to which Blacks are involved in the criminal-legal system, and the outcomes of this interaction. Black criminology makes room for both micro-level and macro-level explanations of criminal offending and encompasses new and existing perspectives of how race operates to increase or decrease the likelihood of Black offending and victimization. See Katheryn Russell-Brown (2018), "Black Criminology in the 21st Century," in James D. Unnever, Shaun L. Gabbidon, and Cecilia Chouhy, eds., *Building a Black Criminology: Race, Theory and Crime* (New York: Routledge, 2018), 101–123.

41 580 US ___ (2017). In *Pena Rodriguez v. Colorado*, the court considered jury bias in a case in which the defendant was convicted of unlawful sexual contact and harassment. After the trial, some of the jurors in his case reported that, during deliberations, another juror made anti-Hispanic comments. On appeal, the US Supreme Court held that, with the goal of protecting the right to a fair trial, courts can consider evidence of overt racial bias if it raises doubt about the fairness of jury deliberations.

42 The Implicit Association Test (IAT) is a popular test for measuring implicit racial bias (and other forms of bias). See implicit.harvard.edu.

43 Jennifer Eberhardt, Phillip Attiba Goff, Valerie Purdue, and Paul Davies, "Seeing Black: Race, Crime and Visual Processing," *Journal of Personality and Social Psychology* 87, no. 6 (2004): 876–893.

44 Ibid.

45 Ibid.

46 US Department of Justice, "The Nation's Two Crime Measures," 2018, https://ucr.fbi.gov.

47 Ibid.

48 "Fatal Force," *Washington Post*, August 10, 2020, www.washingtonpost.com.

49 H.R. 35 Emmett Till Antilynching Act, 2019–2020, www.govtrack.us.

50 US Department of Commerce, "Historical Statistics of the United States: Colonial Times to 1970," 1975, p. 422.

51 Ibid.

52 The murder of James Byrd Jr. in 1998 is perhaps the most well known of the post–civil rights era lynchings. Byrd was kidnapped from a bar in Jasper Texas, by three White men. The men beat Byrd and tied his ankles to the back of a pickup truck and dragged his body for over three miles. Byrd died of his severe injuries. Two of the men, John King and Lawrence Brewer, were members of a White supremacist group. They were sentenced to death row, and Shawn Berry was sentenced to life without parole.

53 In 2016, Congressman Steve King tweeted that "culture and demographics are our destiny. We can't restore our civilization with somebody else's babies" (March 12, 2017). His comments took place during international debates and discussions about Geert Wilders, a far-right candidate for Dutch prime minister whom King endorsed. See Greg Toppo, "Rep. Steve King Blasted for 'Our Civilization' Tweet," *USA Today*, March 12, 2017, www.usatoday.com.

## 2. MEDIA MESSAGES

1 Marshall McLuhan, *Understanding Media: The Extensions of Man* (New York: Signet Books, 1964), 23.

2 See, Violet J. Harris, "In Praise of a Scholarly Force: Rudine Sims Bishop," National Council of Teachers of English, 2007, www.ncte.org.

3 Riva Tukachinksy, Dana Mastro, and Moran Yarchi, "Documenting Portrayals of Race/Ethnicity on Primetime Television over a 20-Year Span and Their Association with National-Level Racial/Ethnic Attitudes," *Journal of Social Issues* 71, no. 1 (2015): 17–38.

4 See, generally, Philip J. Deloria, *Indians in Unexpected Places* (Lawrence: University of Kansas Press, 2004).

5 First Nations Development Institute and Echo Hawk Consulting, *Changing the Narrative about Native Americans: A Guide for Allies* (2018).

6 Peter A. Leavitt, Rebecca Covarrubias, Yvonne A. Perez, and Stephanie A. Fry-berg, "'Frozen in Time': The Impact of Native American Media Representations on Identity and Self-Understanding," *Journal of Social Issues* 71, no. 1 (2015): 39, 41.

7 Christine Hauser, "Land O'Lakes Replaces Logo of Native American Woman," *New York Times*, April 18, 2020, B6.

8 See, e.g., Andrew Newman, "Nike Adds Indian Artifacts to Its Swoosh," *New York Times*, October 3, 2007.

9 See, generally, Lakshmi Gandhi, "Are You Ready for Some Controversy? The History of 'Redskin,'" *Code Switch* (blog), NPR, September 9, 2013, www.npr.org.

10 Samantha Artiga and Kendal Orgera, "COVID-19 Presents Significant Risks for American Indian and Alaska Native People," Kaiser Family Foundation, May 4, 2020, www.kff.org.

11 Larry Elder, "Why Doesn't the News Media Call Naomi Osaka Black?," *Jackson Sun*, January 31, 2019, www.jacksonsun.com.

12 Anemona Hartocollis, "Harvard Does Not Discriminate Against Asian-Americans in Admissions, Judge Rules," *New York Times*, October 1, 2019, www.nytimes.com.

13 David Lat, "Asian Americans v. Harvard: A Closer Look," *Above the Law*, 2019, https://abovethelaw.com.

14 Dave McNary, "Latinos Still Have Highest Moviegoing Rate in the US, but Asians Are Close Behind," *Variety*, April 4, 2018, https://variety.com.

15 See, generally, *Black History: Lost, Stolen, or Strayed* (TV movie; CBS News, 1968); Berkeley Art Center Association, *Ethnic Notions: Black Images in the White Imagination* (text and documentary, 1982).

16 The author's father, Charlie L. Russell Jr., who wrote the play, also wrote the screenplay for *Five on the Black Hand Side* (dir. Williams, 1973).

17 *Do the Right Thing* (dir. Lee, 1989).

18 Tatum Hunter, "These Companies Took Concrete Action in Support of #Black-LivesMatter: Lasting Change Will Require More Than Statements of Support," August 7, 2020, https://builtin.com.

19 Colleen Shalby, "What's the Difference between 'Looking' and 'Finding'? 12 Years after Katrina, Harvey Sparks a New Debate," *Los Angeles Times*, August 29, 2017, www.latimes.com.

### 3. HISTORY'S STRANGE FRUIT

1 Racist laws did not operate in a vacuum. At the same time that slavery and the slave codes existed (and subsequent iterations), scientists in the US and abroad, devised theories and designed studies to prove White superiority. See, e.g., Stephan J. Gould (1996). *The Mismeasure of Man*. W.W. Norton.

2 J. Clay Smith, "Justice and Jurisprudence and the Black Lawyer," *Notre Dame Law Review* 69 (1994): 1077–113.

3 F. James Davis, *Who Is Black?* (University Park: Pennsylvania State University Press, 1991).

4  See, e.g., Smith, "Justice and Jurisprudence and the Black Lawyer," 1105.

5  Ibid., 1105.

6  The South Carolina Supreme Court stated, "The offense of assault and battery cannot at common law be committed on the person of a slave. . . . The peace of the state is not thereby broken, for a slave is not generally regarded as fully capable of being within the peace of the state" 20 S.C.L. 249 (1834).

7  Higginbotham and Jacobs, "The Law Only as an Enemy," 1058.

8  Ibid., 1056.

9  Some states did make the rape of a slave girl under the age of twelve a criminal offense. See, e.g., Thomas Morris, *Southern Slavery and the Law, 1619–1860* (Chapel Hill: University of North Carolina Press, 1996), 306.

10  See, e.g., Kenneth Stampp, *The Peculiar Institution* (New York: Vintage Books, 1956), 214–215; Martin Dulaney, *Black Police in America* (Bloomington: Indiana University Press, 1996), 2.

11  Paul Finkelman, "The Strange Career of Race Discrimination in Antebellum Ohio," *Case Western Law Review* 55 (2004): 373–408.

12  BlackPast, "Mississippi Black Codes (1866)," December 15, 2010, www.blackpast. org.

13  Douglas Colbert, "Challenging the Challenge: Thirteenth Amendment as a Prohibition against Racial Use of Peremptory Challenges," *Cornell Law Review* 76 (1990): 1–128, quote at 41.

14  Gunnar Myrdal, *An American Dilemma* (New York: Pantheon Books, 1944).

15  W. E. B. Du Bois, *Dusk of Dawn* (New York: Harcourt, 1940), 241.

16  Orlando Patterson, *Rituals of Blood* (New York: Civitas, 1999) .

17  Ida B. Wells-Barnett, *On Lynching* (New York: Humanity Books, 2002).

18  Equal Justice Initiative, *Lynching in America: Confronting the Legacy of Racial Terror* (2017), https://eji.org/reports/lynching-in-america/.

19  Ida B. Wells-Barnett, *A Red Record: Tabulated Statistics and Alleged Causes of Lynchings in the United States, 1892-1893-1894* (c. 1895).

20  Arthur Raper, *The Tragedy of Lynching* (Chapel Hill: University of North Carolina Press, 1933), 469–471. Raper notes that there were twenty-one lynchings in 1930, but the text only lists twenty cases. The nineteen with Black victims are included in the table.

21  James Allen, John Lewis, Leon Litwack, and Hilton Als. *Without Sanctuary: Lynching Photography in America* (Santa Fe, NM: Twin Palms, 2000), 25–26.

22  See, e.g., Sherrilyn Ifill, *On the Courthouse Law* (Boston: Beacon, 2007), 798. ("Between 1900 and 1935, courthouse lawns on the eastern shore of were routinely the sites of lynchings or near lynchings, involving the participation of hundreds and sometimes thousands of White onlookers.")

23  S. Res. 39, 109th Cong., 1st sess. (2005).

24 Paula Johnson, "The Social Construction of Identity in Criminal Cases," *Michigan Journal of Race and Law* 1 (1996): 347–489, quote at 366

25  See, generally, Stetson Kennedy, *Jim Crow Guide: The Way It Was* (Boca Raton: Florida Atlantic University Press, 1959).

26  *Loving v. Virginia*, 388 US 1, 5 (1967).

27  Montgomery, Alabama, Ordinance 15–57 (1957).

28  James Loewen, *Sundown Towns: A Hidden Dimension of American Racism* (New York: New Press, 2005).

## 4. RACIAL DISCRIMINATION, RACIAL PROFILING, AND RACIAL MONITORING

1  Besik Kutateladze, Nancy Andiloro, Brian Johnson, and Cassia Spohn, "Cumulative Disadvantage: Examining Racial and Ethnic Disparity in Prosecution and Sentencing," *Criminology* 52 (2014): 514–51.

2  In a meta-analysis of eighty-five quantitative studies of race and sentencing, criminologists Ojmarrh Mitchell and Doris MacKenzie find clear evidence that Blacks and Latinos experience racial discrimination at the sentencing phase, particularly for drug offenses, when compared with Whites. Thus, even after accounting for legal factors (e.g., prior history), on average Blacks and Latinos were sentenced more harshly than Whites.

3  Refer to Appendix A for race-related statistics on population, arrest, and incarceration.

4  Marvin Wolfgang and Bernard Cohen, *Crime and Race: Conceptions and Misconceptions* (New York: Institute of Human Relations Press, 1970), 30–31.

5  Alfred Blumstein, "Racial Disproportionality of US Prison Populations Revisited," *University of Colorado Law Review* 64 (1993): 743–60.

6  See, e.g., Michael Tonry, *Punishing Race: An American Dilemma Continues* (New York: Oxford University Press, 2011); Eric Baumer, "Reassessing and Redirecting on Race and Sentencing," draft manuscript prepared for Symposium on the Past and Future of Empirical Sentencing for Research, School of Criminal Justice, State University of New York at Albany, 2010; see, generally, Ashley Nellis, "The Color of Justice: Racial and Ethnic Disparity in State Prisons," *Sentencing Project*, June 14, 2016, www.sentencingproject.org.

7  US Bureau of Justice Statistics, "Drug Offenders in Federal Prison: Estimates of Characteristics Based on Linked Data," NCJ 248648, Table 3, 2015.

8  517 U.S. 456 (1996).

9  Daniel Georges-Abeyie, "The Myth of a Racist Criminal Justice System?" in Brian MacLean and Dragan Milovanovic, eds., *Racism, Empiricism, and Criminal Justice* (Vancouver: Collective Press, 1990), 11–14.

10  See, e.g., Sheri Johnson, "Racial Derogation in Prosecutors' Closing Arguments," in Dragan Milovanovic and Katheryn Russell, eds., *Petit Apartheid in the Criminal Justice System* (Durham, NC: Carolina Academic Press, 2001), 79–102. See also Nicole Gonzalez Van Cleve, *Crook County: Racism and Injustice in America's Largest Criminal Court* (Oakland, CA: Stanford University Press, 2016).

11  Ibid., Van Cleve, *Crook County*.

12  Erving Goffman, *Presentation of Self in Everyday Life* (Woodstock, NY: Overlook Press, 1973), 112.

13  Katheryn Russell-Brown, *Underground Codes: Race, Crime, and Related Fires* (New York: New York University Press, 2004), 14–15 (includes a "Petit Apartheid Typology" continuum).

14  "DNA Exonerations in the United States," Innocence Project, www.innocenceproject.org (accessed May 14, 2021).

15  For a more detailed discussion of petit apartheid, see Russell-Brown, *Underground Codes*, 5–19.

16  Paul Butler, "Sex and Torture," in *Chokehold* (New York: New Press, 2017), 81ff.

17  See, e.g., Rod Brunson, "'Police Don't Like Black People': African-American Young Men's Accumulated Police Experiences," *Journal of Criminology and Public Policy* 6 (2007): 71–101.

18  Jerome McCristal Culp Jr., "Notes from California: Rodney King and the Race Question," *Denver University Law Review* 70 (1993): 199–212, quote at 200.

19  Gunnar Myrdal, *An American Dilemma* (New York: Pantheon Books, 1944), 542.

20  517 U.S. 806 (1996).

21  Opinion and Order, 08 Civ. 1034 (SAS) (2013), https://ccrjustice.org.

22  Ibid., 2.

23  Michael Bloomberg, "'Stop and Frisk' Keeps New York Safe," *Washington Post*, August 18, 2013.

24  NYCLU, "2019 Annual Report," www.nyclu.org.

25  Chan Tov McNamarah, "White Caller Crime: Racialized Police Communication and Existing While Black," *Michigan Journal of Race and Law* 24 (2019): 335–415.

26  See, e.g., Christina Zhao, "'BBQ Becky,' White Woman Who Called Cops on Black BBQ, 911 Audio Release: 'I'm Really Scared! Come Quick!'" *Newsweek*, September 4, 2018, www.newsweek.com.

27  See, e.g., Melissa Gomez, "White Woman Who Blocked Black Neighbor from Building is Fired," *New York Times*, October 15, 2018, www.nytimes.com.

28  See, e.g., Niraj Chokshi, "White Woman Nicknamed 'Permit Patty' Regrets Confrontation over Black Girl Selling Water," *New York Times*, June 25, 2018, www.nytimes.com.

29  See McNamarah, "White Caller Crime." Author shares the story of Gil Perkins, who had an encounter with a racial hall monitor in front of his home. The woman told Perkins to leave and that he was talking too loud. She concluded by saying, "I'm calling the cops. *And you know what that means for you*" (McNamarah, "White Caller Crime," 369 [emphasis in original]).

30  An Ordinance to Amend Title IX of the Codes of the City of Grand Rapids by Adopting Chapter 175, Articles 1–5, Sections 9.935–9.951 (Ordinance No. 2019).

31  Sophie Quinton, "State Lawmakers Crack Down on Racially Motivated 911 Calls," Pew Charitable Trusts, Stateline blog, July 14, 2020, www.pewtrusts.org.

32 Yazmine C'Bona Levonna Nichols, "Race Has Everything to Do with It: A Remedy for Frivolous Race-Based Police Calls," *Fordham Urban Law Journal* 47 (2019): 153–94.

33 Elizabeth Davis and Anthony Whyde, "Contacts between Police and the Public, 2015," Bureau of Justice Statistics, 2018, NCJ 251145, Tables 1, 3, and 12.

34 Davis and Whyde, "Contacts between Police and the Public, 2015," Tables 11 and 15.

35 See, e.g., Adeiel Kaplan and Vanessa Swales, "Border Patrol Searches Have Increased on Greyhound, Other Buses Far from Border," NBC News, June 5, 2019, www.nbcnews.com.

36 Culp, "Notes from California," 206.

## 5. RACIAL HOAXES

1 Richard Grant, "Mother of All Crimes," *The Independent*, February 25, 1995, 16.

2 Sarah Maslin Nir, "White Woman Is Fired after Calling Police on Black Man in Central Park," *New York Times*, May 26, 2020, www.nytimes.com.

3 A White-on-Black hoax indicates a White person who perpetrated a hoax against someone Black. A Black-on-White hoax indicates a Black person who perpetrated a hoax against someone White.

4 While the women stood outside the house, one of the partygoers, who was upset that they did not finish performing, told them to thank their grandfathers for his cotton shirt.

5 Roni Rabin, "Hoax Fed on Prejudice: Frightened by Notes, Neighbors Suspected Black Family," *Newsday*, October 19, 1990.

6 Ibid.

7 Douglas H. Palmer, mayor of Trenton, New Jersey, press release, January 22, 1995.

8 505 U.S. 377 (1992)

9 508 U.S. 476 (1993).

10 Ibid., 488.

11 Ibid.

12 A slight twist on Justice Oliver Wendell Holmes's language in *Schenck v. United States*, 249 U.S. 47, 51 (1919).

13 "An Act Concerning False Reports to Law Enforcement Authorities," State of New Jersey, Senate (212th Legislature, 1995), No. 1505 (amends N.J.S. 2C: 28–4).

14 Mari Matsuda, "Public Response to Racist Speech," in Mari Matsuda, Charles Lawrence III, Richard Delgado, and Kimberle Crenshaw, eds., *Words That Wound* (Boulder, CO: Westview, 1993), 36.

15 Marc Fleischauer, "Review of Florida Legislation, Teeth for a Paper Tiger: A Proposal to Add Enforceability to Florida's Hate Crimes Act," *Florida State University Law Review* 17 (1990): 697–711, quote at 706n34.

16 Frederick Lawrence, "Resolving the Hate Crimes / Hate Speech Paradox: Punishing Bias Crimes and Protecting Racist Speech," *Notre Dame Law Review* 68 (1993): 673–721, quote at 698.

17 Ludwig Wittgenstein, *Philosophical Investigations*, 3rd ed., trans. G. E. M. Anscombe (New York: Macmillan, 1968), 146E.

18 Charles Lawrence, "The Id, the Ego, and Equal Protection: Reckoning with Unconscious Racism," *Stanford Law Review* 39 (1987): 317–88, quote at 322 (citations omitted).

19 William Raspberry, "Automatically Suspect," *Washington Post*, November 5, 1994, A19.

## 6. WHITE CRIME

1 Richard Delgado, "Rodrigo's Eighth Chronicle," *Virginia Law Review* 80 (1994): 503-548.

2 Uniform Crime Reports, 2019, Total Arrests, Distribution by Race, https://ucr.fbi.gov/crime-in-the-u.s/2019/crime-in-the-u.s.-2019/tables/table-43.

3 Gary Kamiya, "Toni Morrison Tells Publishers They Reinforce 'Racial Half-Truths,'" *San Francisco Examiner*, April 28, 1994.

4 Khalil Muhammad, *The Condemnation of Blackness: Race, Crime, and the Making of Modern Urban America* (Cambridge, MA: Harvard University Press, 2010), 76.

5 Ibid., 271.

6 Edward Sutherland, *White Collar Crime* (New York: Dryden, 1949), 6.

7 Francis Cullen and Michael Benson, "White-Collar Crime: Holding a Mirror to the Core," *Journal of Criminal Justice Education* 4 (1993): 325–47, quote at 334.

8 Ibid., "White-Collar Crime," 332.

9 Uniform Crime Reports, 2018, Nonmetropolitan County Arrests, Distribution by Race, 2019, Table 61, /ucr.fbi.gov; Uniform Crime Reports, 2019, Suburban County Arrests, Distribution by Race, Table 67,ucr.fbi.gov.

10 Andrew Hacker, "Caste, Crime, and Precocity," in Steve Fraser, ed., *The Bell Curve Wars* (New York: Basic Books, 1995), 97.

11 Nazgol Ghandnoosh and Casey Anderson, "Opioids: Treating an Illness, Ending a War," Sentencing Project, December 13, 2017, www.sentencingproject.org.

12 Rose A. Rudd, Puja Seth, Felicita David, and Lawrence Scholl, "Increases in Drug and Opioid-Involved Overdose Deaths—United States, 2010–2015," *MMWR Morbidity and Mortality Weekly Report* 65, nos. 50–51 (2016): 1445–1452, at 1445.

13 See, e.g., Statista, "Number of Mass Shootings in the United States between 1982 and April 2021, by Shooter's Race or Ethnicity," April 19, 2021, www.statista.com.

14 Marvin Wolfgang and Bernard Cohen, *Crime and Race: Conceptions and Misconceptions* (New York: Institute of Human Relations Press, 1970).

15 See Katheryn Russell-Brown, *Protecting Our Own: Race, Crime, and African Americans* (Lanham, MD: Rowman and Littlefield, 2006), for a book-length discussion of Black protectionism.

16 See, e.g., Katheryn Russell-Brown, "Critical Black Protectionism, Black Lives Matter, and Social Media: Building a Bridge to Social Justice," *Howard Law Review* 60 (2017): 367-412.

17  National Science Foundation, "Survey of Earned Doctorates, 2016," 2016, Table 24, www.nsf.gov. Criminology doctorates do not have their own category; they're included within "Other Social Sciences."

18  American Bar Association, "ABA National Lawyer Population Survey 10-Year Trend in Lawyer Demographics," 2020, www.americanbar.org..

19  Janine Jackson, "The Kerner Report Called for More Black Journalists: Major Newsrooms Remain a 'White Man's World,'" *Color Lines*, February 28, 2018, www.colorlines.com.

20  James Q. Wilson, "Crime, Race, and Values," *Society* 30 (November/December 1992): 90–93.

21  Ibid.

22  Ibid.

23  See, e.g., Wesley Skogan, "Crime and the Racial Fears of White Americans," *Annals of the American Academy of Political and Social Sciences*539, no. 1 (May 1995): 59–71; and Sentencing Project, "Race and Punishment: Racial Perceptions of Crime and Support for Punitive Policies," 2015, https://sentencingproject.org.

24  Jesse Jackson's complete statement was, "There is nothing more painful for me at this stage of my life than to walk down the street and hear footsteps and start to think about robbery and then look around and see it's somebody white and feel relieved. How humiliating." Quoted in John DiIulio, "My Black Crime Problem, and Ours," *City Journal* (Spring 1996), www.city-journal.org.

25  Steven D. Levitt and John J. Donohue, "The Impact of Legalized Abortion on Crime," *Quarterly Journal of Economics* 116 (2001): 379-420.

26  Quoted in Brian Faler, "Bennett under Fire for Remark on Crime and Black Abortions," *Washington Post*, September 30, 2005, A5.

27  Andrew Hacker, "Malign Neglect: The Crackdown on African Americans," *The Nation*, July 10, 1995, 49.

28  See, e.g., Derrick Bell, *Race, Racism, and American Law*, 3rd ed. (Boston: Little, Brown, 1992), 29 (quoting speech given by Benjamin Franklin).

29 Associated Press, "Buckley Shocks Abortion Defenders," *Spokesman-Review* (Spokane, WA), June 2, 1996, www.spokesman.com.

30  See Hacker, "Malign Neglect," 45. Hacker recounts a hypothetical exercise he uses with his White students. He gives them the choice between having three hundred dollars in their wallets and having it taken by someone White or having one hundred dollars in their wallets and having it taken by someone Black. The majority of students selected the first choice: "They would gladly play the extra $200 to avoid a black assailant" (46).

31  Derrick Bell, *And We Are Not Saved* (New York: Basic Books, 1987), 245, 246.

## 7. RACE AND CRIME LITERACY

1  See, e.g., Aldon Morris, *The Scholar Denied: W. E. B. Du Bois and the Birth of Modern Sociology* (Oakland: University of California Press, 2015); Elijah Anderson and Douglass Massey, "The Sociology of Race in the United States," in Elijah

Anderson and Douglas Massey, eds., *Problem of the Century: Racial Stratification in the United States* (New York: Russell Sage Foundation, 2001), 3–4.

2  350 F.2d 45 (D.C. Cir. 1965).

3  Judith Shapiro, "From Sociological Illiteracy to Sociological Imagination," *Chronicle of Higher Education*, March 31, 2000, A68.

4  See, generally, Katheryn Russell-Brown, "The Myth of Race and Crime," in Robert Bohm and Jeffrey T. Walker, eds., *Demystifying Crime and Criminal Justice* (Oxford: Oxford University Press, 2005).

5  347 U.S. 483, 493 (1954).

6  Some scholars question the impact of the Court's emphasis on how segregated schools affect Black children. Education scholar Paul Green argues that the Supreme Court's stated reasoning supported a deficit narrative of Black children—that they were psychologically weak:

> While the Brown [decisions] altered the image of African Americans, the Court's decision, far from liberating Blacks from negative images, promoted a new negative stereotype, one acceptable to middle-class Whites, including liberal justices. Though damage imagery imputed black pathology to white oppression rather than biology, the Court provided a medical rationale for the idea of white supremacy. The Warren Court's de-valuing of social science testimony, namely, the argument that damage imagery affected both Blacks and Whites, suggested that only Blacks were harmed by the intangible factors of invidious segregation. Whites, Warren's Court seemed to imply, were socially, emotionally, and psychologically healthy as opposed to the impoverishness and depravity of Blacks.

"The Paradox of the Promise Unfulfilled: *Brown v. Board of Education* and the Continued Pursuit of Excellence in Education." *Journal of Negro Education* 3, no. 3 (2004): 268–84, quote at 273.

7  "Kiri Davis: *A Girl Like Me*," YouTube, 2007, https://www.youtube.com/watch?v=z0BxFRu_SOw.

8  See Katheryn Russell-Brown, "To Combat Racism in Law Enforcement, Start Young," *New York Times*, Room for Debate, September 1, 2014, www.nytimes.com.

## 8. THE SOUL SAVERS

1  Derrick Bell, *Faces at the Bottom of the Well: The Permanence of Racism* (New York: Basic Books, 1992). The year 2020 marked the thirtieth anniversary of Bell's initial iteration of the "Space Traders" tale; see "After We're Gone: Prudent Speculations on America in a Post-Racial Epoch," *St. Louis University Law Journal* 34 (1989–1990): 443–49..

2  See, e.g., James Davis, *Who Is Black? One Nation's Definition* (University Park: Penn State University Press, 1991).

3  Kriston McIntosh, Emily Moss, Ryan Nunn, and Jay Shambaugh, "Examining the Black-White Wealth Gap," Brookings, 2020, www.brookings.edu. Report finds that the typical White family's wealth is ten times greater than the typical Black

family's wealth ($171,000 vs. $17,150). The racial wealth gap has persisted across decades, through recessions and boom times. See also Mehrsa Baradaran, *The Color of Money: Black Banks and the Racial Wealth Gap* (Cambridge, MA: Harvard University Press, 2018).

4 Keith Elder et al., "African Americans' Decisions Not to Evacuate New Orleans before Hurricane Katrina: A Qualitative Study," *American Journal of Public Health* 97, Suppl. 1 (April 2007): S124–S129; Margery Austin Turner and Sheila R. Zedlewski, "After Katrina: Rebuilding Opportunity and Equity into the *New* New Orleans," Urban Institute, 2006, www.urban.org.

5 Gretchen Livingston, "The Rise of Multiracial and Multiethnic Babies in the U.S.," Pew Research, 2017, reports that, in 2015, one in seven children born in the United States were multiracial, a near threefold increase since 1980: www.pewresearch.org.

6 S. Res. 39, 109th Cong., 1st Sess., "Apologizing to the Victims of Lynching and the Descendants of Those Victims for the Failure of the Senate to Enact Anti-Lynching Legislation," 2005, www.govinfo.gov.

7 Erik Ortiz, Kaleigh O'Boyle, and Savannah Smith, "The Next Wave of Statue Removals Is Afoot. See Where They're Being Taken Down across the U.S.," NBC News, June 12, 2020, www.nbcnews.com.

8 See Isabel Wilkerson, *Caste: The Origins of Our Discontents* (New York: Random House, 2020).

9 Monnica T. Williams, "Social Media and Black Bodies as Entertainment," *Psychology Today*, May 31, 2020, www.psychologytoday.com.

10 Katie Benner, "Barr Says Communities That Protest the Police Risk Losing Protection," *New York Times*, December 4, 2019. At an awards ceremony for police, Attorney General William Barr commented that groups who have been critical of the police "have to start showing, more than they do, the respect and support that law enforcement deserves." He stated further, "And if communities don't give that support and respect, they may find themselves without the police protection they need" (see www.nytimes.com).

11 Sarah Picard, Matt Watkins, Michael Rempel, and Ashmini Kerodal, "Beyond the Algorithm Pretrial Reform, Risk Assessment, and Racial Fairness," Center for Court Innovation, 2019, www.courtinnovation.org.

12 Alex Chohlas-Wood, "Understanding Risk Assessment Instruments in Criminal Justice," Brookings, June 19, 2020, www.brookings.edu.

13 For an example of how the Wisconsin Supreme Court decided a constitutional challenge to an algorithmic risk assessment, see *Loomis v. Wisconsin*, 881NW2d 749 (Wisc. 2016) (court held that due process was not violated by the use of an algorithmic risk assessment tool, even though neither the defendant nor the court was informed of the methodology).

14 Ann Carson, "Prisoners in 2018," Bureau of Justice Statistics, 2019, Table 3, www.bjs.gov.

15 See, e.g., Ellis P. Monk, "The Color of Punishment: African Americans, Skin Tone, and the Criminal Justice System," *Ethnic and Racial Studies* 1593 (2019): 42, www.tandfonline.com.

16 Kim Parker, Rich Morin, and Juliana Menasce Horowitz, "Looking to the Future, Public Sees an America in Decline on Many Fronts," Pew Research Center, 2019, www.pewsocialtrends.org (survey shows that nearly one-half of all Whites believe that the United States becoming a majority-minority country will "weaken" American culture).

17 Proposals and debates about reparations for African Americans are not new. See Ta-Nehisi Coates, "The Case for Reparations," *The Atlantic*, June 2014, www. theatlantic.com; Andrea Kristen Mullen and William A. Darity Jr., *From Here to Equality: Reparations for Black Americans in the Twenty-First Century* (Chapel Hill: University of North Carolina Press, 2020); Mary Frances Berry, *My Face Is Black Is True: Callie House and the Struggle for Ex-Slave Reparations* (New York: Vintage, 2006); National Coalition of Blacks for Reparations, "About," www.nco-braonline.org.

18 United Nations, "Universal Declaration of Human Rights," www.un.org.

19 See, e.g., Paul Kivel, "Guidelines for Being Strong White Allies," Racial Equity Tools, 2006, www.racialequitytools.org; Robin DiAngelo, *White Fragility: Why It's So Hard for White People to Talk about Racism* (Boston: Beacon, 2018).

20 The debates by Whites show Derrick Bell's theory of "interest-convergence" in action. In his piece "*Brown v. Board of Education* and the Interest-Convergence Dilemma," *Harvard Law Review* 93 (1980): 518–33, he coined the term to establish the conditions under which racial advancement can take place. Per Bell, racial progress is possible when racial justice, or its appearance, is important to the courts or policy makers: "The interest of Blacks in achieving racial equality will be accommodated only when it converges with the interests of whites" (at 523).

21 See United Nations, "Universal Declaration of Human Rights," Article 13.

## APPENDIX A

1 National Institute of Justice, "Five Things about Violence Against American Indian and Alaska Native Women and Men," US Department of Justice, Office of Justice Programs, 2016, https://nij.ojp.gov.

2 Lifetime likelihood estimates have likely changed since 2001, when the Department of Justice published its most recent estimates.

# SELECTED BIBLIOGRAPHY

Alexander, Michelle. *The New Jim Crow: Mass Incarceration in an Age of Colorblindness* New York: New Press, 2010.

Alfieri, Anthony V. "Lynching Ethics: toward a Theory of Racialized Defenses." *Michigan Law Review* 95 (1997): 1063–104.

———. "Defending Racial Violence." *Columbia Law Review* 95 (1995): 1301–43.

Allen, James, Hilton Als, John Lewis, and Leon Litwack. *Without Sanctuary: Lynching Photography in America.* Santa Fe, NM: Twin Palms, 2000.

Alpert, Geoffrey, Roger G. Dunham, and Michael R. Smith. "Investigating Racial Profiling by the Miami-Dade Police Department: A Multimethod Approach." *Criminology and Public Policy* 6 (2007): 25–56.

Anderson, Carol. *White Rage: The Unspoken Truth of Our Racial Divide.* New York: Bloomsbury, 2017.

Asim, Jabari. *We Can't Breathe: On Black Lives, White Lies, and the Art of Survival.* New York: Picador, 2018.

Austin, Regina. "Beyond Black Demons and White Devils: Anti-Black Conspiracy Theorizing and the Black Public Sphere." *Florida State University Law Review* 22 (1994): 1021–46.

———. "Deviance, Resistance, and Love." *Utah Law Review* 1994 (1994): 179–91.

Banks, R. Richard, Jennifer Eberhardt, and Lee Ross. "Symposium on Behavior Realism: Discrimination and Implicit Bias in a Racially Unequal Society." *California Law Review* 94 (2006): 1169–90.

Barnes, Mario. "Black Women's Stories and the Criminal Law: Restating the Power of Narrative." *UC Davis Law Review* 39 (2006): 941–89.

Barnes, Robin. "Interracial Violence and Racialized Narratives: Discovering the Road Less Traveled." *Columbia Law Review* 95 (1996): 1301–42.

Battle, Nishaun. *Black Girlhood, Punishment, and Resistance: Reimagining Justice for Black Girls in Virginia.* New York: Routledge, 2019.

Bell, Derrick. *Faces at the Bottom of the Well: The Permanence of Racism.* New York: Basic Books, 1992.

———. *Race, Racism, and American Law.* Boston: Little, Brown, 1992.

———. *And We Are Not Saved: The Elusive Quest for Racial Justice.* New York: Basic Books, 1987.

Benjamin, Ruha. *Race after Technology: Abolitionist Tools for the New Jim Code.* New York: Polity, 2019.

Blumstein, Alfred. "Racial Disproportionality of U.S. Prison Populations Revisited." *University of Colorado Law Review* 64 (1993): 743–60.

Bonilla-Silva, Eduardo. *Racism without Racists: Color-Blind Racism and the Persistence of Racial Inequality in the United States.* Lanham, MD: Rowman and Littlefield, 2003.

Brophy, Alfred. *Reconstructing the Dreamland: The Tulsa Riot of 1921.* Oxford: Oxford University Press, 2002.

Browne-Marshall, Gloria J. *Race, Law, and American Society: 1607 to Present.* New York: Routledge, 2007.

Brown-Scott, Wendy. "The Communitarian Law: Lawlessness or Reform for African-Americans?" *Harvard Law Review* 107, no. 6 (April 1994): 1209–30.

Bushway, Shawn, and Anne Morrison Piehl. "Judging the Judicial Discretion: Legal Factors and Racial Discrimination in Sentencing." *Law and Society Review* 35, no. 4 (2001): 733–64.

Butler, Paul. *Chokehold: Policing Black Men.* New York: New Press, 2017.

Carbado, Devon, and Rachel Moran, eds. *Race Law Stories.* New York: Foundation Press, 2008.

Carter, Dan. *Scottsboro: A Tragedy of the American South.* Baton Rouge: Louisiana State University Press, 1969.

Carter, William. "A Thirteenth Amendment Framework for Combating Racial Profiling." *Harvard Civil Rights–Civil Liberties Review* 17 (2004): 39–106.

Chan, Wendy. *Racialization, Crime, and Criminal Justice in Canada.* Toronto: University of Toronto Press, 2014.

Chicago Commission on Race Relations. *The Negro in Chicago: A Study of Race Relations and a Race Riot.* Chicago: University of Chicago Press, 1922.

Clair, Matthew, and Alix Winter. "How Judges Can Reduce Racial Disparities in the Criminal-Justice System." *Court Review* 53 (2016): 158–60.

Coates, Ta-Nehisi. "The Case for Reparations." *The Atlantic,* www.theatlantic.com, June 2014.

Cole, Johnetta Betsch, and Beverly Guy-Sheftall. *Gender Talk: The Struggle for Women's Equality in African American Communities.* New York: Ballantine, 2003.

Collins, Patricia Hill. *Black Sexual Politics: African-Americans, Gender, and the New Racism.* New York: Routledge, 2004.

Cottom, Tressie McMillan. *Thick: And Other Essays.* New York: New Press, 2019.

Crenshaw, Kimberlé, Neil Gotanda, Gary Peller, and Kendall Thomas, eds. *Critical Race Theory.* New York: New Press, 1995.

Crutchfield, Robert. "Warranted Disparity? Questioning the Justification of Racial Disparity in Criminal Justice Processing." *Columbia Human Rights Law Review* 36 (2004): 15–40.

Cullen, Francis, and Michael Benson. "White Collar Crime: Holding a Mirror to the Core." *Journal of Criminal Justice Education* 4 (1993): 325–47.

Culp, Jerome McCristal, Jr. "Notes from California: Rodney King and the Race Question." *Denver University Law Review* 70 (1993): 199–212.

Daly, Kathleen. "Criminal Law and Justice System Practices as Racist, White, and Racialized." *Washington and Lee Law Review* 51 (1994): 431–64.

Davis, Angela J. *Arbitrary Justice: The Power of the American Prosecutor*. New York: Oxford University Press, 2007.

Davis, Angela J., ed. *Policing the Black Man: Arrest, Prosecution and Imprisonment* New York: Pantheon, 2018.

Davis, Angela Y. *Are Prisons Obsolete?* New York: Seven Stories Press, 2003.

Davis, F. James. *Who Is Black? One Nation's Definition*. University Park: Pennsylvania State University Press, 1991.

Davis, Peggy. "Law as Microaggression." *Yale Law Journal* 98 (1989): 1559–77.

Deer, Sarah. *The Beginning and End of Rape: Confronting Sexual Violence in Native America*. Minneapolis, University of Minnesota, 2015.

Delgado, Richard. *The Rodrigo Chronicles: Conversations about America and Race*. New York: New York University Press, 1996.

———. "Rodrigo's Ninth Chronicle: Race, Legal Instrumentalism, and the Rule of Law." *University of Pennsylvania Law Review* 143 (1994): 379–416.

Deloria, Philip J. *Indians in Unexpected Places*. Lawrence: University Press of Kansas, 2004.

DiAngelo, Robin. *White Fragility: Why It's So Hard for White People to Talk about Racism*. Boston: Beacon. 2018.

DiIulio, John. "My Black Crime Problem, and Ours." *City Journal* 6 (1996): 14–28.

Dowd, Nancy. *Reimagining Equality: A New Deal for Children of Color*. New York: New York University Press, 2018.

Du Bois, W. E. B. *The Philadelphia Negro*. New York: Schocken Books, 1967.

Dulaney, Marvin. *Black Police in America*. Bloomington: Indiana University Press, 1996.

Dyson, Michael Eric. *Come Hell or High Water: Hurricane Katrina and the Color of Disaster*. New York: Basic Books, 2006.

Eberhardt, Jennifer. *Biased: Uncovering the Hidden Prejudice That Shapes What We See, Think, and Do*. New York: Viking, 2019.

Eddo-Lodge, Reni. *Why I'm No Longer Talking to White People about Race*. London: Bloomsbury, 2017.

Ellison, Ralph. *Invisible Man*. New York: Vintage Books, 1947.

Ferguson, Andrew. *Rise of Big Data Policing: Surveillance, Race, and the Future of Law Enforcement*. New York: New York University Press, 2017.

Fields, Karen, and Barbara Fields. *Racecraft: The Soul of Inequality in American Life*. New York: Verso, 2014.

Finkelman, Paul. "The Crime of Color." *Tulane Law Review* 67 (1993): 2063–112.

Finkelman, Paul, ed. *Race, Law, and American History, 1700–1990: The African American Experience*. New York: Garland, 1992.

Fleischauer, Marc. "Review of Florida Legislation; Comment: Teeth for a Paper Tiger: A Proposal to Add Enforceability to Florida's Hate Crimes Act." *Florida State University Law Review* 17 (1990): 697–711.

Foner, Eric. *Reconstruction: America's Unfinished Revolution, 1863–1877*. New York: Harper and Row, 1988.

Gabbidon, Shaun. *W. E. B. Du Bois on Crime and Justice: Laying the Foundations of Sociological Criminology*. New York: Routledge, 2016.

Georges-Abeyie, Daniel, ed. *The Criminal Justice System and Blacks*. New York: Clark Boardman, 1984.

Glaude, Eddie. *Democracy in Black: How Race Still Enslaves the American Soul*. New York: Broadway Books, 2016.

Glynn, Martin. *Black Men Invisibility, and Crime*. London: Routledge, 2013.

Gomez, Laura. *Manifest Destinies: The Making of the Mexican American Race*. New York: New York University Press, 2007.

Goodell, William. *The American Slave Code*. New York: American and Foreign Anti-Slavery Society, 1968.

Greene, Wendy. "Splitting Hairs: The 11th Circuit's Take on Workplace Bans against Natural Hair in EEOC v. Catastrophe Management Solutions." *Miami Law Review* 71, no. 4 (2017): 987–1036.

Gutierrez-Jones, Carl. *Critical Race Narratives: A Study of Race, Rhetoric, and Injury*. New York: New York University Press, 2001.

Hacker, Andrew. *Two Nations: Black and White, Separate, Hostile, Unequal*. New York: Scribner, 1992.

Hagan, John, and Celesta Albonetti. "Race, Class, and the Perception of Criminal Injustice in America." *American Journal of Sociology* 88 (1982): 329–55.

Harris, David. *Profiles in Injustice*. New York: New Press, 2002.

Herrnstein, Richard, and Charles Murray. *The Bell Curve: Intelligence and Class Structure in American Life*. New York: Free Press, 1994.

Higginbotham, A. Leon, Jr. *Shades of Freedom: Racial Politics and Presumption of the American Process*. New York: Oxford University Press, 1996.

———. *In the Matter of Color: Race and the American Legal Process*. New York: Oxford University Press, 1978.

Higginbotham, A. Leon, Jr., and Anne F. Jacobs. "The 'Law Only as an Enemy': The Legitimization of Racial Powerlessness through the Colonial and Ante-Bellum Criminal Law of Virginia." *North Carolina Law Review* 70 (1992): 969–1070.

Hindus, Michael. *Prison and Plantation: Crime, Justice, and Authority in Massachusetts and South Carolina, 1767–1878*. Chapel Hill: University of North Carolina Press, 1980.

Ifill, Sherrilyn. *On the Courthouse Lawn: Confronting the Legacy of Lynching in the Twenty-First Century*. Boston: Beacon, 2007.

Ifill, Sherrilyn, Loretta Lynch, Bryan Stevenson, and Anthony Thompson. *A Perilous Path: Talking Race, Inequality, and the Law*. New York. New Press, 2018.

Ignatiev, Noel. *How the Irish Became White*. New York: Routledge, 1995.

Jackson, John L., Jr. *Racial Paranoia: The Unintended Consequences of Political Correctness*. New York: Basic Civitas Books, 2008.

Johnson, Paula. "The Social Construction of Identity in Criminal Cases." *Michigan Journal of Race and Law* 1 (1996): 347–489.

Johnson, Sheri L. "Racial Derogation in Prosecutors Closing Arguments." In *Petit Apartheid in the Criminal Justice System*, ed. Dragan Milovanovic and Katheryn K. Russell, 79–102 Durham, NC: Carolina Academic Press, 2001.

Kaphar, Titus. *Language of the Forgotten*. New Haven, CT: Titus Kaphar, LLC, 2019.

Kendi, Ibram. *How to Be an Antiracist*. New York: One World, 2019.

Kennedy, Stetson. *Jim Crow Guide*. Boca Raton: Florida Atlantic University Press, 1959.

King, Gilbert. *Devil in the Grove: Thurgood Marshall, the Groveland Boys, and the Dawn of a New America*. New York: Harper, 2012.

Klein, Stephen, Susan Martin, and Joan Petersilia. Racial Equality in Sentencing. Santa Monica, CA: Rand, 1988.

Kutateladze, Besiki, Nancy Andiloro, Brian Johnson, and Cassia Spohn. "Cumulative Disadvantage: Examining Racial and Ethnic Disparity in Prosecution and Sentencing." *Criminology* 52, no. 3 (2014): 514–51.

Lawrence, Charles, III. "The Id, the Ego, and Equal Protection: Reckoning with Unconscious Racism." *Stanford Law Review* 39 (1987): 317–88.

Lawrence, Frederick. "Resolving the Hate Crimes / Hate Speech Paradox: Punishing Bias Crimes and Protecting Racist Speech." *Notre Dame Law Review* 68 (1993): 673–721.

Lee, Cynthia. "Race, Policing, and Lethal Force: Remedying Shooter Bias with Martial Arts Training." *Law and Contemporary Problems* 79 (2016): 145–72.

Lee, Orville. "Legal Weapons for the Weak? Democratizing the Force of Words in an Uncivil Society," *Law and Social Inquiry* 26 (2001): 847–90.

Lemelle, Anthony, Jr. *Black Male Deviance*. Westport, CT: Praeger, 1995.

Levinson, Justin, Mark Bennett, and Koichi Hioki. "Judging Implicit Bias: A National Empirical Study of Judicial Stereotypes." *Florida Law Review* 69, no. 1 (2017): 63–113.

Loewen, James. *Sundown Towns: A Hidden Dimension of American Racism*. New York: New Press, 2005.

López, Ian F. Haney. *White by Law: The Legal Construction of Race*. New York: New York University Press, 1996.

Lynch, Michael, and Britt Patterson, eds. *Race and Criminal Justice*. Guilderland, NY: Harrow and Heston, 1991.

Magee, Rhonda V. "The Master's Tools, from the Bottom Up: Responses to African-American Reparations in Mainstream and Outsider Remedies Discourse." *Virginia Law Review* 79, no. 4 (1993): 863–916.

Mann, Coramae Richey. *Unequal Justice: A Question of Color*. Bloomington: Indiana University Press, 1993.

Marable, Manning. *Race, Reform, and Rebellion: The Second Reconstruction and Beyond in Black America, 1945–2006*. Jackson: University Press of Mississippi, 2006.

Markovitz, Johnathan. *Legacies of Lynching: Racial Violence and Memory*. Minneapolis: University of Minnesota Press, 2004.

Masur, Kate. *Until Justice Be Done: America's First Civil Rights Movement, from the Revolution to Reconstruction*. New York: Norton, 2021.

Matsuda, Mari, Charles Lawrence III, Richard Delgado, and Kimberlè Williams Crenshaw, eds. *Words That Wound: Critical Race Theory, Assaultive Speech, and the First Amendment*. Boulder, CO: Westview, 1993.

McIntyre, Charshee. *Criminalizing a Race*. Queens, NY: Kayode, 1998.

McNamarah, Chan Tov. "White Caller Crime: Racialized Police Communication and Existing While Black." *Michigan Journal of Race and Law* 24 (2019): 335–415.

Miller, Jerome. *Search and Destroy: African American Males in the Criminal Justice System*. New York: Cambridge University Press, 1996.

Miller, Reuben. *Halfway Home: Race, Punishment, and the Afterlife of Mass Incarceration*. New York: Little, Brown and Company, 2021.

Mills, C. Wright. *The Sociological Imagination*. New York: Oxford University Press, 1959.

Milovanovic, Dragan, and Katheryn Russell, eds. *Petit Apartheid in the U.S. Criminal Justice System: The Dark Figure of Crime*. Durham, NC: Carolina Academic Press, 2001.

Mincy, Ronald B. *Black Males Left Behind*. Washington, DC: Urban Institute Press, 2006.

Morris, Aldon. *The Scholar Denied: W. E. B. Du Bois and the Birth of Modern Sociology*. Oakland: University of California Press, 2015.

Morris, Thomas. *Southern Slavery and the Law, 1619–1860*. Chapel Hill: University of North Carolina Press, 1996.

Morrison, Toni. *The Source of Self-Regard: Selected Essays, Speeches, and Meditations*. New York: Knopf, 2019.

Morrison, Toni, ed. *Race-ing Justice, Engendering Power*. New York: Pantheon Books, 1992.

Moynihan, Daniel P. *The Negro Family: The Case for National Action*. Washington, DC: US Government Printing Office, 1965.

Muhammad, Khalil. *The Condemnation of Blackness: Race, Crime, and the Making of Modern Urban America*. Cambridge, MA: Harvard University Press, 2010.

Murray, Pauli. States' Laws on Race and Color, Athens, GA: University of Georgia Press, 2016._

Myers, Samuel L., and Margaret Simms, eds. *The Economics of Race and Crime*. Edison, NJ: Transaction, 1998.

Myrdal, Gunnar. *An American Dilemma: The Negro Problem and Modern Democracy*. New York: Pantheon Books, 1944.

Neal, Mark Anthony. *New Black Man*. New York: Routledge, 2005.

Nelson, Jill. *Police Brutality: An Anthology*. New York: Norton, 2001.

Nelson Mandela Foundation. *A Prisoner in the Garden: Photos, Letters and Notes from Nelson Mandela's 27 Years in Prison*. New York: Penguin, 2005.

Nichols, Yazmine Levonna C'Bona, "Race Has Everything to Do with It: A Remedy for Frivolous Race-Based Police Calls." *Fordham Urban Law Journal* 47 (2019): 153–94.

Noble, Safiya. *Algorithms of Oppression: How Search Engines Reinforce Racism.* New York: New York University Press, 2018.

Onwuachi-Willig, Angela, and Mario Barnes. "By Any Other Name? On Being 'Regarded as' Black, and Why Title VII Should Apply Even If Lakisha and Jamal Are White." *Wisconsin Law Review* 2005 (2005): 1283–343.

Pager, Devah. *Marked: Race, Crime and Finding Work in an Era of Mass Incarceration.* Chicago: University of Chicago Press, 2007.

Parmar, A. "Intersectionality, British Criminology, and Race: Are We There Yet?" *Theoretical Criminology* 21 (2017): 35–45.

Patterson, Orlando. *Rituals of Blood: Consequences of Slavery in Two American Centuries.* New York: Basic Civitas Books, 1998.

Perry, Imani. *Breathe: A Letter to My Sons.* Boston: Beacon, 2019.

Peterson, Ruth, and Lauren Krivo. *Divergent Social Worlds: Neighborhood Crime and the Racial-Spatial Divide.* New York: Russell Sage Foundation, 2012.

Peterson, Ruth, Lauren Krivo, and John Hagan, eds. *The Many Colors of Crime.* New York: New York University Press, 2006.

Philips, Coretta, Rod Earle, and Alpa Parma. "Dear British Criminology: Where Has All the Race and Racism Gone?" *Theoretical Criminology* (2019), https://journals.sagepub.com.

Rankine, Claudia. *Just Us: An American Conversation.* Minneapolis: Graywolf Press, 2020.

Raper, Arthur. *The Tragedy of Lynching.* Chapel Hill: University of North Carolina Press, 1933.

Rawls, Anne Warfield, and Waverly Duck. *Tacit Racism.* Chicago: University of Chicago Press, 2020.

Reitzel, John, and Alexis Piquero. "Does It Exist? Studying Citizens' Attitudes of Racial Profiling." *Police Quarterly* 9, no. 2 (2006): 161–83.

Roberts, Dorothy E. "Abolition Constitutionalism." Harvard Law Review 133 (2019): 1–122.

———. "The Social and Moral Cost of Mass Incarceration in African American Communities." *Stanford Law Review* 56, no. 5 (2004): 1271–305.

———. "Deviance, Resistance, and Love." *Faculty Scholarship at Penn Law* 1386): 179–91.

Ross, Thomas. *Just Stories.* Boston: Beacon, 1997.

Russell, Katheryn K. "Development of a Black Criminology and the Role of the Black Criminologist." *Justice Quarterly* 9 (1997): 667–83.

———. "The Racial Inequality Hypothesis: A Critical Look at the Research and an Alternative Theoretical Analysis." *Law and Human Behavior* 18 (1994): 305–17.

Russell-Brown, Katheryn. "Black Criminology in the 21st Century." In Building a Black Criminology, ed. James D. Unnever, Shaun L. Gabbidon, and Cecilia Chouhy, 101–23. New York: Routledge, 2018.

———. *Protecting Our Own: Race, Crime, and African Americans.* Lanham, MD: Rowman and Littlefield, 2006.

———. *Underground Codes: Race, Crime, and Related Fires*. New York: New York University Press, 2004.

Schafer, Judith K. "The Long Arm of the Law: Slave Criminals and the Supreme Court in Antebellum Louisiana." *Tulane Law Review* 60 (1986): 1247–68.

Sheley, Joseph F. "Structural Influences on the Problem of Race, Crime, and Criminal Justice." *Tulane Law Review* 67, no. 6 (1993): 2273–92.

Skogan, Wesley. "Crime and the Racial Fears of White Americans." *Annals of the American Academy of Political and Social Science* 539 (1995): 59–71.

Smith, J. Clay. "Justice and Jurisprudence and the Black Lawyer." *Notre Dame Law Review* 69 (1994): 1077–113.

Stampp, Kenneth. "Chattels Personal." In *American Law and the Constitutional Order: Historical Perspectives*, ed. Lawrence M. Friedman and Harry N. Scheiber. Cambridge, MA: Harvard University Press, 1988.

———. *The Peculiar Institution*. New York: Vintage Books, 1956.

Steele, Claude M., and Joshua Aronson. "Stereotype Threat and the Intellectual Test Performance of African Americans." *Journal of Personality and Social Psychology* 69, no. 5 (November 1995): 797–811.

Steinberg, Stephen. *Turning Back: The Retreat from Racial Justice in American Thought and Policy*. Boston: Beacon, 1995.

Stevenson, Bryan. *Just Mercy: A Story of Justice and Redemption*. New York: Random House, 2014.

Sulton, Anne, ed. *African American Perspectives on Crime Causation, Criminal Justice Administration, and Crime Prevention*. Englewood, CO: Sulton Books, 1994.

Sutherland, Edwin. *White Collar Crime*. New York: Dryden, 1949.

Tassel, Emily F. "Only the Law Would Rule between Us." *Chicago-Kent Law Review* 70 (1995): 873–926.

Troutt, David Dante, ed. *After the Storm: Black Intellectuals Explore the Meaning of Hurricane Katrina*. New York: New Press, 2007.

Ungarte, Francisco. "Reconstruction Redux: Rehnquist, *Morrison*, and the *Civil Rights Cases*." *Harvard Civil Liberties–Civil Rights Review* 41 (2006): 481–508.

Unnever, James, Shaun Gabbidon, and Cecilia Chouhy, eds. *Building a Black Criminology: Race, Theory, and Crime*. New York: Routledge, 2018.

US Bureau of the Census. *Historical Corrections Statistics in the United States, 1850–1984*. Washington, DC: US Government Printing Office, 1986.

———. *Historical Statistics of the United States, Colonial Times to 1970, Bicentennial Edition, Part 2*. Washington, DC: US Government Printing Office, 1975.

———. *Negro Population, 1790–1915*. Washington, DC: US Government Printing Office, 1969.

US Department of Justice. *The Ferguson Report: Department of Justice Investigation of the Ferguson Police Department*. New York: New Press, 2015.

US Department of Justice. *Cuyahoga County Prosecutor's Report on the November 22, 2014, Shooting Death of Tamir Rice, Timothy McGinty, Prosecutor*. Washington, DC, 2015.

US Department of Labor, Bureau of Labor Statistics. *Current Population Survey: Employed Persons by Detailed Occupation, Sex, Race, and Hispanic of Latino Ethnicity, 2005*. Washington, DC.

US House of Representatives. *A Failure of Initiative: Final Report of the Select Bipartisan Committee to Investigate the Preparation for and Response to Hurricane Katrina*. Washington, DC: US Government Printing Office, 2006.

US Sentencing Commission. *Cocaine and Federal Sentencing Policy*. Washington, DC: US Government Printing Office, 1995.

Van Cleve, Nicole Gonzalez. *Crook County: Racism and Injustice in America's Largest Criminal Court*. Oakland, CA: Stanford University Press, 2017.

Verdun, Vincene. "If the Shoe Fits, Wear It: An Analysis of Reparations to African Americans." *Temple Law Review* 67 (1993): 597–668.Walker, Nancy, J. Michael Senger, Francisco Villarruel, and Angela Arboleda. *Lost Opportunities: The Reality of Latinos in the US Criminal Justice System*. National Council of La Raza, 2004.

Weatherspoon, Floyd. "The Mass Incarceration of African-American Males: A Return to Institutionalized Slavery, Oppression, and Disenfranchisement of Constitutional Rights." *Texas Wesleyan Law Review* 13 (2007): 599.

Weitzer, Ronald, and Steven Tuch. *Race and Policing in America: Conflict and Reform*. New York: Cambridge University Press, 2006.

Wells-Barnett, Ida B. *On Lynchings*. New York: Humanity Books, 2002.

———. *On Lynchings: Southern Horrors, a Red Record, Mob Rule in New Orleans*. New York: Arno, 1969.

Western, Bruce. *Homeward: Life in the Year After Prison*. New York: Russell Sage, 2018.

Wilkerson, Isabel. *Caste: The Origins of Our Discontents*. New York: Random House, 2020.

———. *The Warmth of Other Suns: The Epic Story of America's Great Migration*. New York: Vintage Books, 2010.

Williams, Patricia. *Seeing a Color-Blind Future: The Paradox of Race*. New York: Farrar, Straus, and Giroux, 1988.

———. "Spirit-Murdering the Messenger: The Discourse of Fingerpointing as the Law's Response to Racism." *University of Miami Law Review* 42 (1987): 127–57.

Williams, Thomas Chatterton. *Self-Portrait in Black and White*. New York: W. W. Norton, 2019.

Wilson, James Q. "Crime, Race, and Values." *Society* 30, no. 1 (November/December 1992): 90–93.

Wilson, William J. *The Truly Disadvantaged: The Inner City, the Underclass, and Public Policy*. Chicago: University of Chicago Press, 1987.

Wolfgang, Marvin, and Bernard Cohen. *Crime and Race: Conceptions and Misconceptions*. New York: Institute of Human Relations Press, 1970.

Wu, Frank. *Yellow: Race in America beyond Black and White*. New York: Basic Books, 2002.

# INDEX

# ABOUT THE AUTHOR

KATHERYN RUSSELL-BROWN is the Levin, Mabie & Levin Professor of Law and Director of the Race and Crime Center for Justice at the University of Florida, Levin College of Law. She has published numerous books, articles, and essays on race, crime, and justice. She is also the author of three children's books: *She Was the First! The Trailblazing Life of Shirley Chisholm,* winner of the 2021 NAACP Image Award for Children's Literature, *A Voice Named Aretha* (2020), and *Little Melba and Her Big Trombone* (2014).